RENEWALS 458-4574

DATE DUE

GAYLORD			PRINTED IN U.S.A.

ALLEGORESIS

Allegoresis

Reading Canonical Literature East and West

ZHANG LONGXI

Cornell University Press

Ithaca and London

First published 2005 by Cornell University Press

Printed in the United States of America

Library of Congress Cataloging-in-Publication Data

Zhang Longxi.
Allegoresis : reading canonical literature east and west / Zhang Longxi.
   p. cm.
  Includes bibliographical references and index.
  ISBN-13: 978-0-8014-4369-5 (cloth : alk. paper)
  ISBN-10: 0-8014-4369-5 (cloth : alk. paper)
  1. Allegory. 2. Canon (Literature) 3. Literature, Comparative—Chinese and Western. 4. Literature Comparative—Western and Chinese. I. Title.
  PN56.A5Z43 2005
  809'.915—dc22   2005008832

Cornell University Press strives to use environmentally responsible suppliers and materials to the fullest extent possible in the publishing of its books. Such materials include vegetable-based, low-VOC inks and acid-free papers that are recycled, totally chlorine-free, or partly composed of nonwood fibers. For further information, visit our website at www.cornellpress.cornell.edu.

Cloth printing   10 9 8 7 6 5 4 3 2 1

To my father Zhang Xidu,
who first taught me how to read.

Contents

Acknowledgments

The writing of this book has been partially supported by a University of California President's Research Fellowship in the Humanities, which facilitated its start, and by a City University of Hong Kong Strategic Research Grant and a Small-Scale Research Grant, which helped bring it to completion. I am grateful to the two universities with which I have the good fortune to be affiliated for providing me with a pleasant, encouraging, and intellectually stimulating environment in which to work, think, and write.

Many friends have given me much support and valuable help over the years, and, in particular, I would like to mention Daniel Aaron, Anthony C. Yu, Haun Saussy, Richard J. Smith, Ronald Egan, and Lisa Raphals for reading and commenting on the manuscript in its draft stages. Donald Stone, Kang-i Sun Chang, and Ruth apRoberts have backed me up with friendship and ideas. David Glidden has helped me understand the Greco-Roman ideas about the Golden Age and Augustine's subversion of it. I owe much to these friends. Unless otherwise noted, I take responsibility for all the Chinese translations and for some of the French. I am very grateful to David Damrosch for his kind appreciation, strong support, and for sagacious advice that has helped to make this book more coherent. I also want to thank Bernhard Kendler, executive editor of Cornell University Press, whose confidence in the book's worth has been most encouraging; it is deeply appreciated.

A small part of chapter 1 was first presented at an NEH seminar at Rice University and then at the University of Trier, Germany, and appeared in *Chinese Thought in a Global Context: A Dialogue between Chinese and Western Philosophical Approaches*, ed. Karl-Heinz Pohl (Leiden: Brill, 1999). I want to thank Professor Richard J. Smith for inviting me to

Rice and Professor Dr. Pohl for inviting me to Trier for the presentation. Another part of chapter 1 was first published in a special issue of *College Literature* (Feb. 1996), and I want to thank Patrick Colm Hogan and the editors of *College Literature* for allowing me to include that article here in revised form. In some part of chapter 2, I have used ideas and arguments that first appeared in an article published in *Comparative Literature* (Summer 1987). I want to thank the editors of that journal for providing a forum many years ago for my comparative reading of the Song of Songs and Confucian commentaries on the *Book of Poetry*. Part of chapter 4 was first presented as a professorial inaugural lecture at the City University of Hong Kong, then at a conference in Hagen, Germany; it subsequently appeared in *Utopian Studies* (Summer 2002). I am grateful to my audiences in Hong Kong and Hagen, and I want to thank Jörn Rüsen for inviting me to the Hagen conference, and Lyman Tower Sargent for allowing me to use the published article here. All these previously published portions have been revised and expanded.

Some of the ideas in this book were tried out in a six-week graduate seminar on allegory and interpretation in Toronto in March and early April 2004. I am grateful to Professor Amilcare Iannucci for inviting me to be the Distinguished Visiting Fellow for 2003–2004 at the Humanities Centre of the University of Toronto, which gave me the opportunity to teach that seminar at the Centre for Comparative Literature. Of course, I want to thank all my students who attended that seminar with genuine interest and dedication, and also Professors Richard John Lynn and Sonja Arntzen for their friendship and moral support.

My wife Weilin and my children Celia and Caroline have always given me love and support and have patiently waited for the completion of this book. To them I owe much more than just a note of thanks. At the completion of this book, in which I deal with some of the issues in the reading of literature that have interested me since my young student days, I am particularly thinking of my father who initiated me into the wonders of the written word, but left me much too soon, even before I reached my teens. To lose one's parents at a young age is unfortunate, but the little memory left in one's mind may become all the more precious, and it is to the memory of my father that this book is dedicated with my early childhood remembrances and enduring love.

ZHANG LONGXI

Grandeur Villa
Kowloon, Hong Kong

ALLEGORESIS

1

Introduction: The Validity of Cross-Cultural Understanding

Que sai-je?" asks the skeptic, Michel de Montaigne. If the validity of knowledge is a basic question applied to self-understanding, that question may appear far more importunate when one tries to understand things in languages and cultures that are set apart and that form very different identities, traditions, and histories. For cross-cultural understanding, therefore, China may offer a useful test case, because the mere distance between China and the West, in geographical as well as in cultural terms, makes it especially important to examine, first of all, the possibility of knowing: the grounds upon which one can claim to comprehend things, make legitimate use of terms and concepts, and acquire knowledge cross-culturally. Here we may encounter a skepticism that goes deeper than Montaigne's—a skepticism that does not ask, "What do I know?" but more fundamentally, "How do I know?" or "How *can* I know?" The question challenges not just the content but the very possibility of knowing; and it raises doubts about the validity of cross-cultural understanding, the viability of intersubjective transference of consciousness and sensibility.

The aim of this book is to answer the challenging questions as to what and how one knows about different cultures, to inquire into the condition of knowledge that one may acquire beyond one's own linguistic and cultural parameters, and to establish the theoretical ground for the viability of East-West studies. Although discussion of such issues may cover a wide range of topics, it focuses on the reading of literature, the relationship between text and reading, and particularly the question of allegory and allegorical interpretation. Allegory, a trope that many consider to be quintessentially Greek and Western, becomes a suitable test of the possibility of cross-cultural knowledge. Whether the concept of allegory—namely, a text with double-structured meaning—can be usefully deployed in the discussion of texts and interpretations in China as well as the West, or to put it differently, whether allegory can be translated not only linguistically but also conceptually across the gap of cultural differences, will be the main problem investigated in this book.

Chapter 1 establishes some basic notions in order to clear the ground for building a case for allegory in the context of Chinese tradition. Chapter 2 discusses the problem of allegorical interpretation in the reading of two canonical texts influential in the West and East respectively: the biblical interpretation of the Song of Songs and traditional commentaries on the Chinese *Book of Poetry*. Chapter 3 explores the question of allegorical interpretation in terms of its ideological premises; it argues for the importance of literal sense as the ground upon which one may discriminate and evaluate various allegorical readings, while guarding against willful misunderstanding and misinterpretations. Chapter 4 considers utopian and anti-utopian literature as essentially allegorical, because utopia articulates the desirability of a social vision that always lies beyond the reality we know and the language of utopian description, and thus invites us to reach its realm in bold imagination. Ironically, however, the utopian ideal appears to contain the seed of its own dialectical negation, thus giving rise to anti-utopias, which reveal another aspect or layer of the ideal's meaning. Finally, chapter 5 offers some thoughts on the political implications of allegorical reading. Because politics requires commitment and allegiance, as a mode of interpretation, allegoresis can be shown to incur political and ethical responsibilities. After all, the decision to interpret is a decision to take sides that has political consequences.

The discussion of allegory, however, forms part of a larger problem: the viability of cross-cultural understanding. That is why Montaigne's question is so appropriate and why in answering Montaigne we need to investigate texts and interpretations across linguistic and cultural divides, above all, the real and imaginary distances between China and the West.

Of Fish and Knowledge: The Translatability of Terms

Before we look into the matter of cross-cultural knowledge more closely, let us first contemplate the following debate, formulated as a delightfully witty conversation between two ancient Chinese philosophers, Zhuangzi

(369?–286? B.C.E.) and his rival, the captious but invariably outwitted Huizi. Their interesting debate on the validity of knowledge will illuminate the situation of knowing and the known, and thus help us focus on the theoretical assumptions in our own effort at cross-cultural understanding:

> Zhuangzi and Huizi are strolling on the bridge over the Hao River. "Out there a shoal of white minnows are swimming freely and leisurely," says Zhuangzi. "That's what the fish's happiness is." "Well, you are not a fish, how do you know about fish's happiness?" Huizi contends. "You are not me, how do you know that I do not know about fish's happiness?" retorts Zhuangzi. "I am not you, so I certainly do not know about you," Huizi replies. "But you are certainly not a fish, and that makes the case complete that you do not know what fish's happiness is." "Shall we go back to where we started?" says Zhuangzi. "When you said 'how do you know about fish's happiness?' you asked me because you already knew that I knew it. I knew it above the Hao River."[1]

The last statement, that Zhuangzi knew fish's happiness "above the Hao River," as A. C. Graham observes, asserts the relative validity of knowledge, that "all knowing is relative to viewpoint," namely, acquired at a particular locale in one's lived world, related to the circumscribed whole of one's "concrete situation."[2] The emphasis here on the situatedness or circumstantiality is rather significant as it puts knowledge in a real, specific, and historical context and thereby differentiates it from the abstract notion of all-inclusive, transcendental knowledge based on pure reason. Here Zhuangzi appears to have articulated a concept of knowledge completely embedded in historicity and aided by a sort of empathetic imagination, with its claim to truth based on the specific ways in which the knowing subject and the known object are interconnected rather than on the abstract universality of mental faculties. Perhaps this is the kind of knowledge that reminds us of Aristotle's notion of practical knowledge in his distinction between *phronesis* and *episteme*, or practical and theoretical knowledge, a distinction "which cannot be reduced," as Hans-Georg Gadamer remarks, "to that between the true and the probable. Practical knowledge, phronesis, is another kind of knowledge."[3] Thus against the

---

1. Guo Qingfan (1844–95?), *Zhuangzi jishi*, xvii, in vol. 3 of *Zhuzi jicheng* (Beijing: Zhonghua, 1954), pp. 267–68. Hereafter abbreviated as *Zhuangzi*.
2. Graham, *Disputers of the Tao*, p. 81.
3. Gadamer, *Truth and Method*, p. 21. For *phronesis*, see Aristotle, *Nicomachean Ethics*: "That practical wisdom is not scientific knowledge is evident; for it is, as has been said, concerned with the ultimate particular fact, since the thing to be done is of this nature" (VI, 8,

challenge of skepticism, Zhuangzi insists on the cognitive value of his situated knowledge as valid knowledge, even though he may fully admit his all too human finitude and fallibility. But when we speak of Zhuangzi's situated knowledge as *phronesis*, we are inviting the same skeptical challenge; we put ourselves in the same position as Zhuangzi, where, from the skeptic's point of view, the very possibility of knowing becomes highly questionable. It is indeed the same question with which we began, the question or doubt about cross-cultural understanding: Can we speak of Zhuangzi and Aristotle in the same context? Is Zhuangzi advocating knowledge as a kind of *phronesis?* Can such terms and concepts be translated at all? These are the most basic questions we must address before we can claim to attain any knowledge at all across the gaps of languages and cultures.

Like the other similar anecdotal arguments in the *Zhuangzi*, the disputation "above the Hao River" purports to illustrate Zhuangzi's philosophy and present it as superior to its rival positions. What is remarkable about this particular anecdote, as Graham notes, is its playfulness, which "in parodying logical debate is more faithful to the detail of its structure than anything else in *Chuang-tzŭ.*"[4] Graham, however, seems to fall short of our expectation to bring out the full force of Zhuangzi's argument when he remarks that the philosopher in this passage is "making fun of [Huizi] for being too logical," and that Zhuangzi can offer "no answer to 'How do you know?' except a clarification of the viewpoint from which you know."[5] But insofar as practical or moral knowledge is concerned, the viewpoint from which one knows is the only perspective available in human understanding; that is to say, human knowledge is very often situated, conditioned, and its truth very often finite and relative.

Zhuangzi's knowledge about fish is not absolute in the sense that he cannot know fish as only a fish can, but hardly any knowledge worth having is absolute in that sense. Zhuangzi suggests that one does not have to *be* a fish to *know about* fish, for one's knowledge always has something of one's own in it. In Zhuangzi's claim to knowledge, there is surely a sense of playfulness and empathetic enjoyment, a vicarious pleasure that expresses his own happiness in seeing the free and graceful movement of the minnows, which Huizi completely missed or neglected in questioning the logical validity of Zhuangzi's claim. But the crucial point Zhuangzi makes in this passage, as I understand it, is not to counter Huizi's dry logic with a loose and slippery sophism, but to pursue that

---

The Basic Works of Aristotle, ed. Richard McKeon, p. 1030.
    4. Graham, *Chuang-tzŭ: The Inner Chapters,* p. 123.
    5. Graham, *Disputers of the Tao,* pp. 80, 81.

logic vigorously to its very end (or more precisely in this case, to its starting point) where it turns into its own negation. To be thoroughly skeptical about knowledge, Zhuangzi suggests, one must either give up the possibility of asking any question at all insofar as questioning already presumes the certainty of knowing something amiss, or—which comes to the same thing—one must admit that presumed certainty of one's negative knowledge. That is to say, by pushing Huizi's argument *ad absurdum*, Zhuangzi shows that his contender is not logical enough, that the skepticism of knowledge already presupposes, ironically but necessarily, knowledge of a certain kind, and that the answer to "How do you know?" is already implicit in the question, if only because it is asking about something already assumed to be known.

Skepticism and knowledge are thus revealed to be mutually implicated in a dialectical relationship. Notice that for all his doubts about Zhuangzi's knowledge, Huizi never has a moment of doubt about what he knows, namely, that Zhuangzi is not a fish, ergo he does not know fish's happiness. Throughout the conversation, Huizi's negative knowledge, his conviction that there is a difference between Zhuangzi and a fish, between "you" and "I," is stated most positively and assuredly. His skeptical attitude toward knowledge thus rests on his unreflective confidence in his own negative knowledge of the difference of things. For Zhuangzi, however, differentiation is arbitrary and the difference between man and fish is by no means a fact established a priori; thus in positing difference as an unquestioned known fact, Huizi already asserts the possibility of knowledge despite himself. It is Zhuangzi who proves to be truly radical in questioning the very logicality of differentiation, while Huizi never reaches that level of questioning. But if Huizi can have knowledge about Zhuangzi across the gap of intersubjective difference (between "you" and "I"), we must also grant Zhuangzi the knowledge about fish across another gap of intersubjectivity (between "man" and "fish"). And that, in fact, is how Chinese commentators have traditionally read this passage.[6] However counterintuitive it may appear, such a reading follows a stringent logic that refuses to take for granted any conventional notion of difference.

One may protest that the difference between man and fish is of a different kind from that between Zhuangzi and the rival philosopher, and that the former is a greater and more obvious difference than the latter; but in that case we are arguing, like Huizi, on the basis of our conventional

---

6. In his exegesis of this passage, Cheng Xuanying (fl. 637–655) thus rephrases Zhuangzi's retort to Huizi: "If you argue that I am not a fish and therefore cannot know about fish, then how can you, who are not me, know about me? If you are not me and yet can know about me, then, I, though not a fish, can know about fish." *Zhuangzi*, xvii, p. 268.

notions of difference. Instead of doubting the possibility of knowing, we implicitly assert, again like Huizi, differences of various kinds and degrees as given facts already known intuitively. Zhuangzi, however, is far too philosophical to honor such conventional notions. If everything is either a "this" (*shi*) or a "that" (*bi*), he wonders whether there is any real distinction between the two categories except when viewed from a certain perspective. The deictic function of all words and categories is predicated on a certain point of view, a certain center of consciousness from which the rest of the world is seen as differentiated, fragmented, and knowable. But "every *this* is also a *that*; every *that* is also a *this*," says Zhuangzi. "*That* has its sense of right and wrong, and *this* also has its sense of right and wrong. Are there really *this* and *that*? Or are there no such things as *this* and *that*?"[7] Such truly skeptical and relativist reasoning is typical of Zhuangzi, but it serves to destabilize the fixation on difference as the basis of some absolute knowledge.

In his great "synthesising vision" of the universe, Zhuangzi tends to see all things as equal to one another in their primordial, natural, undifferentiated condition, and to regard all differentiation as arbitrarily made to facilitate human understanding.[8] The equality or non-differentiation of things constitutes the central theme of the second chapter of the *Zhuangzi*, and at the end of that chapter, where he recounts a fascinating dream of his, the philosopher claims that he is never sure whether he is dreaming or awake, whether he is a man dreaming of being a butterfly or a butterfly dreaming of being Zhuangzi the philosopher.[9] He is not, however, perversely denying all differences or their usefulness, but he does refuse to attach any special value to difference or the negative knowledge based on it. By revealing the undeclared assumptions of Huizi's argument, he shows that all knowledge, negative as well as positive, has only relative validity, and that the negative moment necessarily contains and depends on a prior moment of the positive knowledge of differentiation. Ultimately, therefore, Graham is right to see the whole debate between Zhuangzi and Huizi as an argument for the relativity of knowledge. From that perspective, then, it would be untenable to insist on either the

---

7. *Zhuangzi*, ii. p. 32.

8. The term "synthesising vision" is Graham's. The theme of the second chapter of the *Zhuangzi*, Graham maintains, is "the defence of a synthesising vision against Confucians, Mohists and Sophists, who analyse, distinguish alternatives and debate which is right or wrong." Graham, *Chuang-tzŭ: The Inner Chapters*, p. 48.

9. See *Zhuangzi*, ii, pp. 53–54. Though less radical in doubting the difference of identities, Montaigne in a different context also asks: "When I play with my cat, who knows if I am not a pastime to her more than she is to me?" "Apology for Raymond Sebond," *The Complete Essays of Montaigne*, 2:12, p. 331.

absolute validity of knowledge or its absolute impossibility, and to make a truth-claim based on negative knowledge would appear just as pretentious as a dogmatic statement of truth.

Relativism, Universalism, and the Rites Controversy

The question of the validity of knowledge, of how to "establish and transmit understanding across the boundaries of language, geography, culture, and time," says David D. Buck, "lies at the very heart of Asian studies," or, one might say, cross-cultural studies in general.[10] Buck identifies cultural relativism and evaluative universalism as the two most commonly used paradigms in Asian studies, and succinctly describes the core of relativist thinking as a skeptical attitude toward "the issue of whether any conceptual tools exist to understand and interpret human behavior and meaning in ways that are intersubjectively valid."[11] But to speak of *human* behavior at all is already to have acknowledged the possibility of intersubjective understanding, or otherwise one can only describe one's own behavior empirically, without ever going beyond the strictly personal and subjective and comparing it with anyone else's to gain knowledge that pertains to the human, that is, intersubjective, condition. Buck's observation, however, concerns understanding across the gap of languages and cultures, which is presumably a much wider gap than that of mere intersubjectivity, and in which the cultural differences involved are assumed to be much greater than differences within the same culture. It is for cross-cultural studies that Buck raises the question whether conceptual tools are available across the gaps of fundamental differences.

In recognizing the importance of linguistic, national, ethnic and other differences and in questioning the viability of using conceptual tools that are intersubjectively valid, Buck's relativist seems to bear some resemblance to Huizi, whose objection to Zhuangzi, as we have seen, is predicated on the recognition of fundamental differences. Zhuangzi, on the other hand, may resemble the universalist in assuming a shared sensibility and common knowledge beyond difference or differentiation. As Buck describes it, however, the universalist position is not really universal but culturally specific, for it is a position related to Western colonialism and imperialism, the ethnocentric position adopted by those Europeans and

10. Buck, editor's introduction, "Forum on Universalism and Relativism in Asian Studies," *The Journal of Asian Studies* 50 (Feb. 1991): 29.
11. Ibid., p. 30.

North Americans who "chauvinistically held that their civilization was superior to others."[12] Here we may see the influence of a predominant relativist paradigm in studying alien cultures and societies, a paradigm that has increasingly gained ground since the 1960s when Western philosophers and cultural anthropologists began to argue for the internal coherence of cultural values and beliefs, the necessity to abandon narrow and ethnocentric Western views and to avoid imposing them on non-Western cultures. This seems to be a morally commendable gesture of cultural critique, by means of which Western scholars genuinely try to dissociate themselves from the racism and cultural hegemony of an embarrassing and erroneous past of Western colonialism.

The change of paradigms in cultural studies, however, proves to be much more complicated than the mere denunciation of colonialism. As Richard Bernstein argues, in the entire range of human and social sciences in recent times, there is a "movement from confidence to skepticism about foundations, methods, and rational criteria of evaluation," and as a result the relativist paradigm reigns everywhere. "There seems to be almost a rush to embrace various forms of relativism. Whether we reflect on the nature of science, or alien societies, or different historical epochs, or sacred and literary texts, we hear voices telling us that there are no hard 'facts of the matter' and that almost 'anything goes.'"[13] Once the old positivistic dogmas concerning reality, objectivity, rationality, and truth are exposed as prejudices and illusions, and once a rigid objectivism or metaphysical realism collapses, nothing seems able to check the swing of the pendulum in the paradigmatic change from objectivism toward relativism.

In this respect, the controversy around Peter Winch's works is quite significant. Drawing on Ludwig Wittgenstein's concept of language games and arguing against the positivistic notion of objective truth, Winch maintains that knowledge or truth does not coincide with any reality outside the language in which that knowledge or truth is expressed, and that different cultures may understand reality differently and may have distinct rules for playing their language games. "Reality is not what gives language sense," says Winch in one of his most controversial essays. "What is real and what is unreal shows itself *in* the sense that language has."[14] If different cultures are all different forms of life engaged in different language games, and if there is nothing outside the various languages to provide an independent basis for description and evaluation, this type of thinking would lead

12. Ibid.
13. Bernstein, *Beyond Objectivism and Relativism*, p. 3.
14. Winch, "Understanding a Primitive Society," in *Ethics and Action*, p. 12.

inevitably to a sweeping cultural relativism that sees various cultures as totally incommensurable, intelligible only to those already living within limits of a specific cultural system. Winch's argument tends to lead precisely to such a relativism, even though he himself maintains that "men's ideas and beliefs must be checkable by reference to something independent—some reality," and he explicitly rejects "an extreme Protagorean relativism."[15] Bernstein tries to disentangle Winch's argument from the very relativism Winch disclaims, but in his own critique, he also points out the controversial aspect of Winch's works that does seem "to entail a new, sophisticated form of relativism."[16] In facing an alien society, says Winch, the social scientist must become a participant in a language game different from his own, and his "reflective understanding must necessarily presuppose, if it is to count as genuine understanding at all, the participant's unreflective understanding."[17] That is to say, the sociologist or anthropologist must suspend his or her own views and must think, feel, and act like a native of the alien society in order to understand it "unreflectively," from the native's point of view.

It is not at all clear, however, how anyone can achieve "unreflective understanding" in thinking about a different culture. If "unreflective" means completely assimilated and internalized to the point of being unaware of the very rules of the language game, one may wonder how anyone can enter and participate in a different game in the first place. It would be nearly as impossible as knowing fish's happiness as a fish does. The desire to escape from one's own prejudice and to assume an alien point of view, as Bernstein notes, simply reenacts "a parallel move in nineteenth-century hermeneutics and historiography, where it was thought that we can somehow jump out of our skins, concepts, and prejudgments and grasp or know the phenomenon as it is in itself."[18] Georgia Warnke also sees a connection between Winch and romantic hermeneutics. "Does Winch suppose, as Dilthey does," Warnke asks, "that social scientists can simply leave their native languages behind them in learning a new one? Or, as in Gadamer's hermeneutics, are the two languages or sets of prejudices brought into relationship with one another and, if so, how?"[19] These are of course crucial hermeneutical questions that Winch's argument prompts us to consider, questions that are particularly relevant to the concept of cross-cultural understanding. It is perhaps

15. Ibid., p. 11.
16. Bernstein, *Beyond Objectivism and Relativism*, p. 27.
17. Winch, *The Idea of a Social Science and Its Relation to Philosophy*, p. 89.
18. Bernstein, *Beyond Objectivism and Relativism*, p. 104.
19. Warnke, *Gadamer: Hermeneutics, Tradition and Reason*, p. 110.

to this relevance that Gerald Bruns alluded when he characterized Winch's works as "deeply involved with the subject of hermeneutics, that is, with its *Sache*—what hermeneutics is *about*."[20] Winch constantly calls our attention to the differences between cultures and languages, but the important hermeneutical question is: How does one achieve understanding beyond and in spite of those differences? His advice to assume a participant's "unreflective understanding," however, does not seem to offer a particularly helpful answer.

In his discussion of understanding alien societies, Winch is "mainly, though not exclusively, concerned about the nature of one man's understanding, in moral terms, of the lives and actions of *others*."[21] In his controversial "Understanding a Primitive Society," he explicitly states that he is trying "to suggest that the concept of *learning from* which is involved in the study of other cultures is closely linked with the concept of *wisdom*."[22] Here questions of hermeneutics become ethical questions as well, as one tries to understand an alien society in order to learn something from it, to expand one's vision, to get rid of one's ethnocentric prejudices, and to acquire moral knowledge about both the self and others. But understanding an alien society already presupposes a certain shared humanity rather than the insistence on difference, and adequate understanding does not entail abandoning one's own cultural values in order to become totally "unreflective" in one's own thinking. Understanding proves to be essential for the project of *Bildung* or self-cultivation, but such learning and self-cultivation can neither be a projection of the self onto the Other nor a complete self-effacement to become the Other: it can only be a moment of mutual illumination and enrichment in what Gadamer calls the fusion of horizons. And that, as I have argued elsewhere, is the only way to learn from different cultures and societies.[23]

The openness to the challenge of others and the fusion of horizons will establish understanding and moral knowledge beyond skepticism and relativism without claiming absolute truth. In fact, it is often the cultural relativist that shows "a deep attachment to metaphysical realism itself," because the relativist argument usually proceeds in a specious line of All-or-Nothing: "First, an impossible demand is made, say, for unmediated

20. Bruns, *Hermeneutics Ancient and Modern*, p. 8.
21. Winch, *Ethics and Action*, p. 2.
22. Ibid., p. 42.
23. See Zhang Longxi, "The Myth of the Other: China in the Eyes of the West," *Critical Inquiry* 15 (Autumn 1988): 108–31. An expanded version appears as chapter 1 of my book, *Mighty Opposites: From Dichotomies to Differences in the Comparative Study of China*.

presentness to reality as it is in itself or for an actual universal agreement about matters of value. Next, it is claimed that this demand cannot be met. Then, without any further ado," as Martha Nussbaum shows in a cogent analysis, the relativist "concludes that everything is up for grabs and there are no norms to give us guidance in matters of evaluation."[24] What Nussbaum proposes as an alternative, or what she calls Aristotelian essentialism, is a list of basic human functioning capabilities that constitute the basis of a notion of goodness in human life without pretending to be either absolute or exhaustively universal. That is also essentially Bernstein's point in arguing for the necessity to break away from the dichotomy of either/or thinking and to move beyond objectivism and relativism.

Insofar as ethics is concerned, one may wonder whether the recognition of cultural difference and its corollary, the relativist attitude, are necessarily tied to a morally superior position whereby one becomes a better person who is more sympathetic to others and has a greater respect for cultural heterogeneity. Conversely, one may wonder whether beliefs in any type of universal rights and values are necessarily related to ethnocentrism and cultural imperialism? If we go back to my earlier suggestion that Zhuangzi seems to resemble the universalist in assuming the possibility of common knowledge beyond fundamental differences, his universalism certainly has nothing to do with the universalism tainted by Western colonialism or imperialism, since Zhuangzi's argument for the commonality of knowledge is based on an egalitarian rather than a supremacist point of view. Indeed, from the perspective informed by Zhuangzi's insights, I will argue that the belief in the possibility of common knowledge and cross-cultural understanding, in the availability of conceptual tools for the interpretation of human behavior across the boundaries of language, geography, culture, and time, can indeed come from a genuine appreciation of the *equal capabilities* of different individuals, peoples, and nations. In other words, a universalist position, like the one grounded in the belief—like Zhuangzi's—in the fundamental equality of things, is not tied to colonialism or ethnocentrism. On the other hand, it is entirely possible and perfectly logical for cultural supremacists to take a relativist position in order precisely to emphasize cultural difference and to insist on the superiority and correctness of their own values over those of others.

We can find an illuminating example in the so-called Chinese rites controversy which marked an early cultural conflict between the East and the

24. Nussbaum, "Human Functioning and Social Justice: In Defense of Aristotelian Essentialism," *Political Theory* 20 (May 1992): 213, 209.

West in the seventeenth century and the first half of the eighteenth, and in which the Catholic Church, its popes and missionaries, the monarchs of Europe, the emperors of China, as well as some leading philosophers of the time, notably Voltaire and Leibniz, were all involved. The rites controversy, as George Minamiki reminds us, has two related aspects. One concerns "the problem of how Western man was to translate into the Chinese language the concepts of the divinity and other spiritual realities" (i.e., the issue of terminology), while the other concerns the problem of "how he was to judge, on a moral basis, the ceremonies performed by the Chinese in honor of Confucius and their ancestors" (i.e., the issue of rites proper). What the controversy exposes are problems in "the whole field of cross-cultural understanding and missionary accommodation."[25]

Insofar as the terminology issue was concerned, the debate arose among the missionaries from a profound difference in opinion with regard to the nature of Chinese language and thinking. Matteo Ricci (1552–1610), the famous Jesuit missionary and head of the China mission, learned the Chinese language and spread the idea that there were "traces of Christianity" in Chinese culture and customs, including "evidences of the cross among the Chinese."[26] He found in ancient Chinese writing the ideas of *tian* (Heaven), *zhu* (Lord), and *shangdi* (Lord on High), and made use of these terms to translate the Christian God. Of the word *tianzhu* (Lord of Heaven) for translating God, Ricci says that the missionaries "could hardly have chosen a more appropriate expression."[27] Obviously he had no doubt about the possibility of translating concepts and terms of Christianity into Chinese, and in *Tianzhu shiyi* [The True Meaning of the Lord of Heaven], his treatise on the Christian doctrine written in Chinese and published in 1604, Ricci tried to present Western religious content in a Chinese garb as elegant as possible. The book "consisted entirely of arguments drawn from the natural light of reason, rather than such as are based upon the authority of Holy Scripture," and it "contained citations serving its purpose and taken from the ancient Chinese writers; passages which were not merely ornamental, but served to promote the acceptance of this work by the inquiring readers of other Chinese books."[28] Here we see Ricci playing the language game according to its rules, but he is by no means unreflective in using an alien language to serve his own purpose, for he does so in order to

25. Minamiki, *The Chinese Rites Controversy*, p. ix. For a recent study of the Rites Controversy that includes detailed discussion of many Chinese documents, see Li Tiangang, *Zhongguo liyi zhi zheng.*

26. Ricci, *The Journals of Matthew Ricci*, pp. 110, 111.

27. Ibid., p. 154.

28. Ibid., p. 448.

win over some high officials at the court of the Chinese emperor and to work toward the eventual Christian conversion of China.

"Ricci's plan for the conversion of the Chinese," as Haun Saussy comments, "involved appropriating the language of the canonical books and official Confucianism to give Catholicism the vocabulary, and incidentally the prestige, it lacked. Converting the Chinese required, as a first step, converting the Classics."[29] For that conversion, linguistic and cultural differences were not of primary interest except as obstacles to be overcome, for Ricci was much more intent on seeing the Chinese as potential fellow Christians and the Chinese language and culture as somehow compatible with the Christian doctrine. His strategy to appropriate the Chinese classics is to argue that they contain the divine revelation of natural religion, which had prepared the Chinese to receive the light of revealed religion.[30] In reading the Confucian classics as compatible with Christianity, the Jesuit Fathers gave the Chinese canonical texts a typological interpretation that separated them from their native context and presented them as shadows and prefigurations of the spiritual reality of Christ and his teachings. Lionel Jensen argues that "Confucius" is not a simple translation of the name of the great Chinese philosopher but a Jesuit invention, "a spiritual confrere who alone among the Chinese had preached an ancient gospel of monotheism now forgotten." Such appropriation of Confucianism and the Chinese classics enabled the missionaries to overcome the cultural strangeness they encountered in late Ming China and, more significantly, "to represent themselves to the natives as the orthodox bearers of the native Chinese tradition, *ru.*"[31]

Filtered through Jesuit interpretation, Confucian moral and political philosophy had a notable impact on the European imagination, and the idea that the Chinese had achieved perfection in natural religion became especially appealing to many philosophers. By the end of the seventeenth century, as Arthur Lovejoy remarks, "it had come to be widely accepted that the Chinese—by the light of nature alone—had surpassed Christian Europe both in the art of government and in ethics."[32] In his enthusiastic

29. Saussy, *The Problem of a Chinese Aesthetic*, p. 36.
30. This view is well reflected in Nicola Trigault's "To the Reader," written in 1615 when he translated Ricci's diary from Italian into Latin and published it in Rome. If he could go back to China and have enough time, says Trigault, he would write about the Chinese and compose "the Code of Chinese Ethics, so that one may understand how well adapted is the spirit of this people for the reception of the Christian faith, seeing that they argue so aptly on questions of morality." Ricci, *The Journals of Matthew Ricci*, p. xv.
31. Jensen, "The Invention of 'Confucius' and His Chinese Other, 'Kong Fuzi,'" *Positions* 1 (Fall 1993): 415. The argument is fully developed in Jensen, *Manufacturing Confucianism*.
32. Lovejoy, "The Chinese Origin of a Romanticism," in *Essays in the History of Ideas*, p. 105.

desire for Europe and China to learn from each other, Leibniz held that "it would appear almost necessary that Chinese missionaries should be sent to us to teach us the use and practice of natural religion (*theologia naturalis*), just as we send missionaries to them to teach them revealed religion."[33] Voltaire's admiration of Confucius was boundless and, in the words of Adolf Reichwein, this Chinese philosopher "became the patron saint of eighteenth-century Enlightenment."[34] Such widespread enthusiasm for a pagan culture, however, was bound to alarm the doctrinal purists in the Catholic Church. Ricci's belief in a common understanding of the concept of the divinity, the idea of the true God shared by peoples in China and the West, soon became the target of severe criticism after his death; it was contested by his opponents as the focus in the rites controversy, and finally condemned in the official decrees issued by several popes from Clement XI in 1704 to Benedict XIV in 1742.

The cultural conflict between the East and the West came to a head in the rites controversy, in which the Catholic Church reasserted the spiritual exclusiveness of the Christian faith and the fundamental cultural difference between Christianity and pagan Chinese culture. Whether the Chinese and the Europeans could possibly have the same idea of God and other spiritual realities across linguistic and cultural differences can be recast as the basic question of translatability, and it is the doctrinal purist's position in the Church that the Chinese language, being a language of matter and mundane concerns, cannot possibly express the spiritual concepts and values of Christianity. The use of the Chinese expression of *shangdi* (Sovereign on High) to mean God and the word *tian* to refer to Heaven were officially condemned by Clement XI in 1704 and again in 1715. Of course, the problem of terminology did not just bewilder the Catholic missionaries alone in their effort to convey Christian ideas in Chinese, for the Buddhist monks had encountered a similar problem earlier in history in translating their sutras from Sanskrit into Chinese, and the Protestant missionaries were again to face this question when they tried to put out their Chinese version of the Bible. The dilemma in translation, as Arthur F. Wright puts it, is a difficult and undesirable choice:

> Select, as equivalents for key terms, native terms which already enjoyed great prestige, and in so doing risk the obliteration of the distinctive meaning of the original concept; or select as equivalents terms which, when used in an explained technical sense, more adequately translate the

33. Leibniz, *Novissima sinica* (1699), preface; quoted in Lovejoy, p. 106.
34. Reichwein, *China and Europe*, p. 77.

meaning of the original, but at the cost of familiarity and prestige and at the risk of uncouthness.[35]

It seems that to translate is always to negotiate between such undesirable choices in the attempt to find conceptual and linguistic equivalents that are, unfortunately, never quite the same. The translation of terms turns out to be nothing more than a compromise reached at the end of this negotiating process, and it is consequently a makeshift, and unacceptable to the staunch purist, who demands nothing less than the unadulterated essence of the original. The frequent complaint is that the Chinese language, which is allegedly too concrete and this-worldly, cannot express the spiritual meanings of the religious concepts of Christianity. "Is there any convenient method of stating the doctrine of the Trinity which does not imply the grossest materialism?" asked one Protestant priest in despair. "Who has been fortunate enough to discover a name for sin which does not dash us on the Scylla of civil crime or engulf [*sic*] us in the Charybdis of retribution for the faults of a former life?"[36]

According to the purist argument, linguistic and cultural differences are so unbridgeable that foreign ideas, especially those of Western religious thinking that have been molded in a long history from the Hebrews and the Greeks to the modern Europeans, are all untranslatable. Not only that, they are simply inconceivable in the Chinese mind and unavailable to the Chinese language. That is roughly the argument Ricci's opponents advanced against his assimilation of Chinese views and terms in propagating Christianity through cultural accommodation. They complained that the Chinese men of letters converted by Ricci remained as Confucian as ever and had no real understanding of Christianity, that "where they appear to speak of our God and his Angels," as the Franciscan Father Antonio de Caballero remarks with obvious impatience and scorn, "they are merely aping the Truth."[37] Caballero's remark takes cultural difference as a matter of right or wrong, truth or deception, and his simian metaphor serves to expose the Chinese converts as fake Christians or inadequate imitators.[38] This should

35. Wright, "The Chinese Language and Foreign Ideas," *The American Anthropologist* 55, no. 5, pt. 2, memoir no. 75 (Dec. 1953): 289.
36. C. W. Mateer, "Lessons learned in translating the Bible into Mandarin," *Chinese Recorder* (November 1908): 608; quoted in ibid., p. 291.
37. Caballero, alias Sainte-Marie, *Traité sur quelques points importants de la mission de Chine* (Paris, 1701), p. 105; quoted in Gernet, *China and the Christian Impact*, p. 33.
38. According to Ernst Robert Curtius, the core of the metaphorical use of *simia* is the idea of bad imitation or pretentiousness. The ape metaphor "can be applied not only to persons but also to abstractions and artifacts which assume the appearance of being something they are not." Curtius, *European Literature and the Latin Middle Ages*, p. 539.

remind us of the ominous implications of the relativist position, the fact that when the cultural supremacists mark the fundamental difference and emphasize that they are different from the non-Western Other, they are in effect saying that they are better and superior, and that they are the original model distorted by inadequate imitations.

Judging from the tenacious grip of Confucianism on the Chinese mind in late imperial China and the negligible number of Chinese converts whom the missionaries succeeded in proselytizing, no one can overlook the enormous gap between Chinese and Western cultural traditions. In fact, the Jesuit approach of cultural accommodation was itself the outcome of a clear recognition of cultural differences, the realization that China was so far away and so different from Europe and had such a long history of its own civilization that it would be impossible to change the millions of Chinese into Portuguese or Italians. According to Bonnie Oh, the policy of cultural accommodation that Ricci implemented in China "took into consideration the high level of civilization in the Asian countries, recognized the futility of trying to make Westerners out of Asians, and demonstrated a willingness to accommodate to the native culture."[39] The policy dictated that the Jesuit missionaries "speak, read, and write the native languages; become an integral part of a particular civilization and behave like the natives of the country"; in short, as Joseph Sebes puts it pointedly, "Become Chinese to win China for Christ."[40] The last clause makes it clear that the Jesuit policy of cultural accommodation was ultimately dictated by their religious agenda of the Christian conversion of China, but that does not change the fact that accommodation was based on the recognition of cultural difference, nor does it rule out the possibility that the Jesuit acculturation might have consequences detrimental to their original agenda or motivation, as the Vatican seemed so to believe.

If their accommodation to Chinese culture and customs was the result of a clear sense of cultural difference, then Ricci and his supporters should perhaps be characterized, in the sense as Buck has defined, as relativist rather than universalist, but such a characterization would contradict Ricci's belief in the translatability of Western concepts and ideas into Chinese, the possibility of shared understanding of the notion of God and other spiritual realities across the boundaries of language, geography, culture, and time. Such a contradiction does not so much reveal a problem with Jesuit accommodation as it shows the limitation and inadequacy of terms like relativism

---

39. Oh, introduction, *East Meets West: The Jesuits in China*, ed. Ronan and Oh, pp. xix–xx.

40. Joseph Sebes, "The Precursors of Ricci," ibid., p. 23.

and universalism used in cross-cultural studies, especially when certain values are attached to these terms. Relativism, the emphasis on cultural differences between the West and the non-West, may indeed suggest an open-minded acceptance of the values of an alien culture, the willingness to see the positive in what is different from one's own tradition. There is, however, nothing inherently benign about a relativist attitude; moreover, as the purist argument in the Chinese rites controversy shows, it is just as possible that the relativist emphasis on difference may serve to legitimize a position of cultural supremacy.

For a doctrinaire like Caballero, cultural difference, the difference between true faith and its poor imitation, is as categorical as the difference between humans and apes, and his metaphor recalls Huizi's assurance of the distinction between man and fish. In this connection, then, we may raise the same question to the relativist as Zhuangzi did: "How do you know that I do not know about fish's happiness?" To put it in a way more relevant to our concerns, how do you know that I do not know about another culture and its concepts? On what basis can you claim to have knowledge about me, but at the same time deny me the possibility of knowing? Put in such terms, the question may help us realize that the purist or the skeptic, far from being a humble and unassuming relativist with a great deal of respect for the alien and the culturally different, assumes a great deal of knowledge about both the self and others, despite the relativist claim that it is impossible to know the others. "Skepticism," as Saussy argues, "requires making even stronger epistemic claims than does naïveté. It requires that the naïve claims be testable, and that itself be capable of doing the testing."[41] Implicit in such skepticism is an unmistakable sense of superiority, even arrogance, a sense that only the skeptic knows both the East and the West and knows them to be fundamentally different and incommensurate.

To recast the question again in terms of translatability, the problem is not whether a particular translation is adequate or not, but whether translation can be accomplished at all. Even if Ricci's use of *tianzhu* or *shangdi* as equivalent Chinese terms for God were bad translations, does that mean that the very idea of God or divinity is inconceivable in the Chinese mind and inexpressible in the Chinese language? Here I am concerned not with vindicating Ricci's choice of terms, but with the implications of the question of translatability. With all sorts of associated connotations embedded in the nexus of Chinese words, *tianzhu*, *shangdi*, or *shen* (spirit, deity, divinity), cannot be strictly *identical* with the word God, but if we

41. Saussy, *The Problem of a Chinese Aesthetic*, p. 10.

are talking about cross-cultural understanding at all, we are talking about the *equivalent*, not the identical. What is identical, anyway? If one cannot step into the same river twice, as the ancient Greeks knew, if we realize that all things exist in a state of flux in temporal as well as in spatial terms, can we still speak of a river as the same river, that is, identical with itself? Obviously not, and yet we speak of the "same river" in the sense of close equivalence or what Saussure calls "synchronic identity" as opposed to real identity.[42] Linguistic and cultural differences between China and the West are obvious, that is, in the etymological sense of "standing in the way" (*ob viam*) like obstacles, and it is the task of translation to clear the way for understanding and communication by discovering equivalent formulations underneath the changing surface of differences. If we insist on complete and absolute identity, then nothing can be translated, and the demand for an unadulterated original essence would preclude translation. From the purist and dogmatic point of view, the only language capable of expressing Christian ideas, insofar as the expression of spiritual meaning is concerned, is a Western language.

But what about the difference among the various Western languages themselves? Is the English word God always exactly identical with the Latin *Deus*? And do these words always precisely translate the Hebrew word *elohim*? If we go on asking, the question of translatability becomes more complicated and the answer less certain. The translation of the Bible into every modern language has never gone unchallenged for all sorts of reasons. William Tyndale had to defend his English translation in the early sixteenth century, and throughout the second half of that century the Catholic polemicists repeatedly accused Protestant translators of "including deliberately heretical mistranslations in their versions."[43] Pushing its logic to the extreme, the purist position would do away with language altogether in order to preserve the concept of God as pure spirit. For a spiritualist theologian, even the biblical Hebrew may appear too concrete, too bound up with the literal sense of the physical world, and filled with too much anthropomorphism to express the pure idea of an abstract God.[44]

---

42. Saussure's notion of "synchronic identity" is in effect equi-valence, that is, equal values to satisfy certain requirements. These are Saussure's examples: "we speak of the identity of two '8:25 P.M. Geneva-to-Paris' trains that leave at twenty-four hour intervals. We feel that it is the same train each day, yet everything—the locomotive, coaches, personnel—is probably different. Or if a street is demolished, then rebuilt, we say that it is the same street even though in a material sense, perhaps nothing of the old one remains." Saussure, *Course in General Linguistics*, p. 108.

43. Gerald Hammond, "English Translations of the Bible," in *The Literary Guide to the Bible*, ed. Alter and Kermode, p. 651.

44. See ibid., p. 647.

As Antoine Berman observes, resistance to translation was first of all "of a religious and cultural order," and "ordered around *untranslatability as a value.*" Just as in the Jewish tradition it is believed that the oral Torah should not be translated into the written language, similarly "the sacred text should not be translated into other languages, lest it lose its 'sacred' character." This has tremendous influence in thinking about secular literature as well, because the rejection of translation, Berman goes on to say, "traverses the whole history of the West, with the dogma, never made explicit and continually refuted practically, of the untranslatability of poetry, without mentioning the famous 'prejudicial objection' against translation in general."[45] This seems to show that the prejudice against translation in the West has always been related to a religious and cultural notion of abstract concepts and transcendental values, the purist notion of untranslatable spiritual essence. One can well imagine how much greater the resistance would be to a translation that attempts to bridge over the cultural gaps between the East and the West, and how much more difficult it would be to answer the question with any assurance, that is, can the Chinese language express abstract, spiritual notions?

The answer to the above question may of course come from all directions, and a negative answer does not necessarily indicate a supremacist attitude. As a Sinologist, Wright recognizes translation as always a compromise and finds the purist view impractical, but in his discussion of the difficulties of translation, he finally agrees with those grumbling missionaries in seeing Western concepts as impossible to translate into Chinese, because "the Chinese was relatively poor in resources for expressing abstractions and general classes or qualities. 'Truth' tended to develop into 'something that is true.' 'Man' tended to be understood as 'the people'—general but not abstract. 'Hope' was difficult to abstract from a series of expectations directed toward specific objects."[46] Here the cultural difference between the Chinese and the Western is formulated as fundamentally distinct ways of thinking and speaking, as the ability, or lack of it, to express abstract ideas.

Jacques Gernet even more straightforwardly endorsed the Catholic purist view, especially that of Longobardi, whose work he considers to be "most interesting for the history of Chinese reactions to Christian theses." In his discussion of the conflict between Christianity and Chinese culture, Gernet traces all the difficulties the missionaries encountered in China to a fundamental difference, "not only of different intellectual traditions but also of different mental categories and modes of thought." In Chinese, he

45. Berman, *The Experience of the Foreign,* p. 187.
46. Wright, "The Chinese Language and Foreign Ideas," p. 287.

declares, it is "so difficult to express how the abstract and the general differ fundamentally, and not just occasionally, from the concrete and the particular. This was an embarrassment for all those who had, in the course of history, attempted to translate into Chinese concepts formed in inflected languages such as Greek, Latin, or Sanskrit. Thus, linguistic structures inevitably pose the question of modes of thought." This statement flies in the face of all Chinese translations of Buddhist sutras in the past and of Western works in more recent times, but for Gernet probably all Chinese translations are nothing more than embarrassing corruption of the original Indo-European ideas. With the assurance of an expert, Gernet asserts that the Chinese language "has the peculiar, distinctive feature of possessing no grammatical categories systematically differentiated by morphology. . . . Furthermore, there was no word to denote existence in Chinese, nothing to convey the concept of being or essence, which in Greek is so conveniently expressed by the noun *ousia* or the neuter *to on*. Consequently, the notion of being, in the sense of an eternal and constant reality, above and beyond that which is phenomenal, was perhaps more difficult to conceive, for a Chinese."[47] In such a formulation, the Chinese language appears to be a language of concrete things and specific objects, a language bogged down in matter and unable to rise above the ground of materiality and literality toward any spiritual height. The judgment is thus not on Chinese translation of particular foreign words and concepts, but on the very nature and ability of the Chinese language as a whole. Given the fact that the relativist views, as Buck observes, are "advanced with much more frequency among Asianists" than universalist ones, it is not surprising that such a view of a concrete and material Chinese language has gained some currency in the circle of sinological studies.[48] A great deal of emphasis has been laid on the cultural difference between China and the West, and the formulation of that difference in terms of a contrast between the concrete and the abstract finds an elaborate counterpart in the study of Chinese literature.

Nature, Writing, and Chinese Poetry

If the Chinese language is not capable of, or relatively poor in, expressing abstract ideas through the medium of linguistic signs and verbal images,

---

47. Gernet, *China and the Christian Impact*, pp. 9, 3, 239, 241.

48. Buck, "Forum on Universalism and Relativism in Asian Studies," p. 32. For recent works that present views more or less similar to Wright's, see Hansen, *Language and Logic in Ancient China*, and Hall and Ames, *Thinking Through Confucius* and a number of other works. For a critique and a different view of the Chinese language, see Graham, "The Relation of Chinese Thought to the Chinese Language," appendix 2, *Disputers of the Tao*, pp. 389–428.

the inevitable inference would be that all it could do is to signify exactly what the signifier refers to, that is, to mean what the word literally says without pointing beyond the literal sense to another level of meaning, either the abstract or the spiritual and transcendental. From this basic assumption follow a number of significant consequences that have exerted a strong influence on Chinese literature studies in the West and have helped shape a notion of that literature as something fundamentally different from what is usually understood as imaginative or fictional creations. Transcendence presupposes distance or difference, and the alleged lack of transcendence in Chinese literature is said to be the result of a primordial continuum of all the phenomena in the natural cosmos, of which Chinese writing or literature is conceived as an integral part rather than a separate and arbitrary human creation trying to represent or imitate nature from the outside at an ontological and aesthetic distance. This is basically how Stephen Owen, for example, interprets the relation between literature and the world in the Chinese tradition. "The term which situates literature in this orderly cosmos is *wen*," says Owen in his exposition of traditional Chinese poetry and poetics.[49] Elaborating on the opening remarks of an early work in Chinese criticism, Liu Xie's (465?-522) *Literary Mind or the Carving of Dragons*, Owen explains that *wen* or "aesthetic pattern" is the ultimate realization or "entelechy" through which the natural order of things becomes visible and known:

> All phenomena have an inherent tendency to become manifest in *wen*, and their manifestation is for the sake of being known and felt; only the human mind is capable of itself knowing and feeling, and of that process, literature is the outward manifest form. Literature thus stands as the entelechy, the fully realized form, of a universal process of manifestation. . . . Insofar as the visual arts merely imitate nature's *wen*, they are subject to the Platonic critique of art as a secondary (or tertiary) phenomenon. But in this formulation literature is not truly mimetic: rather it is the final stage in a process of manifestation; and the writer, instead of "re-presenting" the outer world, is in fact only the medium for this last phase of the world's coming-to-be.[50]

In this formulation, *wen* as writing and literature is not a human invention to imitate nature, but is part of nature or the natural cosmos itself. Differentiated from Western literature as mimesis or representation, Chinese literature becomes the end product of a natural process of manifestation, the form in which elements of the world come together and

49. Owen, *Traditional Chinese Poetry and Poetics*, p. 18.
50. Ibid., p. 20.

become known and visible in a manner as natural, perhaps one might say, as the crystallization of water into ice. As "the medium for this last phase of the world's coming-to-be," the Chinese poet becomes a vehicle or channel through which nature or the world arrives at its manifestation as *wen* or "aesthetic pattern." Now, does this suggest that the Chinese poet, like Ion in Plato's description, becomes the mouthpiece of some sort of a higher authority that constitutes the real source of poetry? Not so, according to Owen, who puts the Chinese poet and poetry in contradis-tinction to their Greek counterparts. If in the Platonic dialogue poetic inspiration comes from gods higher than man and nature, in the Chinese case poetry issues from nature itself, as a natural product. Not only is a literary text naturally formed without the poet's conscious effort, but the Chinese written language, says Owen, the very linguistic constituent of a Chinese text, "is itself natural."[51] While the Western poet creates, in imi-tation of God the first Maker, a fictional world *ex nihilo*, the Chinese poet only "participates in the nature that is," and is concerned not with making up something beautiful yet untrue, but "with the authentic presentation of 'what is,' either interior experience or exterior percept." The Chinese poem thus presents an "uncreated world," and the Chinese poet, follow-ing the example of Confucius, "transmits but does not create."[52]

Perhaps Owen meant to pinpoint the essential difference between Chinese poetry and its Western counterpart, between experiences of reading these two kinds of poetry; or perhaps he was reacting to the kind of sweeping generalizations of certain structuralist criticism that made claims to universal applicability by imposing Western theoretical notions on non-Western literary works. Whatever his intention or motivation for stressing the fundamental cultural differences, he has clearly put Chinese *wen* and Western literature in an untenable opposition, a dichotomy between natural manifestation and human creation. In that conceptual-ization, writing a Chinese poem is almost a natural and certainly imper-sonal process in which the poet hardly plays any creative role, but a role of channeling, a "medium," or that of a scribe who records what is hap-pening right there and then.

We find a similar argument in Pauline Yu's work on reading Chinese poetic imagery. Differentiated from Western literature as imitation of an action, Chinese poetry is understood as "a *literal reaction* of the poet to the world around him and of which he is an integral part." The Chinese poet does not recognize the "disjunctures between true reality and concrete

51. Ibid.
52. Ibid., p. 84; quoting Confucius, *Lunyu*, vii.1.

reality, nor between concrete reality and literary work, gaps which may have provoked censure in some quarters but which also establish the possibility of poiesis, fictionality, and the poet's duplication of his 'heavenly Maker's' creative act."[53] In this view, Chinese culture neither has nor recognizes "disjunctures" and "fundamental ontological dualism," and out of such a tradition Chinese poetry is generated as something seamlessly connected with the real world.

Again, the emphasis on the impersonality and literalness of Chinese poetry purports to reveal the distinct features of Chinese poetry as essentially different from Western literature, but the "fundamental ontological dualism" in this formulation cannot but help reminding us of similar dualistic formulations of cultural difference between China and the West that we have seen in the historical past. How close this sounds to the Christian purist point of view can be seen in Father Niccolò Longobardi's remark that "the Chinese have never known any spiritual substance distinct from matter"[54] and in Gernet's elaboration on the same point that "Chinese thought never had separated the sensible from the rational, never had imagined any 'spiritual substance distinct from the material,' never had conceived of the existence of a world of eternal truths separated from this world of appearances and transitory realities."[55] Here the contrasts between China and the West are similarly predicated on a simplistic notion of Platonic dualism of true and concrete reality, or transcendence and immanence. But if Chinese poetry in such a characterization is exempted from the kind of Platonic critique and censure for being thrice removed from truth, it must also forfeit the claim to poiesis, fictionality, and imaginative creation.

Once the Chinese tradition is seen as radically monistic, and language is seen as inseparable from that which language refers to, then metaphor, fictionality, and above all allegory—the essential features of Western literature—all become quite impossible. How can a Chinese poet create anything fictional and allegorical, anything unreal and distanced from nature, when the Chinese language or *wen* is itself natural? In this "monistic" argument, Chinese poems are "literal responses" to the real world, and their meanings are embedded in the here and now, not pointing to a transcendental or allegorical "Something Else." Owen postulates the following as the first of a number of "propositions" concerning Chinese literature:

53. Yu, *The Reading of Imagery*, p. 35.
54. Longobardi, *Traité sur quelques points de la religion des Chinois* (Paris, 1701), title of section 10, quoted in Gernet, *China and the Christian Impact*, p. 203.
55. Gernet, p. 201.

In the Chinese literary tradition, a poem is usually presumed to be non-fictional: its statements are taken as strictly true. Meaning is not discovered by a metaphorical operation in which the words of the text point to Something Else. Instead, the empirical world signifies for the poet, and the poem makes that event manifest.[56]

Such a proposition has some remarkable implications for practical criticism as Owen has laid out in a methodical contrast of generic expectations between a Western reader's experience with a poem by Wordsworth and a Chinese reader's with a poem by the great Tang poet Du Fu (712–770). Wordsworth writes in a famous sonnet:

> Earth has not anything to show more fair:
> Dull would he be of soul who could pass by
> A sight so touching in its majesty:
> This City now doth, like a garment wear
> The beauty of the morning; . . .

Owen argues that however concretely Wordsworth might portray the view of London seen, as the poet told us, from Westminster Bridge at dawn on September 3, 1802, it is quite inconsequential whether or not he was in fact writing about what he saw at the particular time and place as he specified. "The words of the poem are not directed to a historical London in its infinite particularity," says Owen, but they "lead you to something else, to some significance in which the number of vessels on the Thames is utterly irrelevant."[57] The Western poet is concerned not so much with the historical particularity as with a general meaning that transcends the historical, and the Western reader, cultivated in the same conventions, reads the poem as a fiction addressing something altogether different from London as real and historical presence.

According to Owen, the Chinese reader would adopt a totally different approach towards the poem by Du Fu when he wrote about a river scene flooded over by the moonlight, and compared the old and lonely poet to a solitary bird on the deserted river bank:

> Wind-tossed, fluttering—what is my likeness?
> In Heaven and Earth, a single gull of the sands.

---

56. Owen, *Traditional Chinese Poetry and Poetics,* p. 34. While insisting on the nonfictionality of *shi* or Chinese poetry, Owen does allow a certain degree of metaphoricity or fictionality in some subgenres, especially *yuefu* or songs collected by the official "music bureau." See ibid., p. 53, and a long explanatory note on pp. 292–93.

57. Ibid., p. 14.

This poem, says Owen, "is not a fiction: it is a unique, factual account of an experience in historical time, a human consciousness encountering, interpreting, and responding to the world."[58] The cultural differences between the Chinese and the Western traditions, as the example is intended to show, become manifest in a set of contrasts or dichotomies: Western fictionality versus Chinese factuality, Western creativity versus Chinese naturalness, Western concerns of the general versus Chinese concerns of the particular, Western metaphorical and transcendental meaning versus Chinese literal and historical sense, and so on and so forth. The historical context and the motivation for emphasizing cultural differences have undoubtedly changed since the time of Matteo Ricci, and whatever is now recognized as distinctly Chinese is often appreciated as something unique and valuable precisely because it is non-Western, but still, and perhaps in unexpected ways, the dichotomies and contrasts of Chinese and Western cultural values cannot but remind us of the purist argument advanced in the seventeenth-century rites controversy, especially since the dichotomies today are still predicated on the basic distinction between nature and culture, particularity and generality, the concrete and the abstract, etc. These dichotomies, as Saussy remarks, indicate "a new version, a translation into literary-critical language, of a quarrel as old as the missionary beginnings of European sinology." By setting up similar dichotomies in their effort to emphasize cultural differences, the Catholic purists seemed to have "anticipated the terms of the literary discussion we had before us a moment ago."[59]

To see *wen* or the Chinese written language as "natural" is indeed one of the entrenched misconceptions in the West, an old misconception that began with the missionary beginnings of European sinology, but one that most Sinologists today do not take very seriously. It is Ernest Fenollosa with his amateurish and speculative essay, edited and published by Ezra Pound as *The Chinese Written Character as a Medium for Poetry*, that has given this curious view its undoubtedly most well-known exposition. In that essay, Fenollosa celebrates the concrete materiality of Chinese writing and its power to evoke images of the natural world, a kind of pictorial writing which, as a medium for poetry, he believes to be superior to the abstract Western alphabetic writing. Chinese poetry written in characters presents "shorthand pictures of the operations of nature," says Fenollosa, and in reading such pictographic characters, "we do not seem to be juggling mental counters, but to be watching *things* work out their own

---

58. Ibid., p. 15.
59. Saussy, *The Problem of a Chinese Aesthetic*, pp. 36, 39.

fate."[60] These memorable words effectively express the idea that Western writing is abstract and created arbitrarily in the human mind, whereas Chinese writing is all natural, made of *things* themselves.

Through Pound and his imagistic poetics, Fenollosa's view of the Chinese written language made a distinct impact on much of modern English and American poetry. Reading Fenollosa's essay and reworking his translation of some Chinese poems, Pound realized the implications of Chinese writing for an innovative poetic method. As Laszlo Géfin observes, Fenollosa's essay laid the basis of a new aesthetics, what Pound called an ideogrammic method: "the juxtaposition of seemingly unrelated particulars capable of suggesting ideas and concepts through their relation."[61] David Perkins captures the effect of Fenollosa's essay on Pound in an excellent brief description:

> The Chinese written language, it appeared, was undeviatingly concrete. Every word was an image; the line was a succession of images. Pound must have wondered how he might achieve an equivalent in English. The Chinese poetic line presented images without syntactical directions. Fenollosa's manuscript "Essay on the Chinese Written Character" pointed out that nature itself is without grammar or syntax, so Chinese poetry may be said to come upon the mind as nature does. However the method might be explained, it was a succession of images without the less active, more abstract parts of language that ordinarily connect and interpret them and it afforded speed, suggestiveness, and economy.[62]

The emphasis falls again on the concreteness and naturalness of Chinese writing, on its eschewal of the abstract logic of grammar or syntax for achieving a completely natural effect, which is, so Fenollosa and Pound argued, precisely what poetry should be doing. Insofar as Chinese characters are concerned, Fenollosa and Pound have certainly misunderstood how they actually function, but that, as Géfin argues, is "perhaps the most fruitful misunderstanding in English literature."[63] Of course, the significance of Pound in modern poetry cannot be doubted, and it would be pedantic and pointless to criticize the ideogrammic method on sinological grounds. What I want to show here is not that Fenollosa and Pound have misunderstood Chinese, but that their misunderstanding reflects more than just an amateurish view, that it resulted from a projection of their own desire onto the Chinese language and poetry, and that

60. Fenollosa, *The Chinese Written Character*, pp. 8, 9.
61. Géfin, *Ideogram: History of a Poetic Method*, p. 27.
62. Perkins, *A History of Modern Poetry*, p. 463.
63. Géfin, *Ideogram: History of a Poetic Method*, p. 31.

to see Chinese writing as concrete and natural is a Western illusion and poetic idealization. The charm of Pound's *Cathay*, as George Steiner argues, lies in the fact that it matches and confirms powerful European anticipations of what China looks like in the Western eye, what Hugh Kenner calls a Western "invention of China." Pound is successful in creating the charm of his *Cathay* "not because he or his reader knows so much but because both concur in knowing so little."[64]

In attributing to Chinese characters the power to reveal the mysteries of nature and art, Fenollosa and Pound stand in a long critical genealogy in the Western tradition. As Hwa Yol Jung observes, Fenollosa came from the literary environment of the "American Renaissance" and was especially under the influence of Ralph Waldo Emerson. His fascination with Chinese writing is thus "comparable to Emerson's enchantment with Egyptian hieroglyphics: they all are the 'emblems' of nature beyond whose visual veil there are inscrutable 'golden secrets' which are not readily decipherable to ordinary people."[65] Several centuries earlier, Matteo Ricci had already noted that the Chinese "employ ideographs resembling the hieroglyphic figures of the ancient Egyptians."[66] To see Chinese characters as hieroglyphs seems rather common in the West. Giambattista Vico, for example, remarks that the Chinese "are found writing in hieroglyphs just as the ancient Egyptians did."[67] Ernst Robert Curtius told us that the fascination with hieroglyphics, with emblems and *impresas*, or "pictures without words," has continually occupied the minds of Western humanists since the beginning of the fifteenth century.[68]

Yet no one in modern times knew how to read hieroglyphs until the 1820s when Jean-François Champollion deciphered Egyptian hieroglyphic writing with the help of the bilingual text of the Rosetta stone. Champollion's works marked the beginning of modern Egyptology and made a strong impression on Emerson and his contemporaries, but as John Irwin argues, they did not put an end to centuries of fanciful misreading of the hieroglyphs. For all their scientific force to demystify ancient Egyptian writing, "Champollion's discoveries did not," says Irwin, "topple the metaphysical school of interpretation" which continued, from

64. Steiner, *After Babel*, p. 359. Fenollosa's reading of Chinese characters, Joseph Riddel also notes, is "a purely western idealization." Riddel, "'Neo-Nietzschean Clatter'—Speculation and/on Pound's Poetic Image," in *Ezra Pound: Tactics for Reading*, ed. Ian Bell, p. 211.

65. Hwa Yol Jung, "Misreading the Ideogram: From Fenollosa to Derrida and McLuhan," *Paideuma* 13 (Fall 1984): 212.

66. Ricci, *The Journals of Matthew Ricci*, p. 26.

67. Vico, *The New Science*, p. 32.

68. Curtius, *European Literature and the Latin Middle Ages*, p. 346.

a Christian perspective, to search for the prelapsarian language and read the hieroglyphics as "the language of nature, of natural signs—that world of objects created by God to stand as emblems of spiritual facts."[69] Influenced by Swedenborgian mysticism, Emerson's notion of the hieroglyphics definitely follows the metaphysical approach despite his profound interest in Champollion's works.

In his essays, Emerson remarks that the poet "shall use Nature as his hieroglyphic," and that Nature "offers all her creatures to him as a picture-language."[70] These ideas are evidently echoed in Fenollosa's essay on the Chinese characters, which Fenollosa at one point calls "visible hieroglyphics."[71] Egyptian hieroglyphs and Chinese characters are all "symbolic pictures" or, in Fenollosa's words, "shorthand pictures" of things in nature, and this notion of hieroglyphic writing can be traced back to the medieval symbolism that reads nature, as Hugh of St. Victor puts it, "like a book written by the finger of God."[72] In this connection, then, Fenollosa's fascination with Chinese characters as shorthand pictures can be related to the Christian tradition of allegorical reading that "sees the creation of the world as an establishment of a universal symbolic vocabulary."[73]

Thus from the Catholic purist in the seventeenth century to Fenollosa in the early twentieth, understanding of *wen* or Chinese writing as natural signs can be said to have come full circle, because the appreciation of the Chinese written language as shorthand pictures without grammar is only a small step away from the disparagement of Chinese as being devoid of logic and spirituality. In terms of argument, there is not much difference between Fenollosa's view and that of the Catholic purist; what is entirely different is their attitude, for while the purist despised Chinese for its

69. Irwin, *American Hieroglyphics*, pp. 6, 7. For an early argument that presents Chinese as the first or prelapsarian language of natural religion, see John Webb, *An Historical Essay Endeavoring a Probability That the Language of the Empire of China is the Primitive Language* (London: Printed for Nath. Brook, 1669), and my discussion in "The Myth of the Other."

70. Emerson, *The Complete Works*, ed. E. W. Emerson, 8:65; 3:13; quoted in Irwin, *American Hieroglyphics*, p. 11.

71. Fenollosa, *The Chinese Written Character*, p. 6.

72. Eco, *Art and Beauty in the Middle Ages*, p. 57. Curtius also emphasizes the medieval origin of this symbolic view: "It is a favorite cliché of the popular view of history that the Renaissance shook off the dust of yellowed parchment and began instead to read in the book of nature or the world. But this metaphor itself derives from the Latin Middle Ages," Curtius, *European Literature and the Latin Middle Ages*, p. 319. For the close relation between the metaphysical interpretation of the hieroglyphics and the idea of the book of nature, see also Irwin, *American Hieroglyphics*, pp. 20, 25, 28.

73. Fletcher, *Allegory*, p. 130. Fletcher further notes that "In the seventeenth century, when the meaning of Egyptian hieroglyphics became a much-bruited problem, there was a general adherence to this view that Nature constituted a universal vocabulary of symbols" (p. 130 n.105).

alleged lack of spirituality, Fenollosa admired Chinese for its supposedly hieroglyphic pictorialism.

Sinologists, of course, know better. James J. Y. Liu begins his concise and useful book, *The Art of Chinese Poetry*, by refuting Fenollosa's misconception that "*all* Chinese characters are pictograms or ideograms"; this, says Liu, is a "fallacy" and "seriously misleading." By expounding the six traditional principles for making Chinese characters, he shows that the majority of characters are not pictograms but "contain a phonetic element."[74] That is to say, to read Chinese characters as "shorthand pictures of the operations of nature" is only to misread them, and the presence of a phonetic element in the majority of Chinese characters immensely complicates matters to such a degree that it is no longer meaningful to talk about the difference between the Chinese and Western languages in terms of a neat contrast between natural and conventional signs, or nonphonetic and phonetic writings.

However, *The Art of Chinese Poetry* was first published in 1962, and in his last book twenty five years later, the author changed his mind and, like Owen, he cited Liu Xie to argue that "human *wen* ('writing' or 'literature') is a parallel to natural *wen* ('pattern' or 'configuration,' such as constellations, geographical formations, patterns on animal skins, etc.), both being manifestations of cosmic Dao." He now sees Chinese as fundamentally different from Western languages and commends Fenollosa and Pound for having "sensed intuitively that Chinese characters offered a possible alternative to Western logocentrism." Liu is clearly aware of the inconsistency in his assessment of Fenollosa and Pound, but he insists that his later argument "does not contradict" what he said in *The Art of Chinese Poetry;* it only represents "a shift of emphasis because of changed circumstances."[75] Indeed, this shift reflects the changed circumstances under which he wrote, circumstances that have been influenced by contemporary literary theory and especially deconstruction, given Jacques Derrida's view that the nonphonetic Chinese and Japanese scripts offer "the testimony of a powerful movement of civilization developing outside of all logocentrism," and his high praise of Fenollosa and Pound for accomplishing an irreducibly graphic poetics which was, "with that of Mallarmé, the first break in the most entrenched Western tradition."[76] When we recall David Buck's remarks on the current situation of Asian studies, we can see that these are the circumstances in which cultural relativism, with its emphasis

74. Liu, *The Art of Chinese Poetry*, pp. 3, 6.
75. Liu, *Language-Paradox-Poetics*, pp. 18, 20, 19.
76. Derrida, *Of Grammatology*, pp. 90, 92. For a critique of this view, see Zhang Longxi, *The Tao and the Logos*.

on difference and its doubt about cross-cultural understanding, has become the prevailing paradigm. That a sagacious scholar like James Liu was unable, despite his better knowledge, to resist the temptation of winning glory for Chinese writing as a symbol of *différance* testifies to the powerful influence of the relativist paradigm. As a system of natural signs made of things themselves, the peculiar *wen* or Chinese writing thus constitutes the culturally exotic Other vis-à-vis a conventional, abstract, phonocentric, and logocentric Western writing; it conveniently provides an imaginary ground for all sorts of dichotomies and contrasts in literary and cultural studies that establish entire cultures as self-contained entities—as sharply defined systems with unique and identifiable characteristics.

In *La valeur allusive*, a lengthy discussion of Chinese poetics, the French scholar, François Jullien, offers yet another example of the Western attempt at seeing Chinese literature as a specimen of what he calls *l'altérité interculturelle*, a cultural Other that stands for the opposite of Western tradition. Jullien advocates a "comparatism of difference," arguing that the point of departure of Western sinology, that of examining the Chinese tradition as the Other, is always to "return to the self," that is, to recognize the Western self by differentiating it from the Otherness of the Chinese, and to look at the self from a different angle, from, as it were, the outside. Although Western consciousness may be decentered in this *mise en perspective*, it will also be able to "take a new look at its own questions, its own traditions and its own motivations." Jullien goes on to declare: "The Western Sinologist can also be—quite legitimately—a discoverer of the West; and sinological knowledge would then serve him as a new *organon*." The aim of sinological studies is thus predetermined as the finding of difference, the confirmation of cultural uniqueness, and the highlighting of "intercultural alterity," which makes the Western self clearly recognizable and identifiable vis-à-vis the non-West.

In contrasting the Chinese notion of *wen* as natural sign with the Western notion of literature as the imitation of nature, Jullien also draws on Liu Xie's *Literary Mind* for sterling examples. According to Jullien, Liu Xie is able to integrate the advent of human writing and literature into the entire process of cosmic figuration or manifestation by taking advantage of the rich polysemy of the word *wen*, which does not designate an exclusively human design but shapes and patterns that first unfold in nature. In Liu Xie's discussion, Jullien goes on to say: "While the specificity of literary *wen* is fully affirmed, the relation of derivation between natural *wen* and human *wen* is very consciously elaborated, and thereby the effective complementarity that links the literary work with the beginning of the universe is able to take on its value." Here the emphasis on the connection between Chinese *wen* and the natural universe reminds us of the similar views we have discussed above. Comparing the Chinese *wen*, as Liu Xie expounded it, with the Greek concept of representation or mimesis, Jullien argues that each of these traditions comes to choose a different alternative. "Either it is poetry that 'imitates' nature (as in the case of the classical West) in a movement to 'return' to the world which is the opposite of the independent initiative of art (separated by its original action from the order of nature posited as object); or it is the order of nature that is already 'art' and thus constitutes a precedent with regard to the specific development of the literary text." In Chinese tradition, which makes the second choice here, the human and the natural integrate into a total vision of symbolic networks, and literary texts are not separated from the order of nature as original human creations. "The poem is already woven without the interference of human consciousness as subject; or rather, subjective consciousness is from the very start integrated into the process of mutual interactions that makes the whole of mundane realities alive and able to affect one another."[77] Similar to Owen's reading of Liu Xie, the upshot of Jullien's argument is also the claim that *wen* or Chinese literature is fundamentally different from Western mimesis, that it is not a human creation but an integral part of nature or a natural process of manifestation and that a Chinese poem already exists out there in nature, perhaps like a pebble or a shell on the seashore, which the Chinese poet can readily pick up without the interference of his or her subjective consciousness.

In several other books, Jullien continues the argument for China's radical cultural alterity. In *Detour and Access*, he reaffirms that because of its radical difference in language and history, "China presents a case study through which to contemplate Western thought from the outside—and, in this way, to bring us out of our atavism. I am not claiming," he goes on to add, "that China is totally foreign, but at least it is other." Jullien carefully examines the Chinese predilection for indirect expression, particularly the poetic device *xing*, which he calls the "incitatory" mode of expression. "In this mode," he says, "under the effects of emotion, the *here* of the word and the *there* of the meaning are farthest apart: because of the intensity of the motivation, the words produce an endless beyond, which is why this incitement is also allusive." Thus Jullien fully acknowledges that in Chinese literature and its reading, there is a separation of the word from its meaning, the text from its commentary, the language from its interpretation. Like Greek commentators on the Homeric epics,

77. Jullien, *La valeur allusive*, pp. 8, 35, 52, 65; see also pp. 11–12.

Chinese commentators on the *Book of Poetry* need to make use of such separation of text and meaning to justify the canonical status of some poems that seem to be indecent or licentious on the textual level.

Jullien, however, is quick to make a fundamental distinction between Greek allegorical interpretation and the Chinese commentary tradition. "Basically, Greek and Chinese commentators were faced with the same problem: how to justify a meaning that, because of an ideological shift, they judged literally insignificant if not unacceptable?" He then tries to find the difference between the Greek and the Chinese solutions to the same problem. "But whereas the Greeks sought to salvage this meaning by projecting it onto a spiritual plane, the Chinese saw a historical application in it." The argument here may remind us of the distinction made by Longobardi and others in the rites controversy as we have discussed above, for Jullien again makes the distinction in terms of matter and spirit, the concrete and the abstract, immanence and transcendence. As regards the Chinese separation of text and meaning, Jullien argues:

> True, the social and political world constitutes a reality of another order than that of the images in these poems, images that are most often borrowed from nature; but it does not stand on a different plane. It is just as concrete and particular as they, belonging to the same type of phenomena. As such, it is opposed to any idealized or spiritual world that might mirror the sentient world and transcend it by rising to the plane of absolute being or, at least, of an atemporal and essential generality. Between any natural scene and any situation of the human world, there can be transposition but not allegory. . . . In China, political and moral preoccupations blocked the path to the development of spiritual meaning; and the assignment of a particular reference diverted commentators from a symbolic construction.[78]

Jullien's more recent *Penser d'un Dehors (la Chine)* gives a comprehensive articulation to his views on a variety of topics related to China and Chinese culture. Written in the form of a series of answers to questions posed by Thierry Marchaisse, this book rehearses some of the old questions we find in the rites controversy, for instance, the "triple indifference of the Chinese toward Being, toward God, and toward freedom."[79] The very title of the book, *Penser d'un Dehors (la Chine)* or *Thinking from the Outside (China)*, already expresses Jullien's basic argument in a nutshell: that China, because of its remoteness from Europe geographically and culturally, offers a magic mirror for looking at the European self.

78. Jullien, *Detour and Access*, pp. 9, 155, 169, 173.
79. Jullien with Marchaisse, *Penser d'un Dehors*, p. 264.

"Indeed, if one wants to 'go beyond the Greek framework,' and if one searches for appropriate support and perspective," says Jullien, "then I don't see any voyage possible other than going 'to China,' as one used to say. This is, in effect, the only civilization that is recorded in substantial texts and whose linguistic and historical genealogy is radically non-European." Expanding on Foucault's idea of the Far East as non-Europe, Jullien declares that "strictly speaking, *non-Europe* is China, and it cannot be anything else."[80] From *La valeur allusive* to *Penser d'un Dehors (la Chine)*, then, Jullien has consistently argued for the fundamental incommensurability of Chinese and Western literatures and cultures, his argument being based on his understanding of the nature of *wen*, or the basic characteristics of Chinese language and literature.

But what is Chinese *wen*, and what are we to make of Liu Xie's comment on it in the beginning chapter of *The Literary Mind or the Carving of Dragons?*[81] Written more than fifteen hundred years ago (496–497), this treatise is deservedly famous as the first systematic study of all the different genres of ancient Chinese writing. In his effort to give writing as much prestige and importance as possible, Liu Xie takes full advantage of the polysemy of the word *wen* and relates literary writing to all sorts of patterns and configurations in the phenomenal world until writing as human invention becomes mysteriously connected with natural manifestations of the cosmic *tao*, the overarching principle and ultimate origin of all things. This is how Liu Xie's treatise begins:

> Great is the virtue of writing (*wen*)! Why do we say that it was born together with heaven and earth? The dark blue of heaven and the yellow of earth began the blending of all colors; their square and spheric forms started the differentiation of all shapes. Like a pair of holed disks of jade, the sun and the moon exhibit images attached to the sky; shining with splendor, mountains and rivers mark the contours of the ground. This is indeed the writing (*wen*) of *tao*. Looking upward, we see the radiance

---

80. Ibid., p. 39.

81. According to the first Chinese dictionary, *Shuowen jiezi*, completed by Xu Shen in the year 110, the basic meaning of *wen* 文 is a mark of crisscross strokes. Wang Jun (1784–1854), among many other philological commentators, further explains: "'Crisscross' refers to the lines that pass one another crosswise to make a drawing. In the 'appended words' to the *Book of Changes*, it is said that 'when things are mixed with one another, it is called *wen*.' To mix here means to crisscross" (Wang Jun, *Shuowen judou*, 2:1210). In later usage, however, the character 文 almost exclusively refers to writing or literary writing, while a homophone *wen* 紋 is used to signify pattern or design. For a brief discussion of the prehistory of Chinese writing, see K. C. Chang, *Art, Myth, and Ritual*, pp. 81–87. For a brief summary of the different meanings of *wen* in Chinese texts, see James Liu, *Chinese Theories of Literature*, pp. 7–9, 22–24.

above, and looking below, we detect the latent design; the high and the low take their proper positions, and thus the two Great Standards come to exist. To these only man, in whom inborn intelligence concentrates, can add to form the Three Origins. Man is the flower of the five elements and is indeed the mind of heaven and earth. When there is mind, speech is established, and when there is speech, writing takes a clear form. That is the way that nature is.[82]

The notion that heaven and earth, the high and the low, establish the two Great Standards and that man adds to them to form the Three Origins of the universe comes from commentaries that Confucian scholars of the Han dynasty made on the *Book of Changes*.[83] Drawing on such commentaries and merging *wen* as writing with *wen* as any kind of pattern, configuration, or any discernible shape and form in nature and things, Liu Xie's cosmology and his theory of the origination of literary writing, in the words of Wang Yuanhua in a study dedicated to Liu Xie's work, "assume an extremely confused form."[84] It is confused because Liu Xie has confounded culture with nature. But we can also say that the confusion is deliberate, because by giving writing a cosmic origin, he not only bestows on writing the borrowed authority of nature and expands the concept of writing to a grandiose proportion, but he also subsumes everything natural under the regulation and order of human invention, the *constructed* patterns and designs exemplified by the writings of the ancient sages and of Confucius himself. In his discussion of *tao*, he also mingles two different views, one from the *Laozi* that depicts *tao* as nonactive and running a natural course regardless of human concerns, and the other from commentaries on the *Book of Changes* that put a greater emphasis on the will of heaven and the agency of the sage through whose work of mediation the will of heaven is fulfilled.

In the fusion of the Taoism of Laozi and Zhuangzi with the Confucian ideas in the commentaries on the *Book of Changes*, Liu Xie is very much of a time that blends the authorities of these different views and traditions.

---

82. Zhou Zhenfu (annotator of Liu Xie), *Wenxin diaolong zhushi*, p. 1. Hereafter abbreviated as Liu Xie, *Wenxin diaolong*.

83. See the "appended phrases" and "explanation of trigrams" sections of the *Book of Changes*: "The being of *yi* comes from the Ultimate One, which generates the Two Standards." "The way to form heaven is to have the *yin* and the *yang*; the way to form earth is to have the soft and the hard; and the way to form man is to have benevolence and rightness. There must be the Three Origins and they must be doubled, so in the *Book of Changes* every hexagram is made of six lines" (*Zhouyi zhengyi*, 70a, 81c-82a, in Ruan Yuan [1764–1849], *Shisan jing zhushu*, 1:82, 93–94). For an English translation, see *The Classic of Changes*, trans. Richard John Lynn.

84. Wang Yuanhua, *Wenxin diaolong jiangshu*, p. 60.

Despite his long involvement with Buddhist ideas, Liu Xie's great work of criticism is allied to Confucianism, as many scholars have noted.[85] That is to say, Liu Xie's scale finally tilts toward human writing rather than natural pattern, and things in nature can be said to display recognizable patterns only because they intimate the meaning of the universe as a total order, as emanation from the great *tao*. Thus heaven and earth, mountains and rivers, animals and plants, the entire natural world, and all the things in it, become a gigantic text inscribed in naturally written characters.

If Liu Xie saw nature as generating writing and writing as the manifest form of nature, however, and if he read natural configurations as writing and elaborate patterns, does not his view to some extent lend itself to a comparison with the idea of "the book of nature" so often found in Western texts produced in medieval and Renaissance Europe? Curtius provides numerous examples and offers his illuminating commentaries on this poetic topos. Commenting on the Spanish dramatist and poet Calderón de la Barca, Curtius wrote that "Here too everything writes: the sun on cosmic space, the ship on the waves, the birds on the tablets of the winds, a shipwrecked man alternately on the blue paper of the sky and the sand of the sea. The rainbow is a stroke of the quill, sleep a written sketch, death the signature of life." The entire cosmos appears in Calderón as a book. "The vault of heaven is a bound book with eleven sapphire leaves (the spheres)."[86] If Curtius knew the work of the Chinese critic, he probably would not object to our adding a few more examples from Liu Xie. "Animals and plants all display *wen*," says Liu. "The dragon and the phoenix present good omen with their elaborate design, the tiger and the leopard show the beauty of composition in their bright pelage, clouds and the light at dawn apply colors more subtly than does a master painter, and trees and flowers bring forth the splendor of florescence unaided by any skillful embroiderer."[87] In this view of cosmic writing, *wen* or the Chinese written language is indeed "itself natural," as Owen remarks. "Writing is not constituted of arbitrary signs, created by historical evolution or divine authority; writing appears from observing the world."[88]

That notion of natural writing or nature as writing, however, can hardly be said to characterize Chinese writing as distinct from its Western counterpart, since Western writing was also, at least before the establishment of modern philology and linguistics, considered to be itself a system of natural

85. See Wang Yunxi and Yang Ming, *Wei Jin Nan Bei chao wenxue piping shi*, p. 344.
86. Curtius, *European Literature and the Latin Middle Ages*, p. 344.
87. Liu Xie, *Wenxin diaolong*, p. 1.
88. Owen, *Traditional Chinese Poetry and Poetics*, p. 20.

signs. "In its raw, historical sixteenth-century being," says Michel Foucault in discussing the Renaissance notion of the book of nature, "language is not an arbitrary system; it has been set down in the world and forms a part of it." The metaphor of the book turns the relation of nature and writing around; it transfers a cultural concept to natural phenomena and "forces language to reside in the world, among the plants, the herbs, the stones, and the animals."[89] Foucault describes the book of nature as a vision in which "the face of the world is covered with blazons, with characters, with ciphers and obscure words—with 'hieroglyphs,'" and in which space becomes "like a vast open book; it bristles with written signs; every page is seen to be filled with strange figures that intertwine and in some places repeat themselves."[90] Reminiscent of Owen on Chinese *wen*, Foucault argues that Western language, too, must from this perspective "be studied itself as a thing in nature. Like animals, plants, or stars, its elements have their laws of affinity and convenience, their necessary analogies."[91] Apparently, their difference in cultural background notwithstanding, the ancient Chinese and Westerners before the eighteenth century all traced the origin of language to a remote and nebulous past enshrouded in myths and legends, and credited the creation of writing to a supernatural or divine agency, a mysterious *tao* or an anthropomorphic God as *logos* that impregnated nature with meaning. "Myth, language and art," as Ernst Cassirer observes, "begin as a concrete, undivided unity, which is only gradually resolved into a triad of independent modes of spiritual creativity."[92]

Nevertheless, it is a misleading exaggeration to claim that the book of nature and the concept of language in its raw historical and material being exemplify the mythical premodern *epistemes* that distinguish the mentality of the sixteenth century from the scientific thinking of the seventeenth and that are replaced in a sudden break of the older tradition by a set of new cultural codes, new *epistemes* of a Cartesian rationalism or a Newtonian world view. "The western world's way of perceiving the world," as Ken Robinson puts it, "did not change suddenly on 10 November 1619 when Descartes realized the full significance of mathematics for man's knowledge of the natural world, nor in the autumn of 1665 in Newton's garden at Woolesthorpe when he supposedly recognized that there was a special

---

89. Foucault, *The Order of Things*, p. 35.
90. Ibid., p. 27.
91. Ibid., p. 35. We can compare this notion of language as part or an extension of nature, the idea that language signifies by way of similarities and analogies, with Owen's discussion of analogy and the Chinese notion of *lei*, which he translates as "natural category." See Owen, *Traditional Chinese Poetry and Poetics*, pp. 18, 61, 294.
92. Cassirer, *Language and Myth*, p. 98.

providence in the fall of an apple."[93] Not only did the new scientific and philosophical thinking reach back to medieval times and Greek antiquity, to the technical experiments of the alchemists and astrologers or the speculations of the atomists and natural philosophers, but older ways of seeing the world persisted and became integrated into new ones.

The book of nature, says Robinson, is a shared "common image" at the time, but there emerge two different books from two perspectives: "On one view, which carries over from the Middle Ages to the Renaissance, the book is a remarkable tissue of correspondences or resemblances which require allegorical, mystical-religious reading; on the other, it is written in the language of mathematics, not in the language of Pythagorean and Neoplatonic number symbolism which Renaissance architects had spatialized to embody in their creations the pristine harmonies of the music of the spheres, but in the new mathematics which sharply divided qualities from quantities and saw its province as the latter."[94] In other words, the book of nature does not necessarily fall into the category or vocabulary of the mystical-religious, the archaic concept of language as natural signs coined in divine creation. The same can be said for the Chinese concept of *wen*, which has richer connotations than what Liu Xie allows for in his cosmological reading in the first chapter of his book.

After all, before Liu Xie, in the period of Wei and Jin, *wen* had already acquired the specific meaning of literature as the art of writing.

Bent on highlighting cultural differences as he is, François Jullien also acknowledges that "the Western tradition is not unacquainted with the whole connection by analogy between the order of text and that of nature." He cites some of Curtius's examples of "the book of nature" and finds that notion somewhat comparable with Liu Xie's idea of *wen*, but he goes on to point out two major differences: the first has to do with the "trajectory" or the order in which notions of natural sign and human sign are constructed, because "the Western analogy starts from the book (*the* 'Book') and proceeds from there to conceive of nature, while in China, the idea of *wen* doubtless has first the meaning of natural figuration before signifying 'a graphic sign' and 'a written text.'" The second difference has something cultural or religious to it, because the Western "book of nature," according to Jullien, is just a "rhetorical assimilation," its meaning "is exclusively that of reading and deciphering," while in China, "in the absence of the entire theology of revelation, the natural *wen* can

93. Robinson, "The Book of Nature," in *Into Another Mould*, ed. Cain and Robinson, pp. 86–7.
94. Ibid., p. 89.

be equally conceived as a sign (and as such delivered to a divinatory interpretation), but also prevails spontaneously as a simple effect of figuration,
with a purely aesthetic value."[95]

I rather doubt the "trajectory" Jullien outlines here with such assurance,
for it is questionable whether the Western conceptualization indeed proceeds from book to nature, while in China that order gets "inverted," supposedly started as natural figuration before moving on to human writing. If
we trace the meanings of words to their first roots, it is likely that they will
all turn out to be concrete and "natural." The word "book," according to
the *OED*, is a common Teutonic word "generally thought to be etymologically connected with the name of the beech-tree." If in its etymological
sense a "book" is no less natural than the beech-tree or beechen tablets on
which writing is inscribed, then the Chinese *wen* in its etymological sense
as "a mark of crisscross strokes" is indisputably a sign no less artificial than
those inscribed on the bark of a tree. Whatever Liu Xie has had to say
about *wen*, its basic definition as "a mark of crisscross strokes" is given in
Xu Shen's famous dictionary, *Shuowen jiezi*, which is several hundred years
earlier than Liu Xie's book and a much greater authority for consultation
insofar as Chinese characters and their meanings are concerned.

As for the second difference that Jullien mentions, in China there is
indeed no "theology of revelation," if by that is meant a specifically Christian theology, and a Chinese sign is, of course, different from a Christian
sign. But do we need a Sinologist with all his knowledge and learning to
tell us that China is in Asia, not in *l'Extrême-Occident*, that Chinese is a language different from French or English, and that most Chinese are not
Christians? If Chinese writing as *wen* is a set of natural signs and fundamentally different from Western writing, then why call *wen* writing in the
first place? If, as Jullien suggests by citing Martin Heidegger's "conversation with a Japanese," Eastern notions and ideas are "necessarily distorted
(*dénaturées*) and impoverished as soon as they are transposed in the framework of Western thinking, as soon as they are expressed *in the language* of
the West," one can imagine how enormously ironic and self-defeating it
must be for Sinologists like Jullien to write their books in French, German, or English instead of classical Chinese.

Of course, Jullien argues that the Chinese or Japanese themselves cannot do any better, for native scholars in modern China or Japan have been
Westernized, and once they are "initiated into Western concepts," they
tend to "project, perhaps too directly, categories borrowed from the West
onto their own cultural tradition." In trying to "translate" the notions of

95. Jullien, *La valeur allusive*, pp. 52–3.

their own literary and critical tradition into a modern idiom under Western influence, they tend to *"forget* the proper, original meaning" of those notions.[96] But if those ancient Chinese notions are untranslatable, according to Jullien, even from classical into modern Chinese, then how can he be so sure, as a modern-day Sinologist writing *"in the language* of the West," to *remember* the "proper, original meaning" of those Chinese notions that the modern Chinese themselves have forgotten? On what ground can he claim that his French remembrance of Chinese notions has preserved the essence of the Chinese tradition? Here we seem to have another version of the familiar biblical story of the loss of innocence, one in which classical Chinese in its pure essence assumes the role of the *primitive* or the prelapsarian Adamic language once spoken in the Garden of Eden, which is now hopelessly lost among the fallen native speakers in modern China, and which the Western Sinologist tries in vain to recuperate. Does not this picture strike one as tinted in a distinctly Christian color?

To be sure, the will of heaven is not human, and for Liu Xie, there is no anthropomorphic God behind all those splendid colors, shapes, and patterns in the book of nature, but he also has his share of religious mysticism when he remarks that "The origin of human writing (*ren wen*) began in the Ultimate One," that in antiquity the prototypical map and book emerged miraculously from the Yellow River and the Luo River, brought out of the water by a dragon or a sacred turtle, and that ultimately it is *tao* or "divine reason" (*shen li*) that regulates the manifestation of all patterns and all writing.[97] What is perhaps typically Chinese is Liu Xie's emphasis on the central role of the sages as both human and sacred in the sense that they alone are privileged to know the mysterious *tao* and that the meaning of *tao* becomes manifest in their writings. So he made the claim that "*tao* shows the pattern (*wen*) by way of the sages, and the sages make *tao* manifest in their writing (*wen*)."[98] As Jullien also remarks, human writing becomes essential once it is generated, and the genesis of literary creation depends on "these three fundamental terms: the *tao* as the cosmological-moral totality, the sage as the prime author (and, at the same time, the author par excellence), and the canonical text as the prime text (and, at the same time, the text par excellence)."[99] The centrality of human writing makes it possible for Liu Xie to launch out a detailed discussion of the various literary genres, and the exemplariness of Confucian classics provides the basis for him to conceive of writing not primarily in

96. Ibid., p. 10.
97. Liu Xie, *Wenxin diaolong*, p. 1.
98. Ibid., p. 2.
99. Jullien, *La valeur allusive*, p. 40.

terms of literature or poetry, but as a means to the illumination of *tao*. It is in this context that we can understand why Liu Xie continues to expound, in the second chapter, the idea of seeking models in the works of the sages and, in the third, the idea of devoutly following the examples of the Confucian classics.

Most commentators are quick to point out that it was in reaction to lavishly ornamented form and excessive attention to rhythm and musicality of language, a formalist tendency characteristic of literary writing in his time—the Qi and Liang era—that Liu Xie proposed the idea of following nature in following the classics as models. "The use of writing," he declares, "is indeed that of the branches and twigs of the classics." He then reprehends the tendency of his time in which, as he puts it, "remote from the sages, the norm of writing is broken and scattered. Writers now love the strange and cherish the flashy and the grotesque in language; they apply paint on colorful feathers, and they embellish their writing like putting embroidery on embroidered ribbons and shawls. The farther away their writing drifts from the origin, the more corrupt and inordinate will it become."[100] Most critics would justify Liu Xie's call of "back to nature and the classics" as a necessary antidote to extravagant formalism. In viewing writing as subservient to the illumination of *tao* and calling on writers to follow the classics, Liu Xie strengthened the didactic and moralistic tendency in traditional Chinese criticism; his influence in this respect is yet to be fully evaluated in the study of the history of Chinese literary criticism.

Despite all the talk about the cosmic origin of *wen* in its grandiose and mystifying little preamble, Liu Xie's *The Literary Mind* has, as its primary concern, the art of human writing. Indeed, the most famous chapters of this book offer insights into the writing process as one of literary creation. Chapter 26, for example, gives a vivid description of how writers go beyond the limitations of time and space to envisage things not present at hand:

> "Though my body is by the river and at sea, my mind still resides under the gate of the high palace." This ancient saying characterizes miraculous ideas. The spirit of the ideas in writing indeed stretches far out. So in pensive tranquility, your thoughts may touch things of a thousand years ago, and in quietly changing your countenance, your eyes can see all ten thousand miles. In chanting your poetry, every word you pronounce has the tinkling sound of pearls or jade, and before your eyes, wind and clouds unfold their shape and color.[101]

100. Liu Xie, *Wenxin diaolong*, p. 534.
101. Ibid., p. 295.

The "ancient saying," which Liu Xie quoted, is a phrase from the *Zhuangzi*, and it is used here to demonstrate that the movement of the mind, unlike that of the body, is not restricted by space or a specific location.[102] Thus the phrase is borrowed, as Wang Yuanhua maintains, to give "Liu Xie's definition of imagination."[103] The "miraculous ideas" (*shen si*, literally, divine or spiritual thoughts) is Liu Xie's term for imagination, and his depiction of the author's mind and vision as reaching out beyond the confines of the present time and place clearly indicates "that the activity of imagination has the capacity to break through the limitations of the experience of senses, and that it is a psychological phenomenon unconfined by the physical environment."[104] Aided by imagination, that is, the capability of drawing mental pictures of things long ago, far away, or even nonexistent, the Chinese poet is able to create things not immediately present at hand. That is to say, the Chinese poet does not just pick up a poem as something ready-made in nature and does not just make "strictly true" statements as a literal response to the concrete situation.

Indeed, the belief that Chinese poetry is merely a factual account of real experience is untenable and easily disproved by those hyperbolic expressions so frequently found in Chinese (as in any other) poetry. The use of such basic rhetorical devices makes it impossible to consider poetic language to be factual and strictly true, as Liu Xie himself points out in chapter 37, which is devoted to a discussion of hyperbolic descriptions (*kua shi*). "Thus in speaking of height, the cliff is said to reach to the sky; in stressing closeness, the Yellow River is described as unable to hold a skiff; in emphasizing plentifulness, it is said that the descendants number in the thousands

---

102. See *Zhuangzi*, xxviii, p. 421.

103. Wang Yuanhua, *Wenxin diaolong jiangshu*, p. 105.

104. Ibid., p. 106. Most Chinese critics understand the concept of *shen si* as "imagination." Wang Yunxi, for example, also remarks that in discussing the composition of a literary work, Liu Xie depicts the writer as "immersed in an imagined world and closely related to things of his imagination" (*Wei Jin Nan Bei chao wenxue piping shi*, p. 433). While acknowledging that the concept of *shen si* "evokes the capacity of spontaneous transcendence in thinking, with regard to a person's physical limitation, in space as well as in time," Jullien objects to this Chinese elevation of Liu Xie's concept into "a complete theory of 'imagination'" because in that case, "the notion of imagination would have been born in China a good millennium earlier than with us [in the West]," and also because the word *shen si* [miraculous ideas] "maintains in itself no semantic relation with the idea of 'image.'" Jullien, "Naissance de l'imagination: Essai de problématique au travers de la réflexion littéraire de la Chine et de l'Occident," *Extrême-Orient—Extrême-Occident* 7 (1985): 25. As I have argued earlier about the translatability of terms, in translating Liu Xie's *shen si* into "imagination" (*xiangxiang*) in modern Chinese, we are again dealing with equivalents, not identicals; and it is undeniable that Liu Xie is talking about the mental capacity of evoking things and images not directly present but created in the mind for literary expression, which is what "imagination" means.

of millions; and in underscoring paucity, it is said that not a single survivor is left." Citing these examples from *The Book of Poetry* and other classics, Liu Xie concludes that "though the language is excessive, the meaning is not misleading."[105] The poet, he observes, can either "fabricate writing to express emotions" or "fabricate emotions for the sake of writing," of which he approves the former but not the latter; but whatever his preference, he clearly recognizes literary writing as making or fabrication (*zao*).[106] In other words, Liu Xie realizes that poetry is not to be understood as literally true, and that it expresses the truth of human emotions and the human condition in a manner different from factual accounts.

When we go beyond Liu Xie to examine the question of fact and fiction in the Chinese literary tradition, the alleged Chinese literalism becomes even more dubious. It is a critical commonplace that sorrow and suffering are better suited for poetry than happiness, an idea aptly summed up in Confucius's famous saying that poetry is able "to give vent to one's grievances."[107] Once poets realize that expression of sorrow moves readers and audiences more easily than that of joy, however, such expressions tend to become a poetic topos that may well articulate sufferings fabricated to achieve an emotional effect rather than real grievances. Not every poet is willing to suffer personally in order to write touching poetry. "Consequently we find a situation that has been with us for a long time," as Qian Zhongshu points out in a brilliant essay on this subject, "that poets hope to pay nothing or at least a reduced price for writing good poetry. Thus the young write to lament over their 'old age,' moneybags write to deplore their 'poverty,' and those who live a comfortable life of leisure write to express their 'sorrow of spring' or 'sadness at autumn.'"[108] Of the copious examples Qian cites in his essay, the most amusing one concerns an obscure figure by the name of Li Tingyan, who once sent to his superior a poem that contains this heart-rending couplet: "My younger brother passed away south of the Yangtze River, / My elder brother died in the borderland up north!" His superior was deeply touched and gave him his

---

105. Liu Xie, *Wenxin diaolong*, p. 404.
106. Ibid., p. 347.
107. Liu Baonan, *Lunyu zhengyi*, xvii.9, p. 374. Hereafter abbreviated as Confucius, *Lunyu*.
108. Qian Zhongshu, "Our Sweetest Songs," in *Qi zhui ji*, p. 111. The Chinese title of the essay is the famous quote from *The Analects* that "Poetry can give vent to one's grievances," but the English title Qian himself prefers is not a direct translation but a quote from Shelley's famous poem, "To a Skylark," that articulates the same basic idea the essay discusses: "Our sweetest songs are those that tell of saddest thought." The numerous examples quoted in this essay from both Chinese and Western literatures make a strong case for the universal appeal of the tragic and the sorrowful as both a critical concept and a poetic topos.

condolences, but Li respectfully disclosed that "nothing of the sort really happened, but that was done simply for making neat parallelism with a personal touch." The man of course quickly became a laughingstock, and someone made a mocking sequel to his couplet: "As far as the parallelism is neat, / I don't care having double funerals."[109] Qian Zhongshu's sarcastic comment goes right to the heart of the matter:

> Apparently, this chap Li was writing his poem according to the principle that "words of misery and sorrow may well please," and he knew quite well that poetry should present concrete images and that one should find the proper objective correlative for the emotion expressed. Had his superior not shown his concern and not asked him on the spot, latter-day scholars like us who have been so deeply influenced by positivism may not suspect that this fellow was "making up sorrowful words without feeling sorrow."[110]

The same critical attitude is necessary not just in reading a bad poem like Li's, but in reading the classics as well. One poem from *The Book of Poetry*, mentioned earlier in Liu Xie's discussion of hyperboles, describes the great Yellow River as though it were a small stream: "Who says the River is wide? / It cannot even hold a skiff."[111] Yet another poem from the same canonical book speaks of the Han River, which is much smaller than the Yellow River, as though it were very wide: "Oh, so wide is the Han River / That one can never swim across."[112] The difference here shows not so much the actual width of the two rivers as the ways in which the speakers in the two poems feel about them. To emphasize that homeland is just across the Yellow River to the south, the speaker in the first poem exaggerates the closeness by minimizing the width of the River. In the second instance, however, the width of the Han River is maximized to express the idea that the girl on the yonder bank is simply out of reach. The truth the poems articulate is the psychological truth of feelings and emotions, not factual statement about the rivers. "If based on these poems," says Qian Zhongshu jokingly, "someone would try to figure out the geography and the measurement of the place, and then cite the lines

---

109. The story seems to be very popular among Chinese men of letters, and Qian Zhongshu gives three different textual sources dated from the fourteenth century. On the surface, the story seems to confirm Owen's point that Chinese readers, like Li's superior, tend to read poems as though they were factual accounts, but the point of the story is precisely to discredit such literal reading of fictive (and fictitious) texts. Li's gullible superior certainly does not impress us as a sophisticated reader of poetry.

110. Qian Zhongshu, *Qi zhui ji*, p. 112.

111. *Mao shi zhengyi*, 58c, in Ruan Yuan, *Shisan jing zhushu*, 1:326.

112. Ibid., 14a, 1:282.

to prove that the Han is wider than the Yellow River, that man would indeed be the idiot to whom one cannot confide one's dreams."[113] Of course, no one is so literal-minded as to take such poetic lines as proof of the relative width of the two rivers. Not only cannot such hyperbolic lines be understood literally, but poetry as fabrication can be literally false to the concrete situation or historical reality without being false to the psychological truth it is meant to express.

A good example is a poem entitled "The Old Capital Bridge" (*Zhou qiao*) by Fan Chengda (1126–1193).

> South and north of the Bridge runs the main thoroughfare,
> Where old folks await His Majesty year after year.
> Scarcely holding back tears, they asked the royal envoy:
> "When will our great armies really come back here?"[114]

This is one of the poems Fan wrote in 1170 when he was sent on a diplomatic mission to the court of the Jurchens, a Tungusic nomadic tribe that had taken much of the northern part of the Song territories, and the bridge in the poem is the famous bridge in Bianliang, the old capital of the Northern Song, lost to the Jurchens in 1126 and now under enemy occupation. In his critical notes to this poem, Qian Zhongshu shows how Fan Chengda drew two different pictures of what he had seen in Bianliang. In his diary that covers the same events, Fan writes that "people there have long adopted the barbarian customs, and their attitudes and tastes have all changed." From similar records kept by other emissaries to the Jin court, it is clear that no old folks in occupied territories, even if they were still loyal to the Song, could be audacious enough to make direct contact with the envoy from the Song court and openly request their "great armies" to come and deliver them from foreign rule. And yet, Fan's poem describes them as doing just that. The scene described cannot be true to the poet's real experience, but it gives expression to his own feeling at seeing those old folks, and it may have indeed expressed a secret desire buried in their hearts as he had detected or imagined.

The difference between Fan's poem and his diary, as Qian Zhongshu comments, "makes it clear that to describe realistically in literature does not mean to be overwhelmed by the superficial trivialities of daily life."[115] Even if the poem takes as its material an episode in the author's life and refers to a specific historical moment, as literary writing it nevertheless

---

113. Qian Zhongshu, *Guan zhui bian*, 1:95.
114. Qian Zhongshu, *Song shi xuanzhu*, p. 224.
115. Ibid.

allows for fictional construction that is true to the feelings expressed in the poem, but not necessarily true to the particular situation as the poet himself experienced. Fan Chengda's account of what he saw in Bianliang in different forms, the discrepancy between his diary and his poetic expression, offers an interesting example of how real lived experience in a historical moment is transformed and *fictionalized* in poetry; it allows us to have a glimpse into the interweaving of history and poetry, and the possible presence of fictionality in both types of texts.

History and Fictionality

It is Aristotle who made the definitive statement in the West about the distinction between history and poetry that "the former relates things that have happened, the latter things that may happen. For this reason poetry is a more philosophical and more serious thing than history; poetry tends to speak of universals, history of particulars."[116] Against Plato's dismissal of poetry as imitation not of reality but of the appearance of reality and therefore as "concerned with the third remove from truth,"[117] Aristotle's statement can already be read as a defense of poetry, and it is indeed frequently evoked and reiterated in a long apologetic tradition in the history of Western criticism. The *Poetics*, however, was not widely known in antiquity or the Middle Ages and it did not begin to have a notable impact until the latter half of the sixteenth century. Insofar as history not only records things that have happened but also aims to explain the reason why they have so happened, to offer some kind of a lesson or an insight that goes beyond the particular toward the universal, the distinction Aristotle made cannot be held as rigid and absolute, even though it is generally valid and defensible.

Prior to the eighteenth century, as Hayden White observes, the writing of history "was regarded as a branch of rhetoric and its 'fictive' nature generally recognized."[118] If history indeed records events that take place in specific moments and locations, in writing the narrative of those events, the historian must utilize "precisely the same tropological strategies, the same modalities of representing relationships in words, that the poet or novelist uses."[119] In fact, in the eighteenth century, Johann Martin Chladenius already pointed out the significance of the historian's

---

116. Aristotle, *Poetics* 51b, p. 12.
117. Plato, *Republic* 10.602c, in *The Collected Dialogues*, p. 827.
118. White, *Tropics of Discourse*, p. 123.
119. Ibid., p. 125.

"viewpoint" and the distinction between a historical event and "the concept of the event."[120] Wilhelm von Humboldt in a famous essay defines the task of the historian not as the mere recording of actual events but as the discovery of "the inner causal connection itself" on which "the inner truth" of history rests. In constructing a coherent whole out of the scattered pieces of historical facts, the historian must use his imagination and write as creatively as the poet does, because historical depiction, says Humboldt, is also "an imitation of nature," as poetry is, for both purport to achieve "the recognition of true shape, the discovery of the necessary, and the separation of the accidental."[121]

In contemporary discussions, perhaps the most eloquent critique of the positivist notion of history is advanced by Hayden White, whose works have emphatically established the close relations between historiography and the various literary forms, especially the novel. "The older distinction between fiction and history, in which fiction is conceived as the representation of the imaginable and history as the representation of the actual," White declares, "must give place to the recognition that we can only know the actual by contrasting it with or likening it to the *imaginable*." According to White, what is interesting is not the distinction of history and poetry but what he calls the "fictions of factual representation," that is, how and to what extent "the discourse of the historian and that of the imaginative writer overlap, resemble, or correspond with each other."[122]

In an elegant essay on truth and fiction in the American historical novel, Daniel Aaron also challenges the truth-claim of the dull "clinical monograph" by the positivist "custodians of history," and argues for the value of fictional reconstruction of the sense of history in the novel. "Good writers write the kind of history good historians can't or don't write," says Aaron.[123] The past cannot be fully present in the historical account. "The historian writing from hindsight can never fill in the lost connections," says Aaron with reference to Gore Vidal's controversial literary portrait of Lincoln. "Hence truth is what is best imagined, and the novelist is obviously better qualified than the historian to locate and reattach invisible historical links."[124] In a self-reflective essay on writing about contemporary writers and events, Aaron shows clearly the difficulty

120. Chladenius, "On the Interpretation of Historical Books and Accounts," in *The Hermeneutics Reader*, ed. Mueller-Vollmer, pp. 66, 69.

121. Humboldt, "On the Task of the Historian"; in ibid., pp. 105, 109.

122. White, *Tropics of Discourse*, pp. 98, 121.

123. Aaron, "What Can You Learn from a Historical Novel?" *American Heritage* 43 (Oct. 1992): 62.

124. Ibid., p. 56.

of representing the "true physiognomy" of history, and he wonders "whether the portraits of our living or recent contemporaries can ever be more than impressionistic daubs. One would suppose that the historian-painter, with his model seated before him, ought to achieve a recognizable likeness, but the reverse is often true."[125] Under the pressure of a critical scrutiny that sees both historical and literary narratives as the deployment of language and therefore subject to the same kind of linguistic and literary analysis, the simple distinction between history as factual account and literature as fiction tends to collapse in contemporary Western theory and criticism.

When we look at Chinese literature studies, however, the distinction between history and poetry seems still to function as a working hypothesis that sets up contrasts and dichotomies between Western and non-Western languages and literatures. Here the distinction directly translates into a critical view that sees poetry as characteristically Western on account of its philosophical interest, its representation of the probability rather than actuality, and its concern of the universal rather than the particular, while it sees Chinese poetry as essentially historical because of its being embedded in concrete things and real situations and concerned with literal truth rather than a transcendental meaning. Since in this critical view, history and poetry are put in an opposition as factual account and fictional creation, the "nonfictional" Chinese poetry naturally falls under the category of historical discourse. "The traditional Chinese reader had faith," to quote again Owen's unequivocal statement, "that poems were authentic presentations of historical experience." Whether a Chinese poem does indeed present the authentic historical truth is admittedly a mystery often buried in the remote past beyond recovery, but Owen argues that the "faith" here refers to "the inclinations of readers and of a poet's anticipation of those inclinations."[126] In other words, according to Owen, to consider poetic statements as historically verifiable is the habitual expectation in a Chinese way of reading.

"The Western literary tradition has tended to make the boundaries of the text absolute, like the shield of Achilles in the *Iliad*, a world unto itself," says Owen. "The Chinese literary tradition has tended to stress the continuity between the text and the lived world."[127] Like the contrast between Wordsworth and Du Fu that we saw earlier, Western and Chinese literary texts are here brought into contradistinction as self-contained fiction and

125. Aaron, "The Treachery of Recollection: The Inner and the Outer History," in *American Notes*, p. 11.
126. Owen, *Traditional Chinese Poetry and Poetics*, p. 57.
127. Owen, *Remembrances*, p. 67.

factual account embedded in historical reality. The shield of Achilles that Homer describes in book 18 of the *Iliad*, perhaps the most famous example in Western literature of *ekphrasis* or verbal description of a nonverbal object, is a fictional shield on which a marvelous imaginative picture of both the natural cosmos and the human world are cast in words.[128] The shield becomes a symbol of Western poetry, indeed the symbol of symbols, "a world unto itself," redolent of metaphorical and metaphysical meanings. The Chinese poem, on the other hand, is not an autonomous world at all; it is part of the lived world to which the poem refers and in which both its structure and meaning are grounded.

There is a great deal to be said for the historical grounding of Chinese poetry. History is important not just as the general background or social condition of the writing and reading of literature, but it often serves as the immediate context for the poetic text, the occasion for composing a poem to express feelings and thoughts as responses to that particular occasion. Many Chinese poems are thus occasional poems, of which Fan Chengda's "Old Capital Bridge" quoted earlier may serve as a typical example, because those poems not only arise from a particular moment in the poet's lived experience, but also turn that experience into the very material for poetic variations and reflections. The works of Du Fu are often referred to as a "history in verse," because many of his poems draw a vivid picture of the life and times from what is known as the high Tang to the late Tang, especially the war and suffering around 755 when the corruption at court and the rebellion led by An Lushan, an ambitious general of Turkish origin, precipitated the Tang empire into its speedy decline. One of the uses of poetry, as Confucius has it, is "to observe": to enable the ruler, his officials, and by extension all the literati to see the intimations of the customs and mores of the times by means of poems collected from different parts of the kingdom.

Poetry is thus considered valuable because it can be used "to serve one's father at home and to serve one's king out in the world."[129] The close involvement of poetry with politics in the Chinese tradition and the appreciation of poetry as a sort of mirror of social conditions make the historical grounding particularly important. Much of traditional criticism seems to have been predicated on the assumption that a poem is composed to make a social commentary on the contemporary scene, explicitly or implicitly, and is to be understood as such. As I shall argue, it is precisely this assumption of historical and political relevance of poetic

128. For a theoretical study of this poetic topos and the complexity of verbal and nonverbal representations, see Murray Krieger, *Ekphrasis.*
129. Confucius, *Lunyu,* xvii.9, p. 374.

expressions that entails a kind of allegorical interpretation in the Chinese tradition that tends to read a poetic text as something else, as an encoded text with some sort of a hidden meaning.

To recognize the significance of history in the Chinese literary tradition does not mean, however, that we should take a Chinese poem for a historical document and understand its discourse as "strictly true" statements about the real world. History and reality can enter the world of poetry in many different ways. Chinese poets are not alone in writing on the occasion of a specific moment in their lived experience, for Goethe also called his own works "occasional poems" (*Gelegenheitsgedicht*), to which "reality must give both impulse and material." He told Johann Peter Eckermann: "All my poems are occasioned poems, suggested by real life, and having therein a firm foundation. I attach no value to poems snatched out of the air."[130] According to Helen Vendler, the famous religious and spiritualist poet George Herbert wrote a kind of "private poetry" that usually begins "in experience, and aims at recreating or recalling that experience."[131] Whatever we may think of Goethe's self-description or Vendler's remarks on Herbert, and whatever difference we may find between Goethe's occasional poems and, say, Fan Chengda's, we cannot claim that the connection of poetry with history and lived experience is uniquely Chinese. In the Western tradition itself, that connection has also an impressive presence. Given the much-emphasized distinction between Western imaginative literature and the historical grounding of Chinese poetry, it may be necessary here to examine and recognize the significance of history in the Western literary tradition.

If the shield of Achilles symbolizes the fictionality of Western poetry, we must not forget that there is another shield made by the same god of fire, another famous shield in Western literature as a conscious parallel to the one made for Achilles. I refer, of course, to the shield of Aeneas in Virgil's *Aeneid*, a famous shield cast to symbolize a poetic vision of real history, an *ekphrasis* of historical prophecy. The design on this shield clearly presents Roman history from its legendary beginning in a she-wolf suckling Romulus and Remus to Virgil's own time, the glory of the Roman Empire under Augustus. History is revealed on the shield:

> There the Lord of Fire
> Knowing the prophets, knowing the age to come,
> Had wrought the future story of Italy,
> 　The triumphs of the Romans: there one found

130. Eckermann, *Conversations with Goethe*, p. 8.
131. Vendler, *The Poetry of George Herbert*, p. 5.

> The generations of Ascanius' heirs,
> The wars they fought, each one. (8.626–29)[132]

Compared with the Homeric epic, the *Aeneid* is thoroughly imbued with history. "The scope of the Greek epic falls short of the scope of the Roman *Aeneid*," as Viktor Pöschl remarks. "It was the Roman poet, Virgil, who discovered the grievous burden of history and its vital meaning. He was the first to perceive deeply the cost of historical greatness."[133] The cost here refers to the sacrifice of love and personal happiness, of the private, human interest that Aeneas must surrender for the sake of an impersonal, public cause, the historical mission of the founding of the Roman *imperium*. Much of the tragic pathos in the Virgilian epic derives from this conflict between the personal and the impersonal, the sacrifice of love for the achievement of a great empire. In reading the poem, the attentive reader will notice what Adam Parry calls the continual opposition of two voices, the voice of "the forces of history" and that of "human suffering."[134]

It is interesting to note the two levels of the presentation of time in Virgil's epic, for what is described prophetically as the future destiny for Aeneas is the present historical time for Virgil and his readers, and Aeneas, having seen his future history depicted on the shield, is portrayed as "knowing nothing of the events themselves" (*rerumque ignarus*, 8.730). The prophetic scenes on the shield are thus included, as Francis Cairns suggests, "more perhaps for the readers' enlightenment than for Aeneas,' since they lie in his future and he is said not to comprehend them."[135] With the hindsight of history, Virgil's readers occupy a better position than Aeneas to understand the historical significance of the images carved on his shield, and in reading the *Aeneid*, they would have no difficulty to see Dido, the queen of Carthage, as prefiguring the Egyptian queen Cleopatra, and when the dying Dido utters her bitter curse and calls for an "avenging spirit" rising from her bones (*ex ossibus ultor*, 4.625), they would remember the awesome Carthaginian general Hannibal and the dangerous years of the Punic wars. That is to say, for the Roman readers the poem becomes, in the words of K. W. Gransden, "a prelude to history and to the understanding of history."[136] They would read the Virgilian

---

132. Quoted from Robert Fitzgerald's English translation of Virgil, *The Aeneid*. The number of book and line refers to the Loeb edition of Virgil's original Latin text (Cambridge, Mass.: Harvard University Press, 1967).

133. Pöschl, "Aeneas," in *Modern Critical Interpretations: Virgil's Aeneid*, ed. Bloom, p. 13.

134. Parry, "The Two Voices of Virgil's *Aeneid*"; in ibid., p. 72.

135. Cairns, *Virgil's Augustan Epic*, p. 102.

136. Gransden, "War and Peace," in *Modern Critical Interpretations: Virgil's Aeneid*, p. 141.

epic as both historical and poetic, and the historical elements are absolutely essential to an adequate understanding of the *Aeneid* as poetry.

Virgil and his epic of dynastic history had a tremendous influence during the Renaissance. He established the narrative strategy of what Andrew Fichter calls the Renaissance "dynastic epic," the type of poetry that displays a "consciousness of history" and "reflects the assumption of a historically oriented mind that the present may be regarded as the culmination of a course of events set in motion in the remote past."[137] Like Aeneas, the dynastic hero is *"homo historicus,* the creature of history who, when he comes to know himself as such, is also a creator and a builder. But only as he engages history and sees himself defined by it can he also determine its course."[138] As Fichter shows in a detailed study of Ludovico Ariosto, Torquato Tasso, and Edmund Spenser as Renaissance emulators of Virgil, the Renaissance poet sets out to rewrite the *Aeneid* and in a sense to complete it because Virgil, being a pagan poet without the Christian perspective, could not bring the epic to a conclusion that would satisfy a Christian reader's sense of time and the idea of Providence. Virgil could write about history only in terms of what he had experienced, and the promised return of a Saturnian Golden Age could only be a vague prospect in the remote future. In this, says Fichter, the Renaissance poet sees himself surpassing Virgil:

> The Christian poet-prophet, on the other hand, will claim for himself knowledge of a greater sweep of time. He will see history unfolding from first things to last, according to the divine plan documented in Scripture: the beginning is the universal beginning of mankind and the end is absolute.[139]

From the perspective of Christian eschatology, equipped with an apocalyptic vision, the Renaissance poet will combine the historical with the spiritual, and finally write "a poem moved to a metaphysical plane wholly apart from that on which the *Aeneid* exists." Here the differentiation of the Renaissance "dynastic epic" from Virgil's *Aeneid* by virtue of metaphysical transcendence vis-à-vis the limitations of history may remind us of the supposed dichotomy between Western transcendence and Chinese materiality, but such a dichotomy is quickly put in question when Fichter argues that the real difference between the Renaissance poet and Virgil is not a negation of history in spirituality, not the replacement of Virgil's historical

137. Fichter, *Poets Historical,* p. 2.
138. Ibid., p. 8.
139. Ibid., p. 37.

Carthage and Rome with the allegorical cities of man and God, but precisely the reconciliation of the opposed cities. No "fundamental ontological dualism" distinguishes the Renaissance Christian poet from Virgil. "The Christian poet writes within the framework of a system that abhors and finally denies dualism," says Fichter. "Virgil had written of the conflict of personal love and duty to empire, the antithetical urges between which Aeneas is forced to choose; for Augustine, love is the very foundation of *imperium*."[140] The Renaissance dynastic poem is thus as much a celebration of the earthly power as that of the spiritual Christian love.

When John Milton with his contempt for monarchy and earthly power chose to write a Christian epic of the fall of man instead of an Arthuriad as he had first planned, he certainly made the spiritual dimension overshadow the historical. But in so doing, Fichter argues, he also "brings a literary tradition to full closure."[141] But even with Milton, history is not and cannot be excluded from an adequate understanding. Given his active participation in the political life of his time, the biblical theme of Milton's poetry, "man's first disobedience" or Satan's revolt against God, will often suggest to readers some association with the English Revolution, whatever Milton's own intention might be.[142] From Virgil to Milton and beyond, then, Western poetry is not severed from historical reality at all, but it has made history an essential part of poetic representation as well as an important assumption in reading and interpretation.

When we come back to examine the historical orientation of Chinese poetry, perhaps we can say that it is somewhat closer to Virgil's notion than to the Christian idea of history as the unfolding of God's divine plan. Chinese poetry is mostly short, and for a long and complex narrative structure that may show some semblance to the Western epic and suggest the unfolding of a teleological process, we must look elsewhere, perhaps in the later development of vernacular novels rather than in classical poetry.[143] The difference is surely enormous, but the notion of history as

140. Ibid., p. 10.
141. Ibid., p. 209.
142. For a persuasive historical reading of Milton, see Christopher Hill, *Milton and the English Revolution.* "Milton was not just a fine writer," says Hill. "He is the greatest English revolutionary who is also a poet, the greatest English poet who is also a revolutionary. The poems will not speak for themselves unless we understand his ideas in their context. But the context is historical, and it is very difficult to grasp Milton's ideas without placing them in relation to those of his contemporaries" (p. 4). For Hill, the biblical theme of Milton's poetry is intrinsically historical, for all his major poems, *Paradise Lost, Paradise Regained,* and *Samson Agonistes,* "are deeply political, wrestling with the problem of the failed revolution, the millennium that did not come," p. 362.
143. In Tibetan literature and the literature of other ethnic groups in China, there are long narrative poems similar to the Western epic. In Korean literature, there is a cycle of

the working out of some sort of a divine mandate, with its model already existent in a glorious antiquity, a past Golden Age, is at least in some ways common to both the *Aeneid* and the Chinese tradition.

Unlike the Christian poet, who judges the present in terms of the end of time, the Chinese poet, under the influence of a Confucian idealization of antiquity, tends to assess the present against a perfect beginning, the ideal past under ancient sage-kings. Confucius is especially fond of the customs and institutions of the Zhou dynasty (c. 1122–256 B. C. E.). "Having seen the previous two dynasties, the Zhou has an exuberant culture (*wen*)," says the Master. "I follow the Zhou."[144] Ancient sage-kings and rulers, Yao, Shun, and especially King Wen and the Duke of Zhou, figure prominently in the commentaries on the *Book of Poetry*, and in writing about the historical present, Chinese poets often nostalgically evoke the reign of sage-kings as a yardstick, a paradigm that sets up an unmatched and unmatchable example for the contemporary scene. Thus when Du Fu describes his youthful political ambition as "addressing my lord as Yao and Shun / To bring our mores and customs again to purity," the allusion to sage-kings and a return to the purity of their times is more than a mere convention, for it makes use of a deeply entrenched sense of history to legitimize his political aspirations.[145] The reverence for ancient sage-kings, the idealization of the remote past as the final point of reference in judging contemporary social conditions, constitute what might be called a retro-teleology of history, which in a sense predetermines the nostalgic mood of much of classical Chinese poetry that sees the present as always a falling-off from a better and more balanced past.

If we admit that Chinese poems are, by and large, occasional poems, and that the Chinese literary text is often embedded in the real historical context and continuous with the lived world, we still need to consider whether historical discourse in China is strictly factual and whether Chinese readers past and present do read poetry as history and make no distinction in their expectations when reading the two kinds of texts. In our discussion of hyperbolic expressions, we have seen that competent Chinese readers would not take poetic lines for factual statements, that they would allow poets some kind of a license to exaggerate in order to make their expressions striking and effective. In hyperboles, as Liu Xie notes, "though the

---

dynastic propaganda poetry, the *Songs of Flying Dragons* (*Yongbi och'on ka*), which in many ways resembles the *Aeneid*. See Peter H. Lee, *Songs of Flying Dragons: A Critical Reading*.

144. Confucius, *Lunyu*, iii.14, p. 56.

145. Du Fu, "Twenty Two Rhymes to His Excellency the Left Coadjutor Wei," in Qiu Zhao'ao, *Du shi xiangzhu*, 1:74.

language is excessive, the meaning is not misleading."[146] Historians, however, are not allowed such license and their credibility is called into question when their supposedly factual account seems to exceed the bounds of the probable. In reading the *Book of Documents*, Mencius (371?-289? B.C.E.) dismissed an obviously inflated description of a battle scene, in which the blood shed in the war is said to be able to keep wooden clubs afloat in its steady flow like a river. "It would be better to have no *Book* at all than to believe everything in the *Book*," says Mencius contemptuously of such improbable accounts of history.[147] And yet, when he talks with Xianqiu Meng about the *Book of Poetry*, he shows much more patience and sympathy, and rejects rigid literalism in reading poetic hyperboles. This is one of the important passages in Mencius that has had a tremendous influence on Chinese literary criticism:

> So the interpreter of a poem should not let the words obscure the text or the text obscure the intention. To trace back to the original intention with sympathetic understanding: that is the way to do it. If one should merely understand the text literally, then consider these lines from the poem *Yun han:* "Of the remaining populace of Zhou / Not one single soul survived." Taken as literal truth, this would mean that of all the Zhou people not a single person remained alive.[148]

Instead of demanding that the *Book of Poetry* be discarded for overstatements, Mencius calls the reader's attention to metaphors and rhetorical devices that operate beyond the literal sense of the text, and he advocates a kind of historical sympathy that restores the text in its original context and understands a poem in accordance with the author's intention. His different attitudes toward the *Book of Documents* and the *Book of Poetry* indicate that Chinese readers clearly recognize the generic distinctions between history and poetry, and that they require strict plausibility of historical narratives but exempt poetry from such a requirement.

Wang Chong (27-97?), a great scholar and philosopher of the Han dynasty, used the same two lines from *Yun han* to illustrate what he called "artistic exaggeration" and made some extremely apposite remarks. The poem was about a great drought in ancient time, he explains. "It may be true that the drought was severe, but to say that not a single person remained alive is mere exaggeration." Wealthy people with plenty of food supplies would certainly have survived the ordeal, but the poet used the

---

146. Liu Xie, *Wenxin diaolong*, p. 404.
147. Jiao Xun, *Mengzi zhengyi*, xiv.3, p. 565. Hereafter abbreviated as *Mencius*.
148. Ibid., ix.4, p. 377.

hyperbole "to increase the effect of the text and to emphasize the severity of the drought."[149] Wang Chong argued against all other kinds of exaggeration but tolerated the artistic one, which he considered justifiable if the rhetorical point was to augment the effect of the text and to embellish its message. Here again, a difference is made between poetic license and historical plausibility.

By gathering a wealth of textual evidence, Qian Zhongshu gives the most effective critique of the hackneyed notion of Chinese poetry as "history in verse." Many dialogues and monologues in historical narratives cannot possibly have been recorded either by the historian himself or by anyone else. In *Zuo zhuan* [*Zuo's Commentary on the Spring and Autumn Annals*], for example, Jie Zhitui's conversation with his mother or Chu Ni's monologue before he killed himself, says Qian, "have neither witness when they were alive nor anyone to verify it when they are dead. Despite the commentators' tortuous argument to stitch it together, readers could hardly set their minds at rest or stop voicing their doubts."[150] Chu Ni's last words before suicide, in particular, have left many readers wondering, as Li Yuandu (1821–1887) asked, "who heard them and who recounted them?" But in reading Bo Juyi's "Song of Everlasting Remorse," which also contains improbable reported speech, such questions do not seem to arise.

In that famous work of poetic fantasy, a Taoist adept is sent to find the soul of the emperor's favorite consort and finally meets her in a land of fairies. As a token of love of the emperor and, from the narrative point of view, as a strategy to give the land of fairies and immortals some sense of reality and credibility, the beautiful goddess, who had been incarnated as the royal consort when she sojourned in the human world, gives the Taoist her broken-in-half hairpin, and tells him the words that only she and the emperor could have known, words they had said to each other as a vow of love in the middle of night in the privacy of the inner palace, when no one was around. In reading this, as Qian Zhongshu remarks, "no one seems to have asked dull-wittedly, 'who heard them and who recounted them?' Nor has anyone played the killjoy to accuse the 'Taoist from Linqiong' of lying."[151]

149. Wang Chong, *Lun heng*, p. 84.

150. Qian Zhongshu, *Guan zhui bian*, 1:165. Jie Zhitui, who had followed Duke Wen of Jin for many years in exile, refused to take office when the Duke returned to rule over Jin. He had a conversation with his mother and then went to live in seclusion in Mianshan. See *Chunqiu Zuo zhuan zhengyi*, the 24th year of Duke Xi, 115a, in Ruan Yuan, *Shisan jing zhushu*, 2:1817. Chu Ni was a warrior who, sent by Duke Ling of Jin to murder a good minister Zhao Dun, committed suicide to avoid killing a good man on the one hand and disobeying his orders on the other. See ibid., the 2nd year of Duke Xuan, 165a, 2:1867.

151. Qian Zhongshu, *Song shi xuanzhu*, p. 5 n. 1.

Here again, historical and poetic texts are read in different ways with different expectations. It is therefore biased and untenable, as Qian argues, "to believe that poetry is all verifiable factual account while not to know the fictional embellishment in historical writing, or only to realize that poets use the same techniques as historians while not to understand the poetic quality of historiography."[152] The putative recorded speech of historical characters in *Zuo zhuan*, says Qian, is "in fact imagined speech or speech on behalf of the characters, which becomes, it is not too far-fetched to say, the antecedent of dialogues and dramatic speech in novels and plays of later times."[153] Rather than reading poetry as history, then, we should understand how historiography can itself be read, to some extent and in some ways, as imaginative literature.

The interrelationship between history and narrative fiction has often been discussed in the study of Chinese literature. Henri Maspero studied early Chinese historical romances built around some legendary or celebrated historical figures, and pointed out the often confused relations between such historical romance and historical biography. From King Mu, Chong'er (later the Prince Wen of Jin), to Yan Ying, the wise minister of Qi, and Su Qin, the famous rhetor and political counselor, there is hardly any well-known figure in Chinese antiquity that "has not become the hero of a romance. Imagination being given free rein, imaginary episodes were invented when the real biography seemed insufficient."[154] *Zuo zhuan* provides many examples of a careful rhetorical structure and poetic appeal. Although it is not a novel or historical romance, and its description minimal, its carefully selected events and speeches are arranged to guide the reader to a moral lesson about good and bad, about a benevolent ruler who is wise and kind or a tyrant who is obstinate and cruel. The moralistic and didactic interest of the narrative, as Ronald Egan observes, may explain why the actual process of historical events like the battle between Jin and Chu is described in a few words with no mentioning of the size, training, equipment, morale of the rival forces or any details of how the armies were deployed in the battle fields, while preliminary matters that implicitly predetermine the outcome in moral terms are given a fuller narration. "The emphasis throughout the narrative is on establishing the right and wrong of the situation and on distinguishing the just from the selfish leader," says Egan. "Once this has been

152. Qian Zhongshu, *Tan yi lu*, p. 363.
153. Qian Zhongshu, *Guan zhui bian*, 1:166.
154. Maspero, *China in Antiquity*, p. 360.

done, the outcome of the battle is predictable, and there is a noticeable lack of interest in depicting the main event."[155]

In *Zuo zhuan*, as in Chinese historiography in general, Anthony Yu also argues, one can detect "an attempt to weave a moral pattern wherein not only are the good and bad clearly distinguished but they are also 'encouraged or censured (*cheng'e quanshan*)' accordingly."[156] A moral pattern and didactic interest evidently govern both historical and fictional narratives in China. As Yu shows further, Chinese novels are much influenced by Chinese historical writing, since most novels seek to ground their invented action in dynastic history, and the "popular notion of karmic causality" assumes in novels a function similar to that of the moral pattern in Chinese chronicles, which seeks to explain the practical consequences of speech and action in social and political life. It is in the context of such a conventional historical grounding, Yu argues, that *Dream of the Red Chamber* (the acclaimed masterpiece of Chinese narrative fiction, which is also known as *The Story of the Stone*) stands out as a "sharp contrast to a different and rival mode of writing—history itself," because it consciously reflects on its own structural fictionality and deliberately locates its action outside an identifiable outline of dynastic history.[157]

But what about poetry, the kind of occasional poems that arise from particular historical moments and lived experiences? Are they really nonfictional and, as Owen puts it, readable "as describing historical moments and scenes actually present to the historical poet"?[158] In fact, Owen is far too knowledgeable a reader of classical Chinese poetry to accept the kind of cultural dichotomy we find in some of his own theoretical formulations, and he himself has given a most thoughtful answer to that question. In an article on this particular issue, Owen seeks to put the "historicist" argument in question. "To put it bluntly," he says, "we never see the grounding of a literary text in its history; we see only the formal imitation of such grounding, the framing of the literary text within another text that pretends to be its historical ground, an 'account' of history."[159] Historical grounding turns out to be nothing more than constructing a context for a literary text out of other historical accounts, and the obvious circularity of such textual construction makes it difficult to substantiate any claim to historical truth or

155. Egan, "Narratives in Tso chuan," *Harvard Journal of Asiatic Studies* 37 (Dec. 1977): 335.

156. Yu, *Rereading the Stone: Desire and the Making of Fiction in Dream of the Red Chamber*, p. 40.

157. Ibid., pp. 46, 52.

158. Owen, *Traditional Chinese Poetry and Poetics*, p. 57.

159. Owen, "Poetry and Its Historical Ground," *Chinese Literature: Essays, Articles, Reviews* 12 (Dec. 1990): 107–8.

authenticity. This is an insight that will, when we discuss Han commentaries on the *Book of Poetry* and the influence of that exegetical tradition, prove to be very valuable.

In his poem "On Meeting Li Guinian in the South," Du Fu claims that he used to see the famous singer Li "so often in Prince Qi's house," and that he had heard him singing "several times in the hall of Cui Di."[160] Some commentators have found the claim doubtful since both Li Fan, the Prince of Qi, and Cui Di, a palace chamberlain, died in the fourteenth year of the Kaiyuan reign when Du Fu was only a teenage boy. It was unlikely, they argue, though not impossible, that the young Du Fu could have frequented these noble houses and have seen Li "so often" there in such social gatherings. Commenting on the debate about the reliability of Du Fu's claim, Owen implicitly rejects the notion that one should read a Chinese poem as though it were making "strictly true" statements about the poet's experience in the lived world. It is quite possible, Owen suggests, that Du Fu "might have misremembered, might have allowed his poetic vision of the K'ai-yüan and his own place in it to overwhelm a more sober memory of 'what really happened.'" It is also possible that Du Fu might even have replaced reality with his desire in writing "myths of [his] childhood and youth." Although this is an occasional poem, Owen argues, "there is a world of difference between a poem's *generic* claim to be historically true and actually being historically true."[161] In effect, Owen throws serious doubt on the notion of Chinese poetry as a unique and factual account of real experiences.

In discussing the ambiguous and richly suggestive texts of Li Shangyin's poems, Owen explicitly defines what he calls the "poetic" elements in contradistinction to those that can only be called historical. If historical grounding consists in anchoring the poetic text in specific moments and locales and determinate relations, then the language of classical Chinese poetry clearly shows a tendency to move away from such anchoring, from historical and narrative specificity toward an elimination of functional words and an ellipsis of syntactic relations. What Chinese readers appreciate as *yunwei* or the suggestive lingering taste of the poetic is often something indeterminate and difficult to pinpoint, outside the clearly marked boundaries of historical events. Though there is a generic presumption that the Chinese poem "grows out of and comments on a complete living historical ground," and though that presumption is "often strengthened by the increasing precision of occasional titles

160. Du Fu, in Qiu Zhao'ao, *Du shi xiangzhu*, 5:2060.
161. Owen, "Poetry and Its Historical Ground," p. 109.

and prefaces," says Owen, "what sounded 'poetic' was the withholding of precisely those elements in the language which could provide relatively adequate determination of such a historical ground."[162] Owen's essay on Chinese poetry and its historical grounding evidently makes a subtle and necessary revision of a notion he endorsed in his earlier works, the notion of Chinese poetry as "authentic presentations of historical experience." And here I am in complete agreement with him, for that erroneous notion describes neither the textual condition of Chinese poetry nor the horizon of expectations in most Chinese readers' experiences.

It is true that many Chinese poems were traditionally read as nonfictional and referring to something real and concrete in the poet's lived world. From a critical point of view, however, what is important and interesting is not to accept such traditional "historical" interpretations at face value, but to examine their premises and assumptions, to understand the often political and ideological reasons and motivations that frame, shape, and in a sense predetermine those interpretations. Let us consider the example of Su Shi (1037–1101), the great poet of the Song dynasty, who was often caught in the struggle of competing political rivalries and whose writings often condemned as seditious political satires. In the second year of the Yuanfeng reign (1079), Su Shi was imprisoned for writing allegedly satirical and slanderous poems, and the persecution of the poet on account of his literary writings offers an illuminating case for understanding the censorship and political control of literature and its interpretations. It is known as the notorious "Crow Terrace Poetry Case."[163] Of Su Shi's politically suspect poems, the following simple quatrain on twin juniper trees almost caused him his life in a "historical" reading that deliberately sought to find correspondences between the poetic imagery and its putative referent in the real world:

> Facing one another in dignity, an unassailable pair,
> Their straight trunks rise to the sky without ostentation,
> Their roots reach the nether regions, never bend or twist,
> Known to the dragon alone that lies in hibernation.[164]

Since a dragon, especially a flying dragon, is a symbol of royal power and often identified with the emperor of China, the dragon image in Su

162. Owen, ibid., p. 111.
163. For a discussion of this case in English, see Charles Hartman, "Poetry and Politics in 1079: The Crow Terrace Poetry Case of Su Shi," *Chinese Literature: Essays, Articles, Reviews* 12 (Dec. 1990): 15–44.
164. Su Shi, "Two Poems on the Twin Juniper Trees in Scholar Wang Fu's House," poem no. 2, in *Su Shi shiji*, 2:413.

Shi's poem easily lends itself to a "historical" or political reading. Ye Mengde (1077–1148), one of Su Shi's contemporaries, recounted an anecdote that deserves to be quoted in full:

> When Su Shi was put in the Censorate jail during the Yuanfeng reign, Emperor Shenzong had no intention to inflict severe punishment on him, but the chief minister came to address his Majesty and suddenly accused Su Shi of treason. Shenzong changed his countenance and said: "Shi was indeed guilty, but to me he would not have gone so far. How do you know?" The chief minister thus cited as evidence the couplet from Su Shi's poem on juniper trees: "Their roots reach the nether regions, never bend or twist, / Known to the dragon alone that lies in hibernation." Then he said: "Your Majesty is the dragon flying in heaven, but Shi thinks that Your Majesty does not understand him and turns to seek sympathy from a dragon lurking underground. If this is not treason, what is?" Shenzong replied: "How can you discuss the words of a poet like that? He was writing about juniper trees, and what does that have anything to do with us?" The chief minister was at a loss for words. Zhang Zihou also tried to put in a good word for Su Shi and his punishment was thus reduced. Zihou once told me this and used ugly words in speaking of the chief minister, saying: "Alas! men could harm others like that without fear or misgivings!"[165]

This is a particularly interesting example of the conflict of interpretations because it discloses a number of important things about the reading of poetry and its relationship with political authority. What is immediately relevant to our discussion here is the way Emperor Shenzong dismissed the chief minister's reading that obviously—perhaps too obviously—meant to incriminate Su Shi by interpreting the poem as a statement about the real world and an attack on the emperor. Shenzong's reply immensely complicates the problem of the literal as opposed to the metaphorical or allegorical meanings, because he appears to read Su Shi's poem as literally about juniper trees and sleeping dragons, not related to himself as the "dragon flying in heaven" or to the political reality within which the chief minister tries to frame the poem and its meaning. And yet, Shenzong is not so much reading literally as allowing the metaphors of the juniper trees and the dragon to mean something other than what the chief minister alleged them to mean, and in effect freeing these images from a rigid political reading and its ominous consequences. The dignity and the straightforwardness of the unbending juniper trees may

165. Ye Mengde, *Shilin shihua*, in *Lidai shihua*, ed. He Wenhuan, 1:410. The anecdote can also be found in Cai Zhengsun's (fl. 1279) *Shilin guangji*, p. 260. In Cai's book, many of Su Shi's poems are printed together with their political readings in the notorious "Crow Terrace Poetry Case."

still be read allegorically, as they may be understood, for example, as a praise of Wang Fu the scholar or more generally as a symbol of upright-ness and moral integrity the poet admires, but Shenzong would refuse to identify the specific object of admiration or the referent of the more obscure hidden dragon. His more generous and elastic reading sets the metaphorical meaning free from a fixed signified, and this, the emperor seems to suggest, is the way to interpret "the words of a poet." The chief minister, however, seems to read the poem allegorically as signifying something other than just juniper trees, but his reading aims precisely to eliminate the slippage of metaphorical meaning by supplying a definite signified for every poetic image. That is to say, both Shenzong and the chief minister would not read the poem literally as making true state-ments about juniper trees (and of course not about real dragons), but they differ on the meaning of the structure of poetic imagery as a whole. On the surface, their difference is the result of different reading strategies and assumptions, but that difference is determined by political aims and sympathies that are not clearly articulated in their readings. From the very beginning, as Ye Mengde told us, Emperor Shenzong "had no inten-tion" to punish Su Shi too severely; therefore his more tolerant reading of the poem shows more of his desire to keep a balance between rival politi-cal forces than of his appreciation of Su Shi's literary talent. Shenzong knew very well what the chief minister, a political enemy to Su Shi, was doing in his reading, and his dismissal of that reading has as much to do with politics as with hermeneutics, and indeed in this case politics and hermeneutics are fused together. The accusation made against Su Shi, his arrest, imprisonment, the long and detailed investigation of his poems, and his final release and virtual banishment from the court, in short, the entire "Crow Terrace Poetry Case," offers a revealing example of the dangerous crossing of poetry and politics, a case in which deliberate alle-gorical readings of poetry cannot be fully understood unless they are understood in the context of political and ideological premises. Chinese poetry, now we fully realize, is not literal, nor is it literally understood. It can, and indeed often does, mean *something else*, something other than what the text literally says. The exegetical battle over what exactly that something else is has profound and sometimes threatening implications in the history of Chinese literature.

2

Canon and Allegoresis

Jakob Böhme's mystical works have sarcastically been characterized as a kind of "picnic" in which the author brings the words and the reader supplies the meanings, a characterization that has sometimes been evoked to typify the reading of *all* literature.[1] The claim that meaning is exclusively a readerly contribution seems to articulate, albeit in an exaggerated manner, a received opinion in much contemporary criticism, namely, the idea that the reader plays a decisive role in making sense of the text. Hence it is assumed that the focus of theoretical analysis in criticism should be on *how* meaning is constructed in the reading process, rather than on *what* the textual meaning itself is. The preposterousness of the "picnic" metaphor suggests that this particular model of reading is a caricature in which words and meanings are entirely severed and that the text as mediating ground is missing. Given that a literary work tends to mean more than what it literally says, the relationship between what the text says and how one understands it—say, the tension between the literal and the figurative—always gives rise to complicated hermeneutic problems. This complexity and tension between words and meanings— between text and its reading—may have been deliberately and systematically built into the text itself, in which case we have the text as an *allegory;* or, the tension may be constructed and formulated in the reader's response to the text, in which case we have *allegoresis* as a special mode of

1. See, for example, Northrop Frye, *Fearful Symmetry: A Study of William Blake*, p. 427. Tzvetan Todorov uses the same metaphor to criticize Stanley Fish's notion of reader-response criticism; see Todorov, *Literature and Its Theorists*, p. 187.

interpretation. The opposition between *compositional* and *interpretive* allegories forms two distinct traditions. However, as Jon Whitman argues, in actual reading "it is impossible to treat them in isolation from each other."[2] That is to say, the text is always there as the necessary medium between an author's particular arrangement of words and the reader's interpretation. In this book, I want to use the notion of the allegorical to cover both the compositional and the interpretive sides, since allegory as text and allegoresis as interpretation are so closely connected in the interaction between text and reader.

This interaction is a typical hermeneutical activity of understanding, which can be called, as George Steiner argues, translation in a broad sense. Steiner maintains that translation, properly understood, is a "special case of the arc of communication which every successful speech-act closes within a given language." The problems of translation exist not only between languages on the inter-lingual level but also, and "at a more covert or conventionally neglected level, intra-lingually." Steiner sums up his argument by making this emphatic statement: "*inside or between languages, human communication equals translation.*"[3] In this broad sense of translation, human communication depends on a basic translatability of terms and concepts, which is a prerequisite not just for understanding a foreign language, but even within the same language under a constantly changing situation. That is to say, the efficacy of translation, the rendering of what seems alien into something comprehensible and familiar, is crucial for intersubjective as well as cross-cultural understanding.

Given the skeptical and relativist attitude that challenges the viability of cross-cultural understanding, however, it is translation *between languages* that is most often seriously questioned. Whether allegory and allegoresis can be translated between Western and Chinese languages is a much-debated issue. Some critics and Sinologists have denied that translatability, and it is my contention that the concept of the allegorical is indeed possible to translate across linguistic and cultural boundaries. Much of the argument in this book will inquire into the condition of that translatability and will produce textual evidence to support that translatability across cultures. The translation of terms such as allegory and allegoresis is not just a technical problem of transferring a set of words from one language to another, but above all a theoretical issue of finding conceptual equivalents that make such a transfer possible, of identifying crucial aspects of those concepts that

2. Whitman, *Allegory*, p. 31.
3. Steiner, *After Babel*, p. 47.

seem to be sufficiently general and common in different languages and cultural traditions.

Quintilian's often-quoted characterization of allegory as a text that "presents one thing in words and another in meaning" is perhaps the simplest and one of the earliest definitions.[4] Such a simple definition has the advantage of being able to provide the most basic element of allegory without further complicating it to accommodate its later development, especially in biblical exegesis, where allegory is turned into a much more specific but also much narrower concept. To Quintilian's basic definition I shall return often. My main concern is to inquire into the translatability of terms, though it is not so much to find some common features in Chinese and Western texts than to reveal a similar interpretive framework within which the very concept of allegory takes shape. To put it differently, in seeing allegory as a sort of double structure of text and meaning, I am interested in the conditions of such double structuring: the linguistic, literary, and especially the ideological reasons (moral, political, religious, and so forth) for reading a text as something other than what it literally says. By looking into both the Chinese and the Western canonical literatures and their commentaries, I try to show the commonality of using certain interpretive strategies, and especially similar relationships between interpretation and ideology in different traditions.

This is not to say that a text in its plain sense has no ideological underpinnings, or that the literal sense is fixed and unproblematic— identifiable as a primary source from which the allegorical can be clearly separated as secondary extrapolations. I shall have occasion later to delineate more precisely the contours of the literal and to discuss its complexity, but I do want to make the argument—though at this point it can only be made as a preliminary one—that a notion of the literal needs to be established as an important basis for appropriate understanding and plausible interpretations, and also for the protection of a text from willful distortions and manipulations. I remain unpersuaded by hermeneutic nihilism, which is really a version of cultural relativism, namely, the specious argument that all understanding is misunderstanding, and that all reading is but manipulation, determined by pervasive and coercive power relations. I do not accept the ground rule of hermeneutic nihilism that text and interpretation are all free plays in which "anything goes," and that as a result there is

---

4. Quintilian, *Institutio Oratoria*, VIII.vi.44, 3:327. For a brief account of the various definitions of allegory, see Whitman, *Allegory*, especially Appendix 1, "On the History of the Term 'Allegory,'" pp. 263–68.

no legitimate ground on which one can protest against any manipulation, however unjustified, as misreading or misinterpretation.[5]

It may well be that in some cases reading can be all fun and free play, as the "picnic" metaphor in reading Böhme seems to suggest. For me, however, it is important to remember that there are other cases and occasions, like the so-called "Crow Terrace Poetry Case," briefly discussed at the end of the previous chapter, where we see conflicting interpretations of Su Shi's poem thinly disguising different political interests and motives, where reading can be deadly serious and carry dangerous implications in real life, where the "political" has a much stronger meaning than just textual manipulations, and interpretation has much more at stake than the business of going for a picnic and bringing to the words whatever meaning one finds palatable.

Reading the *Song of Songs*

When we recall Quintilian's definition of allegory as saying one thing and meaning another, there is already a clear sense of discrepancy between text and reading, the sense that linguistic and pictorial signs can have different meanings: a literal sense and some other sense beyond the literal. The idea of allegory thus indicates the problematic relationship between the sign and its referent: a relationship of disconnectedness rather than a seamless continuity or perfect representation. In the medieval development of this theory of signs, the Holy Scriptures are thought to contain four meanings, of which the nonliteral ones impart a spiritual message beyond what the biblical text literally says, sometimes even opposed to, or at the cost of, what it literally says. Crucial to this notion of allegory is the prerequisite distance between signifier and the signified, the literal sense and the transcendental meaning, the material medium and the spiritual content, a distance that constitutes the very structure of allegory in the Western tradition.

When we look into the question of allegorical structure cross-culturally, however, we immediately face the challenge of an argument, presented by some scholars in Chinese studies, which claims that no such distance is conceivable in the Chinese language and that no such spiritual

5. In a critique of Paul Valéry's idea of the incompleteness of an artwork, Gadamer argues that the notion that one way of understanding a work "is no less legitimate than another," that "there is no criterion of appropriate reaction," simply leads to "an untenable hermeneutic nihilism," *Truth and Method*, pp. 94–95.

or metaphysical transcendence exists in Chinese thinking or philosophy, and that as a result no allegory can be found in a Chinese text. "Western allegory," to quote Pauline Yu again as one example, "cannot be taken at face value as a literal record of actual events; rather, it is a system of signs whose very meaning consists in asserting their fictiveness and their function as signifiers for something beyond the text."[6] But to mean "something beyond the text," following the logic of Yu's argument, is precisely what Chinese words cannot do, because a Chinese poem, as she puts it, registers "a *literal reaction* of the poet to the world around him."[7] The literalism of the Chinese language and Chinese poetry is here contrasted to the figurality of the Western language, a figurality exemplified by allegory as the trope of tropes. Therefore, whether allegory and allegorical interpretation do cross over the Chinese-Western boundaries is crucial to the whole question of cross-cultural comparisons. What we encounter here is the notion of fundamental incommensurability between Chinese and Western languages, cultures, and literatures, but surely the talk of incommensurable Chinese and Western ways of thought is highly problematic. Such "grandiose generalisation about Greek, or Chinese, ways of thought," as G. E. R. Lloyd points out, ignores internal variety by making "the unjustified assumption of a *uniformity* in the relevant characteristics across different domains and at different periods."[8] Rather than trying to answer directly the question of whether allegory is possible in Chinese, I would like first to take a look at a Western allegory, or more precisely, a text that has been understood in the Western tradition as supremely allegorical: the Song of Solomon in the Bible. I believe that to know how a text, especially a canonical one, comes to be interpreted allegorically will help us understand the nature of allegoresis and its cross-cultural translatability.

One thing about the Song of Songs that signals its special status in the Bible is the fact that its canonicity is far from unassailable. The problem obviously arises from the text of the Song, which is a beautiful expression of passionate love portrayed with sumptuous erotic imagery and couched in an astonishingly sensuous language. Eroticism and sexuality manifest themselves in the metaphorical language of the Song of Songs to an extraordinary degree. "Sexual experience is properly ineffable," as Ruth apRoberts argues, "and in the Song of Solomon the very extravagance of the figures is a confession of the failure of ordinary speech, and at the same

---

6. Yu, *The Reading of Imagery*, pp. 20–21.
7. Ibid., p. 35.
8. Lloyd, *Adversaries and Authorities*, p. 5.

time more evocative of that experience than one would have imagined."⁹ From richly metaphorical depictions of the female body to the impassioned avowal of love, the Song, as Francis Landy remarks, "appeals to the sensual ear as much as to the intellect; the reader may be baffled by the words and still respond to their emotional and physical connotations; in fact the difficulty reinforces this appeal to an uncritical pleasure."¹⁰ In the religious context of the austere and august Holy Scriptures, however, the words Landy chooses to describe the effect of the Song—"sensual," "emotional and physical," "an uncritical pleasure"—may all appear highly suspect. Let us look at two famous verses from the last chapter of the Song in the King James Version, which may give us a very good idea of the musical quality of its melodious language:

> Set me as a seal upon thine heart, as a seal upon thine arm: for love is strong as death; jealousy is cruel as the grave: the coals thereof are coals of fire, which hath a most vehement flame.

> Many waters cannot quench love, neither can the floods drown it: if a man would give all the substance of his house for love, it would utterly be contemned. (8:6–7)

In these beautiful lines, love, death, and jealousy are not abstract notions, but they come alive in such incredibly vivid images and are arranged in such a rhythmic sequence that George Saintsbury, a renowned English critic at the end of the nineteenth century, took these two verses to be the "perfect example of English prose rhythm" in all of English literature.¹¹ With its perfect rhythm, its sensuous appeal, and the promise of "uncritical pleasure," the Song of Songs undoubtedly deserves to be placed among the most refined pieces of love poetry in world literature, and yet its inclusion into the Holy Bible must give us pause in taking it to be the same kind of human writing as secular love poems. As part of the biblical canon, the Song of Songs must have some kind of a spiritual meaning congenial to the nature of the canon of which it forms a part, and yet its very language seems to insist on the sensuality of erotic love that threatens to obscure the spirituality and makes its inclusion into the biblical canon problematic.

In fact, it is precisely the presence of a love song in the Bible that has raised a hermeneutic problem for all exegetes throughout the centuries,

9. Ruth apRoberts, *The Biblical Web*, p. 49.
10. Landy, "The Song of Songs," in *The Literary Guide to the Bible*, ed. Alter and Kermode, p. 306.
11. Saintsbury, "English Prose Style," in *Miscellaneous Essays*, p. 32.

Jews and Christians alike. The problem is not that the Canticle sings of love, but that it surpasses many secular love poems in its praise of female beauty, its unmistakably erotic imagery, its "Oriental" sensuality, and the conspicuous absence of God from the entire text. In some other translations, such as the *Jerusalem Bible*, the name of God does appear once in 8:6 where the Hebrew word *šalhebetyah*, which corresponds to "a most vehement flame" in the Authorized Version, is rendered as "a flame of Yahweh himself." But as Marvin Pope remarks, "to seize upon the final consonants *yh* as the sole reference to the God of Israel in the entire Canticle is to lean on very scanty and shaky support."[12] The language of the Song is simply indistinguishable from the language of secular love. It speaks of day break and spring, of the desire and joy of love, the physical charms of the beloved, jewels and spices, wine and milk, the dove, the rose, the lily, the sweet-smelling myrrh, the grape vines, the apple and the fig tree, the roe and the young hart, but surprisingly, it does not speak the usual biblical language of law and covenant, the fear and worship of God, or sin and forgiveness. The Song of Songs is thus unique in biblical context, and that uniqueness must be explained. Its textual sensuality must be contained in some way, and indeed the history of its interpretation is a long record of debates and controversies.

The canonicity of the Song has not gone unchallenged. At the council of Jamnia toward the end of the first century, the rabbis discussed the holiness, or lack of it, of the two books ascribed to Solomon, the Song of Songs and Ecclesiastes. Rabbi Judah argued that the Song of Songs defiled the hands—that is, was taboo or sacred, hence canonical—while Ecclesiastes did not. Rabbi Jose then expressed his doubt about the propriety of including the Song in the canon, but Rabbi Aquiba made a powerful plea, saying that "No man of Israel ever disputed about the Song of Songs, that it did not defile the hands. The whole world is not worth the day on which the Song of Songs was given to Israel, for all the Scriptures are holy, but the Song of Songs is the Holy of Holies." He angrily denounced those who treated this holy Song as an ordinary song and chanted it in "banquet houses." That does not mean, however, that the Song had until then remained outside the canon, for "the issue was not whether the book was included in the Canon, but whether it should have been."[13]

Perhaps the proceedings at Jamnia were not mainly concerned with the problem of canon, but biblical scholars today, as Frank Kermode notes, "still appear to accept the date, ca. 100 C.E., as about right for the closure

---

12. Pope, ed. and trans., *The Anchor Bible: Song of Songs*, p. 671.
13. Ibid., p. 19.

of the canon." And for the Jewish Bible, the process of canon closure means precisely to draw the distinction "between books which 'defiled the hands' because of their sacred quality, and 'outside' books which presumably failed this test."[14] Among Christians, similar doubts and disputes about the Canticle also arise from time to time. For example, Calvin's fellow reformer Sebastian Castellio revived the view of Theodore of Mopsuestia, which had been condemned by the Roman Church at the council of Constantinople in 550, that the Song was Solomon's rejoinder to popular protest against his unconventional marriage to an Egyptian princess, and therefore it dealt with nothing but earthly affections. An eighteenth-century rationalist, William Whiston, even asserted that the Song "exhibits from the beginning to the end marks of folly, vanity, and looseness," that "it was written by Solomon when He was become Wicked and Foolish, and Lascivious, and Idolatrous."[15] Many of those who question the canonicity of the Song tend to take its literal sense seriously and read it as a song about secular love or as Solomon's colloquy with his mistress. As such, they regard it as unworthy of inclusion in the Holy Scriptures. For them, the literal sense of the Song is incompatible with its canonical status.

From Jewish Midrash to Christian Allegorization

The fundamental way to justify the canonicity of the Song of Songs, for both Jews and Christians, has always been an exegetical move to read the Canticle as a text that says one thing but means another. The rabbis hold that Solomon's works, including the Song of Songs, belong to the category of *mashal*—a text that enables one to understand the Torah. "By reading Song of Songs, Proverbs and Ecclesiastes as *meshalim*," as Daniel Boyarin remarks, "the midrash is claiming that they are not hermetic texts, 'locks to which the key has been lost,' but hermeneutic keys to the unlocking of the hermetic Torah."[16] Thus reading a verse from the Song of Songs, the midrashist would understand it as a gloss on a verse from Exodus or some other book in the Pentateuch. For Boyarin, however, this linkage of verses or biblical intertextuality differentiates midrash from allegorical interpretation because midrash is not, he insists, a "translation of the verse to another level of signification"; it is rather "the establishment of an intertextual connection between two

14. Kermode, "The Canon," in *The Literary Guide to the Bible*, p. 601.
15. Quoted in *The Anchor Bible: Song of Songs*, p. 129.
16. Boyarin, "The Song of Songs: Lock or Key? Intertextuality, Allegory and Midrash," in *The Book and the Text*, p. 216.

signifiers which mutually read each other."[17] But allegory does not, as we shall see in more detail, necessarily translate a verse or a text to "another level of signification," and to read the Song of Songs *as a mashal* or a hermeneutic tool for understanding the Torah is already to read it as a text that means something other than its obvious meaning. In this particular case, the Song and Exodus surely do not form a pair of equal signifiers that "mutually read each other," but rather the Song is taken to be the signifier that refers to Exodus as its signified: when we read the Song of Songs, we are supposed to be really reading about Exodus, but not the other way round. The Song of Songs, not Exodus, is the mashal, the "hermeneutic key" to unlock the hermetic Torah; the former is the "lighter saying" that serves to illuminate the latter, which is the weightier, more important "darker saying." Their relationship is thus hierarchical, not reciprocal, because the significance of the Song of Songs resides in its usefulness as a tool for understanding the Torah. That is to say, it is the *use* of the Song to reveal a meaning beyond and higher than its own that justifies its canonical status as part of Scripture. Applying Quintilian's basic definition to this case, then, we may say that the rabbis already read the Song of Songs allegorically.

In fact, in discussing the hermeneutic rules of the *Aggadah*, Saul Lieberman translates *mashal* precisely as allegory: "*Mashal*, i. e. parable or allegory or symbol." Lieberman writes that "the *mashal* is already used in the Bible; as an allegory it is common in the *Midrash*. Very often the interpretation by way of *mashal* is undoubtedly the only true explanation of the text. But some allegories are obviously far from the real meaning of the text."[18] The mashal is thus a story serving an exegetical purpose, a parable or fable that leads to the understanding of something other than what its narrative literally says. In a detailed and thorough study of the mashal in rabbinic literature, David Stern gives a nuanced discussion of the relationship between mashal and allegory. The mashal, says Stern, is a parabolic narrative with an "ulterior purpose," a story with a message that is implied but never openly stated. Indeed, "the mashal's effectiveness in persuading its audience of the truth of its message lies in its refusing to state that message explicitly, thereby making the audience deduce it for themselves."[19] The presence of an indirect message makes the mashal doubly exegetical: it not only serves to interpret the Torah but also invites interpretation of its own text.

17. Ibid., p. 219.
18. Lieberman, *Hellenism in Jewish Palestine*, p. 68.
19. Stern, *Parables in Midrash*, pp. 8, 9.

In this respect, the mashal is indeed rather similar to allegory, but much of modern scholarship on meshalim or parables, under the influence of Adolph Jülicher's late nineteenth-century seminal work on Jesus' parables in the New Testament, would insist on the fundamental difference between mashal or parable and allegory, and tend to play down the significance of the mashal's allegorical features. Stern suggests that this tendency toward dissociating mashal from allegory is partly due to the influence of "the conventional nineteenth-century view of allegory as an artificial, intrinsically inauthentic mode of language, and hence as a particularly unsuitable medium for Jesus' divine speech."[20] But the opposition between allegory and symbol is largely the result of a polemical contention in the nineteenth-century romantic period for creative perfection and critical authority. In the effort to dissociate the mashal from allegory, Stern argues, one may "detect a nostalgic yearning for language as a virtually unmediated presence, for an almost revelatory experience of divine fullness. . . . The proponents of the claim that parable is not allegory are really expressing a desire for a word, perhaps The Word, that will somehow exist in a realm beyond the interventions of interpretation, within a magic circle impervious to the intrusions and interferences of an interpreter."[21]

That notion of the mashal or parable as unmediated presence is of course very close to the theological notion of the symbol in what Walter Benjamin calls "the theosophical aesthetics of the romantics."[22] Once we abandon that polemical construction of the unmediated presence of the symbol and the representational disjuncture of the allegory, however, we can argue, as Stern does, that "the mashal *is* to some extent allegorical. But the mashal is allegorical—or as I would prefer to call it, referential— only to the extent that it must allude to the ad hoc situation that gives it a concrete meaning."[23] This is a more persuasive and nuanced argument than the denial of any allegorical significance of the mashal, as it acknowledges the subtle difference between parable and allegory without subscribing to the old dichotomy between symbol and allegory or making the difference absolute and incommensurate. The point is that the mashal has the double function of being a text that needs interpretation and that is a tool for interpreting another, more important text. That is to say, the mashal is allegorical in nature; and the Song of Songs as a mashal exemplifies that allegorical nature.

20. Ibid., p. 11.
21. Ibid., p. 12.
22. Benjamin, *The Origin of German Tragic Drama*, p. 160.
23. Stern, *Parables in Midrash*, p. 16.

When we look at the actual text of the Song of Songs and how it has been traditionally interpreted, there is little doubt that the Song has often been read as saying one thing but meaning another. Interpretations of the Song fall into either an allegorical or a literal mode, of which the former, as Marvin Pope observes, is not only the older one but also the more successful and pervasive one. Allegoresis "prevailed both in the Synagogue and the Church."[24] Indications of this approach can be seen in the Talmud and in rabbinic interpretations, and allegoresis is carried on by the Targum or the Aramaic translations of the Old Testament, by medieval Jewish mysticism as well as patristic hermeneutics. When Rabbi Aquiba insisted at the council of Jamnia that the Song of Songs is the Holy of Holies, says Pope, he "must have understood the Song allegorically."[25] In fact, in the Hebrew Bible itself, there are already passages that cry out for allegorical interpretations. In the Book of Hosea, for example, God came to Hosea and said to him: "Go, take unto thee a wife of whoredoms and children of whoredoms: for the land hath committed great whoredom, departing from the Lord" (Hos. 1:2). What God asked the prophet to do here is to reenact, symbolically or allegorically, the relationship between God and Israel of his time. But did God really request Hosea to marry a woman that was, according to Deuteronomy 22:21, supposed to be stoned to death for "playing the whore in her father's house"? Whatever one may think of the meaning of this passage, the literal sense of this biblical text is rather disconcerting, and allegorical interpretation becomes almost a necessity.

In the Jewish tradition, the Song of Songs is understood as celebrating the love between God and Israel. Such a claim obviously has to be substantiated through an interpretation that would relate what is described in the scriptural text either to God or to Israel as his beloved, or to heroic figures in Israel's legendary history. In the *Midrash Rabbah*, for instance, verses from different books of Scripture are constantly linked together, and sometimes the words of one text are displaced by those of another. The text of the Song in 4:5 says: "Thy two breasts are like two young roes that are twins, which feed among the lilies." In the midrash, the "two breasts" here are not literally understood but are displaced by historical references, for they are identified as Moses and Aaron on the grounds that "just as the breasts are the beauty and the ornament of a woman, so Moses and Aaron were the beauty and ornament of Israel."[26] Verse 7:2

---

24. *The Anchor Bible: Song of Songs*, p. 89.
25. Ibid., p. 19.
26. *The Midrash Rabbah*, ed. Freedman and Simon, 4:198.

reads: "Thy navel is like a round goblet, which wanteth not liquor," and the midrashist interprets the "navel" of the beloved as referring to the Sanhedrin on the grounds that when it met, the members of this supreme Jewish council sat in a semi-circle, forming a center of such great importance in the Jewish community that "just as the embryo so long as it is in its mother's womb lives only from its navel, so Israel can do nothing without their Sanhedrin."[27] As we see, in commenting on the scriptural text, the midrashist presents a reading that in some way corresponds to the literal sense in a parallel structure, for instance, "Moses and Aaron" and "Israel" are parallel to the "two breasts" and "woman," thus effectively translating what the text literally says into something of a very different sphere, of the history and religion of ancient Israel. However strange it may sound to the gentiles, such parallel identification is nonetheless justifiable if Israel is indeed the beloved woman in the Song; but when commenting on verse 2:7, "I charge you, O ye daughters of Jerusalem," the midrashist does not identify the beloved either with Israel the nation or with individual Israelites, but identifies her with God Himself.[28]

Now, how can the beloved be allegorically both God and Israel in one and the same Song? In the host of rabbinic exegeses, however, such inconsistencies are by no means rare, and yet they apparently did not bother the ingenious midrashist at all. In fact, in a passage from the Talmudic tractate Hagigah, a passage attributed to Rabbi Eleazar ben Azariah, we have some interesting self-conscious reflection on the problem of the conflict of interpretations. That passage depicts Jewish rabbis as sitting in assemblies, studying the Torah and making mutually exclusive claims about the meaning of its words. Hearing their contradictory opinions, the puzzled student is bound to ask, how should one go about learning the Torah? The Talmudic passage offers the following response to that question:

> Should a man say: Since some [rabbis] pronounce unclean and others pronounce clean, some prohibit and others permit, some declare unfit and others declare fit—how then shall I learn Torah? Therefore Scripture says: All of them "were given from one shepherd." One God gave them, one leader (i.e. Moses) proclaimed them from the mouth of the Lord of all creation, blessed be He, as it is written, "And God spoke *all* these words" (Exod. 20:1). Therefore make your ear like the hopper and acquire a perceptive heart to understand the words of those who pronounce unclean and the words of those who pronounce clean, the words

27. Ibid., 4:281.
28. See ibid., 4:112.

of those who prohibit and the words of those who permit, the words of those who declare unfit and the words of those who declare fit.[29]

The answer is, basically, to be open to all the conflicting interpretations and accept all of them as valid. Hence this passage provides a particularly interesting example of the kind of interpretive plurality in midrash. This is not to say, however, that no criterion or authority exists in midrash, and that in rabbinic interpretation "anything goes." As Stern argues, all the conflicting interpretations in midrash find legitimation in a common divine origin, for they all are "part of Torah, part of a single revelation. They all were once spoken by the mouth of one shepherd, Moses, who in turn received them all from one God."[30] That is to say, whatever conflict there is, it is contained and finally resolved in a divine perspective. What differentiates midrashic polysemy from indeterminacy in contemporary literary theory, says Stern, is precisely this shared divine perspective, "the divine presence from which all the contradictory interpretations derive."[31] Thus midrash is both endlessly open and perpetually closed, both free and determined, and all its multiple interpretations are produced under specific exegetical conditions in response to specific questions in the world.

In discussing the multiplicity of midrashic interpretations, Gerald Bruns also emphasizes the situatedness of midrash, its communal and social function. The midrashist is not just reading one verse with reference to another, but he always tries to apply the sense of the Torah to "the life and conduct of those who live under its power." Like a case in legal hermeneutics, this emphasis on the application of the text to specific social conditions entails "the political meaning of midrash as well as its spiritual purpose."[32] Here the context of interpretation is not just textual but also social and ideological. Moreover, midrash as situated knowledge, that is, as a powerful instrument for using Scripture to deal with present issues, says Bruns, "is *phronesis* as well as *techne* because what matters in midrash is our responsiveness to the claims of the text, where responsiveness means knowing not only how the words of the text work but also how they are to be applied in this or that situation, how they are to be internalized and put into practice."[33] Therefore, in reading the Song of Songs as referring to the Pentateuch and singing about the love between

29. Babylonian Talmud, Hagigah 3a-b; quoted in Stern, *Midrash and Theory*, p. 19.
30. Stern, p. 20.
31. Ibid., p. 22.
32. Bruns, *Hermeneutics Ancient and Modern*, p. 105.
33. Ibid., p. 118.

God and Israel, the midrashist is trying to consolidate the religious beliefs of his community and to show, by linking up the prophetic books and wisdom writings with the first five books of Moses, the spiritual values of all Scripture. That is to say, biblical intertextuality is much more than just the connection and mutual illumination of signifiers.

In connecting the words of all Scripture to make an intertextual network of cross references, the midrashist is typically concerned with textual details, with particular words or phrases. Multiple interpretations arise from this exegetical tendency of what Stern calls "atomization."[34] In an introductory essay on midrash, James Kugel also points out this tendency and clearly explains how this attention to textual details results in contradictory rabbinic interpretations:

> What the midrashist addressed himself to was not first and foremost the book as a whole, i. e. not the allegory itself—"Granted, it is a love song about God and Israel"—but single verses, isolated in suspended animation. If the precise wording of a verse suggested an interpretive tack that would violate the overall allegorical frame, the midrashist sometimes picked up the suggestion nonetheless. For the same reason, of course, midrashic collections do not scruple at assembling different solutions to the same "problem" in a verse, even though they may contradict one another: it is not that one is right and the others wrong, but that all are adequate "smoothings-over."[35]

In other words, one can hardly say that midrash is already full-fledged allegory, only that "the overall allegorical frame" operates distantly as the legitimating divine perspective. The chief interest of the midrashist lies in ironing out textual irregularities in single verses rather than in structuring a coherent account of the meaning of entire texts. For him it is not so much the overall structure as the rich details that constitute the sacredness of Scripture. Nothing is superfluous, and yet nothing is obvious, and therefore a correct understanding must be obtained by making ingenious connections between single verses, by manipulating words and their syntactic relations, and thereby explaining away any dissonance between the Jewish religion and the sacred book on which it stands. In his exegetical practice, the midrashist often exploits the resources of the literal to the utmost so as to reinforce his own reading of a particular verse, but he need not always stick to an overall allegorical structure. Such a structure appears

---

34. *Midrash and Theory*, p. 20.
35. Kugel, "Two Introductions to Midrash," *Prooftexts* 3 (May 1983): 146.

only gradually when exegeses of single verses merge into the shape of a consistent totality in the later development of rabbinic interpretations.

In the Aramaic translation and interpretation of the Song, known as the Targum to the Song of Songs (ca. 636–638), the divine love motif, long existent in the rabbinic tradition and particularly promoted by Rabbi Aquiba, is fully developed into a fairly consistent allegorical narrative of Jewish history from Exodus to the impending advent of the Messiah. For example, the text of 1:5 reads: "I am black, but comely, O ye daughters of Jerusalem, as the tents of Kedar, as the curtains of Solomon." The Targumic elaboration of this verse, as Raphael Loewe recapitulates it, identifies the speaker who is at once black and comely with Israel in her ancient historical context:

> "When . . . the house of Israel made the golden calf, their faces turned black as the Ethiopians . . . but when they returned in penitence and their sin was forgiven them, the effulgence of the glory of their faces did increase to be bright as that of the angels, both in virtue of their penitence and because they made curtains for the tabernacle, and so the Presence of the Lord came to dwell amongst them: and [also because] Moses, their teacher, had gone up to heaven and had effected peace between them and their King." The three basic elements in the Targum's exegesis are thus *black* in sin, *fair* in penitence, and the reconciliation effected by means of the *curtains* of the tabernacle with "Solomon"—that is, with the King of peace.[36]

The Targum in its accepted form emerged partly from the development of the motif of divine love in the Jewish tradition and partly as a response to Christian allegorization. For verse 1:5, as Loewe observes, the Christian allegorist Origen used an interpretive scheme similar to that of the Targum which sees *black* as sin, "but after penitence—which for Origen is the equivalent of conversion—blackness is no longer a defect but a mark of beauty."[37] Although the midrashist always puts emphasis on individual words and textual details, midrash as a whole undoubtedly goes beyond the literal sense of words to relate the biblical text to the situation at hand in a figurative or allegorical reading. Again, Jewish interpretations of the Song of Songs provide the most illuminating examples of such midrashic readings. Although earlier rabbinic interpretations may not have the fully developed form of allegoresis, the motif of divine love, which constitutes the core of allegorical interpretation of

36. Loewe, "Apologetic Motifs in the Targum to the Song of Songs," in *Biblical Motifs: Origins and Transformations*, ed. Altmann, p. 175.
37. Ibid.

the Song of Songs, did exist from the start in the Jewish tradition, in the reading of the Song as a mashal, and then in the Targum to the Song as an allegory of the history of Israel.

Having taken the motif of divine love from rabbinic interpretations, the early Christians give it a new twist and read the Canticle as representing the love between God and the new Israel, namely, the Church. The New Testament is filled with references to the Old, and the way Christians can relate the Old Testament to their new religion is to try to find figures or types of Christ in the Jewish Bible. That is how Paul reads the Torah or the Mosaic Law which, he declares, is meaningful only because it has "a shadow of good things to come" (Heb. 10:1). That is also how he reads Genesis 2:24 when he writes in the Epistle to the Ephesians: "Husbands, love your wives, even as Christ also loved the church, and gave himself for it. . . . For this cause shall a man leave his father and mother, and shall be joined unto his wife, and they two shall be one flesh. This is a great mystery: but I speak concerning Christ and the church" (Eph. 5:25–32). In such a typological reading, the Genesis story of the union of Adam and Eve becomes meaningful only because it foreshadows and refers to the love between Christ and the Church. According to Jean Daniélou, this theme of divine love is the same as that "in the Canticle of Canticles which represents the union of Yahweh and Israel in a paradisaical setting, under the symbolic form of the union of man and woman." What Paul does here is to show "how this union is realized in Christ and the Church."[38] Following Paul's hermeneutic principle of eschatological typology and reading all the themes and motifs of the Old Testament in terms of the New, the early Christian exegetes had no difficulty in substituting the Church for Israel as the receiver of God's love.

Philo, Origen, and the Anxiety of Interpretation

Christian allegorization flourished in Alexandria where Hellenistic culture provided an important backdrop for the exegesis of biblical texts. Greek philosophers, notably the Stoics, had long been engaged in allegorical readings of the Homeric epics in order to find out the deeper meanings that underlie the myths and to justify the sometimes seemingly indecent or irresponsible behavior of the gods. According to K. J. Woollcombe, Greek allegorization assumes two different forms: "(1) positive allegorism, the object of which is to elucidate the undersenses

---

38. Daniélou, *From Shadow to Reality*, p. 20.

of the myths, and (2) negative allegorism, the object of which is to defend morally offensive passages." In contrast, "the main object of Christian allegorism has always been to elucidate the secondary, hidden meaning of the Old Testament, rather than to defend its primary and obvious meaning against charges of immorality."[39] Some scholars, J. Tate in particular, have argued that the function of Greek allegorism was "originally not negative or defensive but rather (as with Anaxagoras, Metrodorus, etc., in later times) positive or exegetical."[40] In appropriating the mythical language of the poets, the philosophers read into Homer and Hesiod all sorts of philosophical ideas and theories, and allegorism is nothing less than such "reading of scientific or quasi-scientific doctrines into the mysterious language of tradition."[41] More recently, however, Robert Lamberton reaffirms that much of the interpretive literature on Homeric epics that have come down to us is indeed of the "defensive" kind, but Homer and Hesiod as the first poets enjoyed a unique position of honor and respect among the Greeks who, as a matter of principle, held anything old and ancient in great veneration. Even though some passages in Homer may shock or offend the sense of propriety, says Lamberton, "tradition demanded that this response somehow be made compatible with the dignity of the divine and the respect due the text itself by virtue of its antiquity."[42]

Whether positive or negative, whether to find profound undersenses couched in mythical language or to defend the poets against charges of immorality, philosophical allegorism, as Jon Whitman observes, produced the same effect: "the poetic text turned into a mere fiction hiding underlying philosophic truths."[43] The philosophers' attack on Homer was well known, as it culminated in Plato's condemnation of poetry in the *Republic*. According to Curtius, allegorical interpretation emerged as the "compromise" the Greeks found to mediate between philosophy and poetry in their ancient quarrel, for the Greeks "wished to renounce neither Homer nor science."[44] But if Greek allegoresis served to defend Homer against his detractors, it is the Greek-speaking Jews of the Diaspora and Christians of the early Church who felt the need to adopt allegoresis for an apologetic and tendentious presentation of the Bible

---

39. Woollcombe, "The Biblical Origins and Patristic Development of Typology," in *Essays on Typology*, ed. Lampe and Woollcombe, pp. 51, 52.
40. Tate, "On the History of Allegorism," *The Classical Quarterly* 28 (April 1934): 105.
41. Ibid., p. 107.
42. Lamberton, *Homer the Theologian*, pp. 15, 11–12.
43. Whitman, *Allegory*, p. 20.
44. Curtius, *European Literature and the Latin Middle Ages*, p. 204.

against the background of a rich and highly developed pagan culture.[45] Especially in Alexandria, the great center of learning and Hellenistic culture in late antiquity, allegorical interpretation was used by Jewish writers to show not only that their tradition was worthy of comparison with that of the Greeks, but that it was actually superior to Greek philosophy and contained its source.

Philo of Alexandria is famous for his allegorical readings of the Pentateuch and for making Moses the source of all philosophy, law, and wisdom. He was vastly knowledgeable in Greek writings and applied a philosophical allegoresis to the Bible, and his influence on Christian patristic hermeneutics was great and profound. When Philo found similarities between Greek philosophy, which was based on human reason, and God's divine teaching, which was revealed to Moses and passed on by him, Philo declared that those similarities suggested: "a dependence of Greek philosophers upon Moses," that Heraclitus might be "snatching" ideas from Moses "like a thief," and that Plato had also "borrowed from the Prophets or from Moses."[46] Therefore, allegoresis that had been created for reading Homer was borrowed by Philo to read the Hebrew Bible, and in such allegorical readings, the emphasis is always on the spiritual, transcendental meaning rather than the literal sense. For Philo, everything in Scripture can be understood allegorically, but the literal sense of the biblical text must be rejected whenever it would make "the inspired words of God" seem "base or unworthy of their dignity."[47] If such a hermeneutic principle applies to any anthropomorphic description of God in the Bible, it certainly does to the sensual appeal of the Song of Songs, in which the portrayal of physical charms of the female body and explicit sexuality must be rejected on the literal level and understood allegorically. In the case of the Song of Songs, then, the positive and negative aspects of allegorism cannot be separated from one another, and the apologetic motif is as important as the elucidation of a deeper meaning. Indeed, the apologetic motif is substantiated and legitimated only through such an elucidation.

This can be seen clearly in Origen's *Commentary and Homilies on the Song of Songs*, which are characteristic of the Alexandrian allegorical method and command great admiration in later writers like Jerome. The *Commentary*, in particular, as Daniélou observes, is "the most important of Origen's works, as far as getting to know his ideas on the spiritual life is concerned. It is also the one that had the greatest influence on other writers; through

45. For a brief discussion of the Jewish and Christian apologetics, see Curtius, pp. 211–13.
46. Wolfson, *Philo*, 1:141, 160.
47. Ibid., 1:123.

Gregory of Nyssa and St. Bernard, it introduced a new method of symbolizing the mystical life."[48] Many of Origen's writings are now lost, mainly because they were condemned by Emperor Justinian I in 543, and his *Commentary and Homilies* on the Song survive only in partial Latin translations. We may, however, get some idea of the tremendous importance of his works, especially those on the Song of Songs, from Jerome's famous tribute that "while Origen surpassed all writers in his other books, in his *Song of Songs* he surpassed himself."[49] Despite his later rejection of many of Origen's theological views, Jerome did not revise this high estimation, and in reading the Song as an allegory of divine love, he closely followed Origen's interpretation. Jerome chose to translate the two *Homilies* instead of the major *Commentary*, probably because in the *Homilies* the bride in the Song is identified with the Church, while in the *Commentary* this identification always goes hand in hand with the interpretation that the marriage also symbolizes the mystical union of Christ and the soul. It is owing to Rufinus that we now have the Latin version of Origen's *Commentary*.

Origen began his *Commentary* with a generic definition of the Song as "an epithalamium, that is to say, a marriage-song, which Solomon wrote in the form of a drama and sang under the figure of the Bride, about to wed and burning with heavenly love towards her Bridegroom, who is the Word of God."[50] The last part of this definition is crucial as it determines that the nature of love is "heavenly" and that the bridegroom is "the Word of God." The bride, according to Origen, is either the Church or the soul of individual Christians. He firmly based his allegorization on the Pauline dichotomy of the letter and the spirit (2 Cor. 3:6) or the spiritual and the carnal (1 Cor. 3:1). When Paul contrasted the letter of the Mosaic law with the spirit of Christian faith, declaring that the epistle of Christ was "written not with ink, but with the Spirit of the living God; not in tables of stone, but in fleshy tables of the heart" (2 Cor. 3:3), he was concerned not so much with positing an exegetical rule as with defining the Christian position with regard to Judaism in terms of a Christocentric theology. In rejecting Jewish legalism, Paul contrasted it with the new Christian faith not merely as letter and spirit, but as death and life.

This dichotomy, however, soon became a hermeneutic principle not only of how to conceive of Judaism from the Christian perspective, but also how to read Scripture allegorically in its spiritual sense. On the basis of this principle, Origen was able to insist that the description of physical charms

---

48. Daniélou, *Origen*, p. 304.
49. Origen, *The Song of Songs: Commentary and Homilies*, p. 265.
50. Ibid., p. 21.

in the Song "can in no way be applied to the visible body, but must be referred to the parts and powers of the invisible soul."[51] He declared that "just as the human being consists of body, soul, and spirit, so does Scripture which God has arranged to be given for the salvation of humankind."[52] In actual exegesis, Origen almost exclusively emphasized the spiritual meaning and claimed, following Philo, that concerning Scripture "all of it has a spiritual sense, but not all of it has a bodily sense. In fact, in many cases the bodily sense proves to be impossible."[53] He insisted that the literal or bodily sense should simply be eliminated from the Song so that the spiritual meaning might unfold itself before the discerning eyes of the faithful and that the sexual elements might be minimized. Origen argued that the three books attributed to Solomon were so arranged in the Old Testament that the Proverbs taught first the subject of morals, then Ecclesiastes discussed natural things and warned against vanity, and finally the Song of Songs dealt with the subject of contemplation. In this divinely inspired Song, Solomon "instils into the soul the love of things divine and heavenly, using for his purpose the figure of the Bride and Bridegroom, and teaches us that communion with God must be attained by the paths of charity and love."[54]

The search for the *sensus spiritualis* is undoubtedly a positive object in itself, but the apologetic motif is also quite evident in Origen's deep concern that the Song should first be carefully interpreted and properly seasoned with allegory before it is offered as spiritual food to the Christian reader. Or rather, it is the reader who must be properly prepared and adequately educated before he touches the Song. Otherwise there is "no small hazard and danger" in this sacred book, for the untrained reader may regard the book as giving him a sort of carte blanche for debauchery:

> For he, not knowing how to hear love's language in purity and with chaste ears, will twist the whole manner of his hearing of it away from the inner spiritual man and on to the outward and carnal; and he will be turned away from the spirit to the flesh, and will foster carnal desires in himself, and it will seem to be the Divine Scriptures that are thus urging and egging him on to fleshy lust!

> For this reason, therefore, I advise and counsel everyone who is not yet rid of the vexations of flesh and blood and has not ceased to feel the passion of

51. Ibid., p. 28.

52. Origen, "On First Principles, Book Four," 2.4, in Froehlich, *Biblical Interpretation in the Early Church*, p. 58.

53. Ibid., p. 67. For Philo's influence on Origen concerning the literal and the allegorical, see Wolfson, *Philo*, 1:158–59; also Daniélou, *Origen*, pp. 178–90.

54. Origen, *Commentary and Homilies*, p. 41.

his bodily nature, to refrain completely from reading this little book and the things that will be said about it.[55]

We can almost feel Origen's anxiety throbbing in this "advice and counsel." He seemed to feel abhorrence at the thought that a holy book in the Bible could in any way encourage physical love and lead the reader to the lusts of the flesh. This ascetic attitude is of course widely shared by the Church Fathers. When Jerome wrote to advise the education of a little girl named Paula, who had just been born in Rome in 401, he not only suggested that the future reading of the infant must be confined to the Bible and the orthodox Fathers, but he also prescribed a carefully planned route for her Bible reading: "Beginning with the Psalms, Proverbs, Ecclesiastes, and Job, she should pass on to the Gospels, Acts, and the Epistles. Then back to the Prophets and other Old Testament books. Only when well grounded in all these may she look into Song of Songs; if she tackled it too soon, she might jump to the mistaken, damaging conclusion that its theme is physical love."[56] For the pious and ascetic Father, love in its human sense is sin, and whatever is physical, sensuous, and pleasurable seems inherently dangerous. Anxious to guard the Song of Songs against its detractors and against any suggestion of carnal desire, Origen practiced allegorical interpretation in order to reveal the spiritual meaning of the text and thereby to dismiss all charges of pernicious influence and immorality. In that sense, then, allegoresis is not only an apologetic but also a *charitable* or benevolent interpretation of any part of the canonical text that might be seen as arousing physical, sensuous, and pleasurable reactions.

In Origen's allegorical reading, the epithalamium is the bodily form of the Canticle, and its spiritual meaning intimates the mystical union of Christ and the Church or Christ and the soul. We have seen that the midrashist interpreted the "two breasts" of the bride (4:5) as representing Moses and Aaron; similarly in commenting on verse 1:13, "he shall lie all night betwixt my breasts," Origen tells the reader to understand the "breasts" as "the ground of the heart in which the Church holds Christ, or the soul holds the Word of God."[57] When the text speaks about the "bed" in the sense of her body she shares with her lover, he urges the reader to "understand this in the light of the figure that Paul also uses when he says that *our bodies are members of Christ.*"[58] When the depiction of the love scene seems explicit, as in 2:6, "His left hand is under my head, and his right hand

55. Ibid., pp. 22–23.
56. Kelly, *Jerome: His Life, Writings, and Controversies*, p. 274.
57. Origen, *Commentary and Homilies*, p. 165.
58. Ibid., p. 173.

doth embrace me," he promptly warns the reader not to take it literally: "you must not understand the left and right hands of the Word of God in a corporeal sense, simply because He is called the Bridegroom, which is an epithet of male significance. Nor must you take the Bride's embraces in that way, simply because the word 'bride' is of feminine gender."[59] In the second *Homily*, Origen further explains that "the Word of God has both a left hand and a right"; therefore, the meaning of the verse is that "He may cause me to rest, that the Bridegroom's arm may be my pillow and the chief seat of the soul recline upon the Word of God."[60] In such an ascetic allegorical reading, the male-female relationship is aptly evaporated, all sensual imagery effaced, and any possible suggestion of eroticism utterly eliminated together with the literal sense of the biblical text.

For Origen, as noted earlier, everything in Scripture has a spiritual meaning but not necessarily a literal one; in reading Scripture, therefore, it is vital to find out the spiritual meaning beyond the bodily sense. Moreover, spiritual truth is concealed and can be attained only through allegorical interpretation because, says Origen, "the Word used actual historical events wherever they could be accommodated to these mystical (meanings), hiding the deeper sense from the multitude."[61] Here Origen was indebted to Philo, who had claimed that the allegorical meaning "loves to hide itself," and "only those who are qualified both by natural abilities and moral character and by preliminary training are to be instructed in the method of the allegorical interpretation of Scripture."[62] Of course, the emphasis on the hidden mystical nature of spiritual truth empowers the allegorist as guide to correct understanding of the Bible, as one initiated in the secret of God's message and capable of leading others to the circle of initiation. In Origen's writings, this emphasis on the mystery of spiritual meaning is reinforced by the dichotomy of letter and spirit, or shadow and reality. Relying on such a principle of typological thinking, Origen's allegoresis everywhere emphasizes the spiritual meaning and its revelation at the cost of suppression of the letter.

To understand Scripture correctly, as Origen puts it in summary, one must realize that "there are realities whose meaning cannot be properly expressed by any words of human language; it is affirmed by a simpler act of intellectual comprehension rather than by any properties words may have. . . . What [divine writings] say should not be judged by the lowliness of the verbal expression but by the divinity of the Holy Spirit who

59. Ibid., p. 200–201.
60. Ibid., pp. 297–98.
61. Origen, "On First Principles," 2.9, in *Biblical Interpretation in the Early Church*, p. 62.
62. Wolfson, *Philo*, 1:116.

inspired their composition."[63] For Origen and those who followed him, it seems that the written word should be cast off and forgotten in order to free the spirit of the Logos from the shell of human language. As a mode of interpretation that leads from the text to a deeper meaning beyond, allegoresis as Origen used it, becomes eventually the erasure of language for reaching to the Logos as pure presence of the divine.

From midrash or rabbinic interpretation to Origen's excessively allegorical reading, much of traditional commentaries on the Song of Songs share the same interpretive strategy of *displacement*, that is, displacing the text of the Song and its richly suggestive and erotic imagery with something else that is theologically proper and meaningful. The systematic displacement of textual elements makes it possible to read the canonical text as saying one thing but meaning another, and it constitutes the crucial strategy for all allegorical interpretations. In displacing the literal sense with a spiritual meaning, allegoresis makes the Song of Songs congenial with the other books of the Bible and thereby justifies its canonicity. On the other hand, however, as our further discussion of the implications of allegorical readings will show, such displacement also tends to make the canonical text susceptible to misreading and misinterpretations.

Reading the *Book of Poetry*

The way biblical exegetes use allegorization to read the Song of Songs as a theologically meaningful and morally edifying text and to justify its canonicity bears striking similarities to the way many traditional Chinese scholars read the Confucian canon, *Shi jing* or the *Book of Poetry*. This is especially true for the first part of *Shi jing* known as *Guo feng* or "airs from the various states." As the first anthology of Chinese verse allegedly compiled by Confucius himself (a legend the great historian Sima Qian [145?-90? B.C.E.] recorded in Confucius's biography), the *Book of Poetry* occupies an extremely important place in ancient Chinese culture, comparable to that of the Homeric epics or the Bible in the Western world.[64] "As Greek

63. Origen, "On First Principles," 3.15, p. 78.

64. The legend that Confucius has a hand in the compilation of the *Book of Poetry*, that he selected some three hundred poems out of a pool of three thousand ancient songs, has a particular moralistic ring to it as it indicates that the great sage has included only those songs that conform to moral propriety and excluded those that are lascivious and deviating from the norm. Though backed by the authorities of great Han historians Sima Qian and Ban Gu (32–92), this legend was later seriously questioned by many writers and scholars. Kong Yingda (574–648) of the Tang Dynasty already proclaimed Sima Qian's words "unbelievable" (*Mao shi*, in Ruan Yuan [ed.], *Shisan jing zhushu*, 1:263). On the other hand, however, though

poets and philosophers often cited Homer to endorse their argument or as the Christians hold the Old and the New Testaments as their guide in life," says Zheng Zhenduo, a famous Chinese bibliophile and literary scholar, "so would our ancient statesmen and literati turn to a verse or two from the *Book of Poetry* as ground for their views in debate or admonition, or as evidence in their promulgation or argument."[65] To many scholars who know both the Chinese tradition and the canonical books in the West, similarities of the canon and the method of its exegesis, and more specifically the comparable status of Homer, the Bible, and the Chinese classic as Zheng mentioned, suggest themselves naturally.[66]

As an anthology of the earliest songs in China, the antiquity of the *Book of Poetry* undoubtedly contributed to its canonization, but the word *jing*—referring to a classic or canonical book—is not used in early texts to refer to this anthology, which is simply mentioned as *Shi* (Poetry) or *Three Hundred*, the rounded-up number of poems in the anthology. The word *jing* was not added to the title until the Warring States period (475–221 B.C.E.).[67] Once canonized, however, this anthology of ancient songs was elevated to such a high position of social significance that it was expected to teach the perfection of morality. "A classic," as Liu Xie puts it, "is exposition of the eternal and ultimate *tao* and unalterable great teachings."[68] For poems that do not explicitly deal with religious or moral issues in some sanctioned orthodox fashion, however, canonicity may well prove to be a burden, because the text often seems to lack relevance or fails to deliver the expected meaning or canonical significance. In such

---

not necessarily believing in the authenticity of the legend, many have nonetheless appealed to it to underscore the prestige and importance of the *Book of Poetry* as one of the canonized Confucian classics. For discussions of the questioning of this legend, see Jiang Boqian, *Shisan jing gailun*, p. 188; and Zhou Yutong, "Confucius," in *Zhou Yutong jingxueshi lunzhu xuanji*, p. 355.

65. Zheng Zhenduo, *Chatu ben Zhongguo wenxue shi*, 1:36.

66. For a cross-cultural study of different exegetical traditions, see Henderson, *Scripture, Canon, and Commentary: A Comparison of Confucian and Western Exegesis*.

67. See Zhou Yutong, "Classics, Classical Studies, and the History of Classical Studies," in *Jingxueshi lunzhu xuanji*, p. 650. Jiang Boqian provides a brief survey of the meanings of the word *jing* and finds Zhang Binglin's (1860–1936) explanation most sensible and satisfying, which defines *jing* as etymologically the string that ties bamboo slips together into scrolls for writing in ancient China. Based on that explanation, Jiang concludes that "what is called *jing* was originally the general name for all books, but it becomes the term for a special class of books that are revered in later time as canon or classics" (*Shisan jing gailun*, p. 3). In that sense, then, *jing*, like the word Bible, originally means book, but more specifically a *canonical book* or *scripture*. That is why I have translated *Shi jing* as the *Book of Poetry* rather than *Classic of Poetry*, though many scholars prefer the latter translation.

68. Liu Xie, *Wenxin diaolong*, p. 18.

cases, the expected or prerequisite canonical meaning or function of the text must be supplied by tightly controlled interpretations.

When poetry is thought to give us divine knowledge, virtue, and wisdom, we cannot read it as mere poetry or literature but interpret it instead as religion, ethics, or philosophy. That is to say, we do not read it as a text with more or less autonomous self-referentiality, but as an allegory that says one thing but means something quite different from its literal sense—a "true" meaning beyond the text, accessible only through elaborate commentaries and exegeses. Of course, no text is free from interpretation, but allegoresis is not just any interpretation: in the case of Song of Songs or the *Book of Poetry*, it is a strong interpretation that often ignores, or even does violence to, the letter of the text in order to make it fit within the framework of a religious, moral, political, or philosophical system. It is often the case that meaning in allegorical interpretation does not so much arise from one's reading as it precedes one's reading; indeed, it provides the very context of one's reading. To some extent, it is not something one learns from and about the text, but the confirmation of something one already knows before one reads: the ideas, beliefs, and expectations one has with regard to the canonical text and its meaning.

In Greek antiquity, as Curtius reminds us, the poet was at once sage and educator; poetry should therefore tell of the truth: it should teach as well as delight. Acting so often like mere human beings, however, Homer's gods cannot always be revered as paragons of virtue. If there is any pedagogic merit in Homer's works, as the Greeks believed there should be, it must exist somewhere beyond the literal sense of the text and could only be revealed through allegorical interpretation. Moreover, in the rise of scientific thinking of Ionian natural philosophy, the demand for truth put old mythology in question and formed the ground for denouncing poetry as lying. It was again allegorical interpretation that helped settle the dispute between philosophy and poetry and that justified the canonicity of Homer. Beyond or beneath the surface of the Homeric text, the allegorists claim, there is another speech with a proper sense, containing a profound moral teaching. "From the first century of our era onwards," says Curtius, "allegoresis gains ground. All schools of philosophy find that their doctrines are in Homer, as Seneca mockingly remarks."[69] In late antiquity, not only did allegoresis become "*the* way of talking about Homer, and an integral part of that *paideia*," as James Kugel also notes, but "Scripture too lent itself to such a reading . . . a special sort of informed reading, one keen to the text's 'other

69. Curtius, pp. 205–6.

speaking.'"[70] Allegoresis thus became the predominant way of reading Homer and the Bible as canonical texts, and this, as we shall see, was also the case with the Chinese *Book of Poetry*.

From the dozen or so references in the Confucian *Analects* to the first anthology of Chinese poetry, we can see clearly what was to become the orthodox line in traditional Chinese criticism: a moralistic and utilitarian tendency to read literature as an instrument of achieving moral perfection both in individual cultivation and in the social order. In this basic idea of the use of poetry for pedagogic purposes, we may already find the ground for allegoresis in the Chinese tradition. Confucius once told his son: "If you do not study *Poetry*, you will have nothing in your speech."[71] The idea that familiarity with poetry will make one more refined in speech is also the point Confucius made when he remarked: "If you speak without any embellishment (*wen*), your words will not go far enough."[72] The use of the *Book of Poetry* as a primer of rhetoric reminds us of the pedagogic function of Homer in ancient Greece and the attitude toward classical literature in early Christianity as set forth by Augustine, who maintained that Christians should read pagan and secular poetry and learn about the various rhetorical devices solely for acquiring the necessary equipment for better understanding the Scriptures. For Augustine, the knowledge of tropes like allegory, irony, antiphrasis and so on "is necessary to a solution of the ambiguities of the Scriptures, for when the sense is absurd if it is taken verbally, it is to be inquired whether or not what is said is expressed in this or that trope which we do not know; and in this way many hidden things are discovered."[73] For Confucius, the study of poetry serves no overtly religious purpose but prepares one for polished moral suasion or diplomatic discourse, or generally for better skills of communication in the performance of civic duties.

In a famous passage urging his students to study the *Book of Poetry*, Confucius defines the functions of poetry as *xing* (the affective function of giving rise to high spirits), *guan* (the cognitive function of revealing social conditions and changes), *qun* (the communal function of reconciling different interests of social groups), and *yuan* (the cathartic function of giving vent to one's sorrow or grievances with a view to appealing to the authorities for rectification).[74] Given the practical value he has in

---

70. Kugel, "The 'Bible as Literature' in Late Antiquity and the Middle Ages," *Hebrew University Studies in Literature and the Arts* 11 (Spring 1983): 30.

71. Confucius, *Lunyu*, xvi.13, p. 363.

72. *Chunqiu Zuo zhuan zhengyi*, in *Shisan jing zhushu*, 2:1985.

73. St. Augustine, *On Christian Doctrine*, 3.29.41, p. 104.

74. See *Lunyu*, xvii.9, p. 374. The interpretation and consequently the translation of the

mind, he gives hardly any consideration to the aesthetic value of poetry. "If someone can recite all the three hundred poems, but cannot fully communicate with others when entrusted with administrative responsibilities, or fails to respond to changing situations when sent as an envoy to foreign states, no matter how many poems he can memorize, what use can he make of them?"[75] Having acquainted ourselves with this typical Confucian pragmatism, we may understand why the Master's overall comment on the *Book of Poetry* sounds more apologetic than complimentary: "Of the three hundred poems one can sum up the substance in one phrase: herein there is no evil."[76] That is indeed the highest tribute Confucius paid to poetry, a comment at least less militantly censorious than Plato's attack on poetry as deceptive fiction and a morally pernicious influence.

The Confucian *Analects* contains a few passages where brief and somewhat opaque remarks are made on verses quoted from the *Book of Poetry*. Let us take a look at two such passages in some detail. The first is a conversation between Confucius and his disciple Zigong, whom the Master calls by his given name Ci:

> Zigong said: "How about being poor but not fawning, and being rich but not haughty?" The Master said, "That's fine; however, it is not as good as being poor but taking pleasure in the Way, and being rich but gladly observant of the rites."
> Zigong then asked: "*Poetry* has it: 'As if cut, as if carved, / As if chiseled, as if polished.' Is that referring to what you have just said?" The Master answered, "Ah, Ci, now at last I can discuss *Poetry* with you, for being told one thing past, you are able to know what is to come."[77]

In the first paragraph, Zigong asked his teacher about the qualities or qualifications of a virtuous man: he wondered whether one was already good enough if one was poor but not fawning, or rich but not haughty. Confucius added to these the ideas of moral cultivation and following the ancient rites as the way to that cultivation. Zigong then cited some lines from the *Book of Poetry* to illustrate Confucius's meaning: a typical way of

---

four functions defined by Confucius is still a matter of debate. D. C. Lau's version reads: "An apt quotation from the *Odes* may serve to stimulate the imagination, to show one's breeding, to smooth over difficulties in a group and to give expression to complaint" (*The Analects*, p. 145). James J. Y. Liu translates the same passage as "It can be used to inspire, to observe, to make you fit for company, to express grievances" (Liu, *Chinese Theories of Literature*, p. 109). For a more detailed discussion of the four terms, see Liu, ibid., pp. 109–111.

75. *Lunyu*, xiii.5, p. 285.
76. Ibid., ii.2, p. 21.
77. Ibid., i.15, pp. 18–19.

using poetry in pre-Qin texts. The Master was evidently impressed and considered Zigong the initiated one who knew how to make connections between what was said explicitly and what was implied, and how to understand the hidden meaning beyond the obvious. The connection between the quoted lines and the topic under discussion, however, is not immediately clear. The stanza of the poem in which those lines appear reads:

> Look at that curve of River Qi,
> Lush are the reeds and bamboo.
> There is a handsome gentleman,
> As if cut, as if carved,
> As if chiseled, as if polished.
> Oh he is noble; he is strong,
> Oh he is bright; he is renowned.
> There is a handsome gentleman,
> Oh, never can I forget him.[78]

In their original context, the lines Zigong quoted seem to form part of a love song: they describe a "handsome gentleman" and portray his finely shaped figure. In the conversation between Confucius and his student, however, these lines are made to mean something quite different that bears on the issue of moral perfection. As many commentators have pointed out, here Zigong seems to have drawn an implicit analogy that just as materials like bone, ivory, jade, and stone can be turned into precious objects by being cut, carved, chiseled, and polished, so can good natural dispositions ("not fawning" and "not haughty") be improved upon through moral cultivation ("taking pleasure in the Way" and "observant of the rites").[79] Thus cutting, carving, chiseling, and polishing become figures or metaphorical expressions of the arduous training and self-cultivation in studying the classics, which will turn men with promising natural qualities into fine and virtuous gentlemen. When analogies of this kind are established, poetic lines are literally lifted out of their context and put into a new environment in which they acquire a meaning very different from what they originally may mean.

Let us now turn to the other passage, in which we find Confucius using exactly the same words to praise another student of his, Zixia, named Pu Shang, for making unexpected connections between verses quoted from the *Book of Poetry* and, again, the topic of moral perfection.

---

78. *Mao shi*, 53a, in *Shisan jing zhushu*, 1:321.
79. See Liu Baonan's (1791–1855) collated commentaries, in *Lunyu*, p. 19.

Zixia asked: "'Her lovely smile dimpling, / Her beautiful eyes turning, / Plain silk for colorful patterns.' What does all this mean?" The Master said, "Painting colors after making the plain background."

Zixia then said, "Do the rites likewise come afterwards?" The Master said, "Oh, Shang, it is you who have enlightened me on this! Now at last I can discuss *Poetry* with you."[80]

The use of the lines quoted from the *Book of Poetry* in this case is even more puzzling. Indeed, there seems some suggestion that even Confucius was a little surprised by Zixia's interpretation, as he acknowledged to have been "enlightened" by his student. Zixia, on his part, was apparently not satisfied with Confucius's plain answer to the question he had raised about those poetic lines. He then took the initiative to give his own explanation and related the quoted lines to "the rites." Here the connection between the lines and moral perfection depends on the idea of sequence of things that come before and after. In Zixia's analogy, the rites, like colors, come afterwards, presumably following the Confucian virtues of benevolence and righteousness as the plain background. The third line that provides the basis of Zixia's analogy, "Plain silk for colorful patterns," does not appear in the *Book of Poetry* as we now have it, whereas the first two lines, which do appear in a poem from the anthology, describe the beauty of a woman and have nothing to do with ancient rites. These verses can be forced into a connection with moral virtue only by a strained interpretive act, a not particularly ingenious sleight of hand.

The Use versus the Reading of Poetry

What we see above in the *Analects* is the kind of forced reading known as *duan zhang qu yi* (taking meaning out of a broken stanza), which, as Qian Zhongshu points out, is a common phenomenon in ancient China,

---

80. Confucius, *Lunyu*, iii.8, p. 48. The precise meaning of the third line quoted and consequently that of Confucius's laconic answer are rather uncertain. I have followed one way of reading them in my translation, which basically agrees with D. C. Lau's (See Confucius, *The Analects*, p. 68). The third line quoted, however, can also be understood as "White brings final touch to colors." Confucius's answer would then be something like the following: "In painting, white comes afterwards." This means, as the famous Han commentator Zheng Xuan (127–200) explains, that "painting is the making of patterns. In painting, one first applies various colors, and then distributes white space among the colors to form patterns. This is a metaphor for the perfection of a beautiful woman by following the appropriate rites, even though she already has the qualities of beauty with her dimpling smile and lovely eyes" (*Lunyu*, iii.8, pp. 48–49). Zheng Xuan, of course, is making explicit what Zixia obliquely refers to in that brief conversation.

something "often perpetrated by the ancients and repeatedly seen in classical writings. All are ancient 'phrases and verses' borrowed to express present 'feelings and things.'"[81] In such a practice of free association, almost anything can be read into anything else, and we constantly find an analogy or parallelism being constructed in the reading that displaces the literal sense of the text. That may strike us as remarkably similar to the use of verses from the Song of Songs as *meshalim* in rabbinic interpretation or the Christian allegorization of classical literature, especially Virgil's works, which, "once yanked out of context," as Kugel observes, are rendered "capable of being attributed new, evangelical, significance."[82] In such cases, the quotation of poetic lines is very rarely the complete text (except when the poem is extremely short, composed of a few lines), but a "broken stanza," a verse or two out of the original context so that the meaning of the quoted lines can be manipulated to suit the purpose at hand. In the passages discussed above, the governing principle is to relate everything to the Confucian moral teaching, which provides a new framework for understanding verses quoted from the *Book of Poetry*, regardless of what meaning they may have in the original poem as a whole. The important point here, as Donald Holzman remarks, is "not that Confucius emphasizes the morality of the poem; it is that he deforms the poem so that it can be *used*."[83]

The *use* of poetry as opposed to the *reading* of poetry is a crucial issue, particularly in the light of the rather common practice in ancient China of "taking meaning out of a broken stanza." Here the distinction between use and reading hinges on whether one acknowledges the textual integrity of the poem under discussion and respects that integrity. The many examples in pre-Qin texts, especially *Zuo zhuan*, seem to suggest that the use of poetry for diplomatic or other purposes was indeed a very ancient practice, and it therefore appears questionable whether one should posit a "first," literal sense of the poem predating its alleged later distortion in allegoresis. This is indeed a significant question, but the practice of using or quoting poetry in ancient China presupposes the existence of a body of poetry already created separately from the practice of citation; that is to say, poems necessarily predate the use of poetry. Moreover, poems are not single words or phrases that do not have definite meanings until they are used as building blocks in a particular context. On the contrary, a poem is a text already constructed with coherence of

81. Qian Zhongshu, *Guan zhui bian*, 1:224.
82. Kugel, "The 'Bible as Literature' in Late Antiquity and the Middle Ages," p. 34.
83. Holzman, "Confucius and Ancient Chinese Literary Criticism," in *Chinese Approaches to Literature from Confucius to Liang Ch'i-ch'ao*, ed. Rickett, p. 32.

meaning, the totality of semantic values and syntactic relations. In short, poems are words already in use. The meaning of a poem is surely not context-free, but it is the totality of the poem itself, the way words and phrases are put together in a specific order and interrelationship that constitutes the basic or primary context for its interpretation. In that sense, then, any figurative or allegorical meaning must be based on the literal sense of the text, and any use of poetry that does violence to that primary context would constitute a breaking of the poem's textual integrity.

Not surprisingly, the poem used in a diplomatic exchange or other such practical discourse in pre-Qin China was often a "broken stanza," bits and pieces that might be bent in one way or another to suit the occasion. If poems in the first Chinese anthology existed only to be used, then, they would have no meaning independent of their subservience in religious ritual, moral suasion, diplomatic oration, or political maneuver, and it would indeed be pointless to talk about their aesthetic values. But the fact that poems were quoted out of context and used for practical purposes in ancient times does not invalidate our effort to examine their aesthetic values from a literary point of view; indeed, it is probably their aesthetic values and rhetorical force that stimulated the practice of citation in the first place. Those ancient Chinese who quoted lines or stanzas out of context knew that they were using fragments of poems for purposes unrelated to the poem as a whole. Lupu Kui in *Zuo zhuan* acknowledged as much when he referred to such a practice as "reciting poetry as broken stanzas" (*fu shi duan zhang*).[84] That is to say, poetry as a literary construct distinct from its practical use was an idea fully recognized in pre-Qin antiquity.

The use of poetry as broken stanzas was not, however, the whole story. When the Great Preface to the *Book of Poetry*, that cornerstone of the entire commentary tradition, defines poetry as the articulation of the poet's intent at heart, as Haun Saussy notes, it "interprets the familiar 'Poetry expresses intent' of the *Book of Documents* as a statement about poetic meaning, not about the uses to which poetry might be put; its assumptions are therefore different from those of the *Tso Commentary's* nobles and diplomats."[85] That is to say, textual integrity was already assumed in traditional commentaries, and instead of proclaiming the legitimacy of the use of poetry, the commentators were making claims to the intention of the poet as basis for their interpretation. Therefore, it is only fair to examine and judge the merits of the Great Preface and the other

84. *Chunqiu Zuo zhuan zhengyi*, 298a, in *Shisan jing zhushu*, 2:2000.
85. Saussy, *The Problem of a Chinese Aesthetic*, p. 86.

traditional interpretations according to the criteria they themselves have assumed. Many critics in the modern period are doing just that. "The Great Preface is meant to explain the *Book of Poetry*," Zheng Zhenduo argues. "We must therefore follow the poems as the primary texts and must not misread the poems on the grounds of the Preface. Insofar as the Preface agrees with the meaning of the poems, we would respect it; but if the Preface violates the meaning of the poems, we should definitely reject it no matter how old it is and who its author is, whether Confucius or someone else."[86] Indeed, much of modern scholarship on the *Book of Poetry* depends on the discrimination of the meaning of poetry in its own context from the use of poetry out of context, and it is for the use, or rather the abuse, of poetry that modern critics have taken traditional commentators to task.

The historian Gu Jiegang's (1893–1980) survey of the pre-Qin reception of the *Book of Poetry* still remains probably the most exhaustive and informative study of this particular issue. Gu acknowledges that during the Spring and Autumn period (c. 722–481 B.C.E.), the widely circulated verses quoted out of context were used, very much in the manner of set phrases and proverbs, to express whatever meaning the users intended. The conversations between Confucius and his disciples quoted above from the *Analects* can thus be seen as typical examples of the way poetry was used at the time, but such a practice of "citing poetry as broken stanzas," Gu argues, is not literary criticism per se and was never meant to be. The ancients who used poetry in such a way did not claim to make commentaries on the *Book of Poetry* or individual poems as such. Moreover, Gu identifies Mencius's famous remarks concerning the reading of poetry as a crucial moment when the use of poetry turns into a search for textual meaning, that is, from a "non-poetics of quotation" during the Spring and Autumn period to a poetics of authorial intention that dominates traditional Chinese criticism since the period of the Warring States (c. 475–221 B.C.E.). Mencius told Xianqiu Meng that "the interpreter of a poem should not let the words obscure the text, or the text obscure the intention. To trace back to the original intention with sympathetic understanding: that is the way to do it."[87] With "back to the original intention" assigned to the interpreter as at once the task of interpretation and its measurement, Mencius put an end to the random use of poetry practiced during an earlier period, and that, says Gu, marked "the inception of poetics" in the Chinese literary tradition, even though Mencius himself often interpreted verses from the *Book of*

86. Zheng Zhenduo, "Reading the Mao Preface to the *Book of Poetry*," in *Gu shi bian*, ed. Gu Jiegang et al., 3:397.

87. *Mencius*, ix.4, p. 377.

Poetry no less arbitrarily than his predecessors.[88] According to Mencius, then, a poem and its meaning are governed by the poet's intention, and a good reader who "knows the sound" (*zhiyin*) is supposed not to let his reading violate the text or the original intention, but he should recuperate the poet's original voice as it is inscribed in the poem.

A problem arises, however, when poems and their apparent meanings or authorial intentions do not easily corroborate the moral values that Confucian commentators would like all canonical literature to impart. As one may expect of any anthology of ancient songs, the *Book of Poetry* contains a large number of poems dealing with the joy as well as the pain of love, and such poems do not lend themselves easily to a moralistic reading. The *locus classicus* in any discussion of the *Book of Poetry* is the very first song in the anthology, "*Guan ju*," a love song, perhaps an epithalamium, over which Confucian commentators have woven a heavy layer of elaborate moral-political exegesis. Let us first look at the text in a literal translation:

> *Guan, guan,* cry the fish-hawks
> On the islet of the river.
> The pretty and good girl,
> The gentleman loves to woo her.
>
> High and low grows the waterplant,
> Left and right we catch it.
> The pretty and good girl,
> Awake or asleep he seeks her.
>
> He seeks her but to no avail,
> Awake or asleep he thinks of her;
> Longing for her, and longing,
> He turns and tosses all night.
>
> High and low grows the waterplant,
> Left and right we gather it.
> The pretty and good girl,
> With zither and lute we greet her.
>
> High and low grows the waterplant,
> Left and right we choose it.
> The pretty and good girl,
> With bell and drum we cheer her.[89]

---

88. Gu Jiegang, "The Place of the *Book of Poetry* during the Period of the Spring and Autumn and the Warring States," in *Gu shi bian*, 3:363.

89. *Mao shi*, 5b-6b, in *Shisan jing zhushu*, 1:273–74.

Confucius himself has chosen to comment on this poem, and his commentary smacks of the condescending generosity the great pedagogue must have felt when he smiled at this harmless little song, in which, the Master certified, "there is joy without licentiousness, and sorrow without self-inflicted harm."[90] That is to say, emotions expressed here are all right and proper, tame and moderate, under good control and conformable to the Confucian idea of decorum. As commentators later picked up the suggestion of moderated emotion and stretched it into an elaborate reading, the moralistic line thickened in interpretation that understood the poem either as a critique of the improper behavior of King Kang and his queen (11th century B.C.E.) by setting up the image of proper courtship, or conversely as an encomium of the virtuous queen of King Wen (d. 1027 B.C.E.). The poem, according to the Han commentators Mao Heng and Zheng Xuan (127–200), is about "the moral virtue of the queen." Kong Yingda (574–648) of the Tang dynasty develops the idea further and argues:

> "*Guan ju*" expresses the idea that what pleases the queen is her pleasure of finding the good and pure girl for her own lord, what concerns her is her anxiety to present good ladies to the lord and to take no pride in her own beauty, and what makes her sad is that ladies in secluded and obscure places are not promoted. Her desire is to find those with virtue and talents and have all of them serve the king; she takes great pains and thinks a great deal about this, and she never wants to harm the good. That is the meaning of "*Gu ju*."[91]

Comparing the commentary with the poem itself, we find that such a reading has little to do with the actual text, but has a great deal to do with Confucian moral and political philosophy. In this explanation, any emotion in excess becomes licentiousness. "When a man loves a woman too much, he becomes lecherous; and when a woman exceeds the proper bounds in seeking a man's favors, she becomes wanton in her own fairness," even if the emotion involved is marital love between husband and wife.[92] This may remind us of the ascetic Christian view that passion is in itself sinful, even though marriage is excusable if it is appropriately oriented toward procreation. As C. S. Lewis observes, such an asceticism is quite relevant to the allegorization of love in medieval literature, because "according to the medieval view passionate love itself was wicked, and did

90. *Lunyu*, iii.20, p. 62.
91. *Mao shi*, 5a–b, in *Shisan jing zhushu*, 1:273.
92. Ibid., 5b.

not cease to be wicked if the object of it were your wife . . . *omnis ardentior amator propriae uxoris adulter est,* passionate love of a man's own wife is adultery."[93] The fish-hawks, according to the Confucian commentators, love one another but live separately, and they provide an appropriate metaphorical initiation (*xing*) into the theme of the poem, namely, the proper relation between the king and the queen. The commentators claim that because the virtuous queen is content to stay in seclusion, like the good birds sitting in their nest, and abstain from excessive intimacy with her husband, she sets a good example to help shape the moral order of the world.

> When man and wife observe the separation of the sexes, father and son will remain close to each other. When father and son remain close to each other, the king and his minister will have mutual respect. When the king and his minister have mutual respect, all at court will be fair and just. When all at court is fair and just, the king's benevolent influence will shape the whole world.[94]

The emphasis on the ethico-political effect of such a short song is truly staggering, and to most modern readers such an interpretation seems completely tedious, far-fetched, and unwarranted by the text.

Most Western Sinologists recognize the long tradition of moralistic exegesis as "allegorical" and feel quite uncomfortable with it. Ironically, however, many of them failed to step out of the huge shadow of this exegetical tradition, even though they consciously tried. Among earlier translators, for example, James Legge considered the traditional view "not worth while to discuss," namely, the notion "that the subject of the piece is Wen's queen, and that it celebrates her freedom from jealousy, and her anxiety to fill his harem with virtuous ladies." Nevertheless, traditional commentaries have evidently influenced Legge's translation, of which the first stanza reads:

> Hark! from the islet in the stream the voice
> Of the fish-hawks that o'er their nest rejoice!
> From them our thoughts to that young lady go,
> Modest and virtuous, loth herself to show.
> Where could be found, to share our prince's state,
> So fair, so virtuous, and so fit a mate?[95]

93. Lewis, *The Allegory of Love,* pp. 14–15.
94. *Mao shi,* 5b, 1:273.
95. Legge, trans., *The She King or the Book of Ancient Poetry,* p. 59.

Compared with the more literal version I gave above, it becomes quite obvious that the "girl" becomes "that young lady" and that the "gentleman" (*junzi*, a "respectable man") becomes "our prince." There is no hint in the original text that the lady is to "share our prince's state," which is totally unjustifiable unless one presumes that indeed "the subject of the piece is Wen's queen."

Similarly, in his French and Latin translations of 1896, Father S. Couvreur takes the poem as sung by palace ladies in praise of the queen: "*Les femmes du palais chantent les vertus de Tai Séu, épouse de Wênn wâng.*" The first stanza in his French version thus reads:

> *Les* ts'iu kiou (*se répondant l'un à l'autre, crient*) kouan kouan *sur un îlot dans la rivière. Une fille vertueuse (T'ai Seu), qui vivait retire et cachée (dans la maison maternelle), devient la digne compagne d'un prince sage (Wenn wang).*[96]

Here, the virtuous lady is described as hiding in her mother's house, and the phrase "*devient la digne compagne d'un prince sage,*" like Legge's "to share our prince's state," owes more to traditional exegesis than to the actual words of the poem.

Twentieth-century Sinologists who are more sensitive to the literary value of the *Book of Poetry* tend to reject the moralistic rationalization in traditional commentaries. In his prose translation (1942–46), Bernhard Karlgren makes a special effort to be "as literal as possible" and contributes immensely to this tendency toward reading the *Book of Poetry* as an anthology of early Chinese poetry valuable in itself without all the trappings of Confucian moralism. Arthur Waley, whose translation appeared in 1937, attempts to dissociate the anthology from Confucius, arguing that "the songs are indeed 'Confucian' in the sense that Confucius (who lived c. 500 B. C.) and his followers used them as texts for moral instruction, much as Greek pedagogues used Homer. There is no reason to suppose that Confucius had a hand in forming the collection."[97] The reference to the pedagogic use of Homer is noteworthy, as is his later reference to the allegorical reading of the Bible. Waley's translation thus tries to rid the poem of traditional commentaries and follows closely the wording of the original text.

The difference between earlier and more recent translations becomes evident when we compare the first stanza in Waley's and Karlgren's translations with those by Legge and Couvreur quoted earlier. First, Waley's version reads:

96. Couvreur, *Cheu King: texte chinois avec une double traduction en français et en latin*, p. 5.
97. Waley, trans., *The Book of Songs*, p. 18.

> "Fair, fair," cry the ospreys
> On the island in the river.
> Lovely is this noble lady,
> Fit bride for our lord.[98]

The following is Karlgren's:

Kwan kwan (cries) the ts'ü-kiu bird, on the islet of the river; the beautiful and good girl, she is a good mate for the lord.[99]

Both versions are fairly close to the literal sense of the text, though Waley's "noble lady" and the word "lord" in both versions may sound more elevated than the original words in Chinese (*shunü* and *junzi*). There is, however, no suggestion of a royal consort and her moral virtues. In an appendix on "allegorical interpretation," Waley acknowledges that allegorization and the use of poems "for a variety of social and educational purposes which had nothing to do with their original intention" actually helped preserve the songs, especially the love songs, which "could only be used for moral instruction if interpreted allegorically." He then remarks that allegorical interpretation is not confined to traditional Chinese commentaries: "Parts of our own Bible have been explained on similar lines, particularly the Song of Solomon and certain of the Psalms." He hails the "enormous advances" in sinological studies since Marcel Granet's 1911 French translation of some of the love songs, because that translation rejects traditional exegesis and has discovered the "true nature" of those poems.[100] I should add that since the end of imperial China in the early twentieth century, to read the love songs in the *Book of Poetry* as love songs, that is, as literary texts with no hidden meanings of moral and political significance as traditionally laid out by Confucian commentators, is also the typical way most Chinese readers approach this ancient book in modern times.

Scholars and critics tend to see traditional commentaries as unwarranted moral and political overinterpretation imposed on poetry without considerations of its literal meaning or aesthetic values. "The susceptibility to allegorization in the traditional *Shih Ching* scholarship," as C. H. Wang puts it, "is a manifest distortion of this classic anthology, a distortion both of its genetic character and of the original definition of *shih* in general."[101]

---

98. Ibid., 81–82.
99. Karlgren, trans., *The Book of Odes*, p. 2.
100. *The Book of Songs*, pp. 335, 336, 337.
101. Wang, *The Bell and the Drum*, p. 1.

Applying Milman Parry and Albert Lord's theory of oral verse-making to the Chinese classic, Wang argues that the ancient poems recorded in the *Book of Poetry* were originally composed and transmitted orally, of which a variety of set phrases or "formulas" are important component parts, and that the earliest definition of *shi* or poetry, as seen in the *Book of Documents*, clearly relates poetry with music and dancing. It is debatable whether Wang has successfully applied the theory worked out by Parry and Lord to the anthology of ancient Chinese poetry. Yet his study of the Chinese classic as formulaic poetry in an oral tradition also continues the general trend in Chinese scholarship of the 1930s and the 1940s—from the work of Gu Jiegang and Zheng Zhenduo to Wen Yiduo. This is an important body of work that takes a different orientation in *Shi jing* scholarship from the tendency toward allegorization in much of traditional commentaries.

But can we characterize the Confucian commentary tradition as allegoresis? Is there allegory in Chinese literature? If allegory presupposes the transcendence of the literal level toward a different level of metaphysical presence and necessarily points to something abstract, invisible, and of a spiritual nature, is it true that all these are inconceivable and out of the question in a Chinese context? In considering possible ways to answer these questions, let us first recall one more time Quintilian's basic definition: "*Allegory*, which is translated in Latin by *inversio*, either presents one thing in words and another in meaning, or else something absolutely opposed to the meaning of the words."[102] Notice that Quintilian does not specify that what is said and what is meant, which is to say, the vehicle and the tenor of an extended metaphor (another way to define allegory) necessarily belong to two realms opposed to one another—the concrete world of historical reality versus the abstract world of spiritual truth. The one thing said and the other meant can be any two things of different kinds, whatever the kind.[103]

Quintilian's discussion with classic examples makes this abundantly clear. In examining the use of various rhetorical devices to achieve the effect of jest, he cites Cicero's joking remark on Marcus Caelius that "he had a good right hand, but a weak left," by which Cicero meant that Caelius "was better at bringing charges than at defending his client against them." Here the right hand, the one that holds the sword, stands for attack or bringing charges, and the left hand, which carries the shield, stands for the ability to defend. Both the vehicle and the tenor are, so to

102. Quintilian, *Institutio Oratoria*, VIII.vi.44, 3:327.

103. Quintilian remarks that a "continued *metaphor* develops into *allegory*" (ibid., IX.ii.46, 3:401). Cf. Saussy: "Allegory in the technicist and—*sit venia verbo*—pagan sense of the ancient rhetors says one thing and means another, whatever the thing said and the thing meant may be." *The Problem of a Chinese Aesthetic*, p. 28.

speak, of this world, referring to a real person and his abilities, and yet Quintilian considers this an example of *"allegory* in [Cicero's] witticism."[104] After giving the definition of allegory quoted above, Quintilian cites a few examples as illustrations. The first one is from Horace's ode that "represents the state under the semblance of a ship, the civil wars as tempests, and peace and good-will as the haven"; it is again firmly grounded in the real world of Roman history.[105]

The other type of allegory, in which what is meant is "absolutely opposed to the meaning of the words," has nothing to do with transcendental philosophy or theology, either, but it involves, says Quintilian, "an element of irony, or, as our rhetoricians call it, *illusio,*" that is, ironic statements that "censure with counterfeited praise and praise under a pretence of blame."[106] In fact, as they are so close to antiphrasis, mockery, and sarcasm, some writers do not consider them species of allegory but just tropes, "for they argue shrewdly that allegory involves an element of obscurity, whereas in all these cases our meaning is perfectly obvious."[107] For Quintilian and the ancient rhetorical tradition he represents, allegory is clearly not tied to a metaphysical or theological *sensus spiritualis.*

Even in the Christian concept of allegory, the literal and the allegorical do not necessarily dwell on different semantic levels, either. The medieval fourfold interpretation of the Bible, as Morton Bloomfield observes, does not always move the spiritual meaning away from the literal to a totally different level of transcendence or metaphysical presence.

> The moral or tropological level, for instance, does not refer to another reality revealed by words, but is actually *seen in the meaning itself.* When Isaac displays the virtue of obedience as he willingly lies on the altar at his father's command, the tropological meaning is right in the primary level of meaning: obedience to the command of one's superiors. Furthermore, in personification-allegory the allegorical meaning (or most of it) is in the literal sense itself. When Lady Holy Church appears in Passus I of the B Text of *Piers Plowman,* her allegorical significance is not the Christian significance of what Holy Church stands for, it is Holy Church right then and there.[108]

104. Quintilian, *Institutio Oratoria,* VI.iii.69, 2:477.

105. Ibid., VIII.vi.44, 3:327.

106. Ibid., VIII.vi.54–55, 3:333. Many poems in the Chinese anthology are also understood by the commentators as fundamentally ironic as either praise or blame in an indirect way of speech. For a detailed discussion of this ironic mode of praise or blame in the *Book of Poetry* and its relation with allegory, see Saussy, *The Problem of a Chinese Aesthetic,* pp. 91–96.

107. Quintilian, *Institutio Oratoria,* VIII.vi.58, 3:335.

108. Bloomfield, "Allegory as Interpretation," *New Literary History* 1 (Winter 1972): 313.

In the West, perhaps the symbolism of the Eucharist best represents the allegory of the theologians, in which wine and bread are not to be understood as real food at all but symbolize the blood and the body of Christ, where blood and body are not used in the usual bodily sense. "The material bread is of no benefit to those who eat it, even if the way they eat it is not unworthy of the Lord," says the great allegorist Origen. "What is of benefit to them is the word spoken over the bread." Though not exactly denying the efficacy of the sacrament as such, Origen here certainly emphasizes the spiritual significance of the Eucharist over the material objects with which the ritual is performed. "Spiritual eating," as Daniélou observes, "is plainly asserted to be superior to material."[109] Yet any ritual *qua* ritual must have a symbolic meaning beyond the material form of the sacrament. That is certainly true of the Eucharist, but isn't it also true of the ancient Chinese rites that Confucian scholars often talked about? Are Chinese rites merely concrete and material? Confucius surely did not think so. As if he had anticipated our question, he warned against a literal-minded understanding of the rites and music as only material paraphernalia in ritual processions when he posed this rhetorical question: "When we say 'the rites, the rites,' are we just talking about jade and silk? When we say 'music, music,' are we just talking about bells and drums?"[110] For Confucius, the meaning of the rites and music certainly resides beyond the material form of the ritual; it is not about the jade and silk, or the bells and drums. For Confucius, moral perfection is possible precisely because we can draw a symbolic, immaterial meaning out of the concrete form of a ritual. Obviously it is the same or equivalent ability of abstraction that constitutes the basis of any symbolic operation of language as well as the allegorical understanding of texts. The relevant question we may explore is not whether Western ritual is symbolic but Chinese rites are not, but what different contents the ritualized forms may express in the different cultural traditions.

Allegory and Historical Contextualization

It is certainly possible that a text with no intended allegorical meanings is read allegorically; and this is true in China as it is in the West. In denying the possibility of allegory in Chinese poetry, some scholars argue that ancient songs in the *Book of Poetry* are not in themselves allegorical; but

109. Daniélou, *Origen*, pp. 64, 65.
110. *Lunyu*, xvii.11, p. 375.

one may answer that neither are the Homeric epics. Erich Auerbach maintains that "the Homeric poems conceal nothing, they contain no teaching and no secret second meaning. . . . Later allegorizing trends have tried their arts of interpretation upon him, but to no avail. He resists any such treatment; the interpretations are forced and foreign, they do not crystallize into a unified doctrine."[111] This is evidently a modern opinion, but in Greek antiquity, as Jon Whitman remarks, even though "Homer himself writes no allegorical work, his twofold perspective of gods interacting with men promotes the earliest systematic tendencies of the two allegorical traditions—the one procedure seeking to analyze the constituents of the divine world, the other seeking to articulate the categories of the human one."[112] Much the same can be said of the Bible as well. Stephen Barney argues that "since allegoresis is a matter of critical response rather than a work's intrinsic nature," the allegorical exegesis of the Bible has very little to do with the nature of biblical texts: "there is little if any allegory in the Bible, most Biblical allegoresis is not based on the actual allegorical character of the Bible."[113] Nevertheless, as allegorical interpretations of Homer and the Bible clearly show, there is nothing to prevent generations of interpreters from reading a text as an allegory, perhaps not a consciously constructed allegory, but rife with different layers of meaning nonetheless.

The question is, then, whether traditional Chinese commentaries on the *Book of Poetry* are instances of allegoresis? Whether the commentators read moral and political meanings into poetic texts that resist such allegorization? François Jullien maintains that even though Chinese commentators had to legitimize the canonical status of the *Book of Poetry* and "sought another meaning at the heart of the poetic text," that other meaning "does not refer to *another level*, as in Greek allegory; it is entirely extracted from the contextual, historical reference assigned to each poem."[114] It is true that much traditional Chinese interpretation tries to put the poems in a historical context, arguing, for example, that the love song "*Guan ju*" we quoted earlier praises the virtue of a particular historical figure, the queen of King Wen. On closer examination, however, such contextualization is only a means to an end rather than the end itself. We may raise a number of questions. Why did texts in the *Book of Poetry* need to be contextualized in the first place? What was the condition of the

111. Auerbach, *Mimesis*, pp. 13–14.
112. Whitman, *Allegory*, p. 14.
113. Barney, *Allegories of History, Allegories of Love*, pp. 41, 43.
114. Jullien, *Detour and Access*, p. 57.

poems before they were "contextualized"? By whom and how were the poems contextualized?

In the case of the *Book of Poetry*, the purpose of contextualization was obviously to justify the canonicity of this ancient collection of songs, just as in the case of the Song of Songs elaborate allegorical readings were produced to defend its canonicity and justify its inclusion in the Holy Scriptures. In the Chinese commentary tradition, the ultimate purpose of putting a poem into a quasi-historical context is more than just to view it as some "literal vignette" of the past; it is rather to transform the poem into a model of propriety and good conduct, something that carries an extraordinary ethico-political import, as we have seen in the commentaries on "*Guan ju*," the very first song in the anthology. After all, the sum of Confucius's own comments on the *Book of Poetry* is moralistic rather than historical.

More importantly, the past into which the poems are contextualized is not just any part of history, but the legendary model or the very ideal of history, the reign of King Wen, who was the founder of a splendid culture of which Confucius saw himself as both preserver and reviver.[115] The well being of a state, Confucius believed, depended on following the way of King Wen and returning to the observance of the rites created in that lost Golden Age. This belief became the final frame of reference in traditional commentaries, the principle that guided Confucian commentators in their reading of ancient poetry. As the Great Preface to the *Book of Poetry* puts it: "The ancient king used poetry to regulate the proper bond between husbands and wives, to mold filial piety and respect for the elder, to strengthen human relationships, to accomplish education and good influence, and to adjust social customs."[116] Therefore, we can conclude that such contextualization is an interpretive strategy that Chinese commentators used to justify the canonicity of the *Book of Poetry*, a strategy that relates the poems to an ideal history that embodies all the essentials of Confucian moral teachings.[117]

---

115. See Confucius, *Lunyu*, iii.14: "Having seen the previous two dynasties, the Zhou has an exuberant culture. I follow the Zhou" (p. 56); and ix.5: "When besieged in Kuang, the Master said, 'Now that King Wen is gone, is not culture (*wen*) to be found here with me? If heaven wills that this culture be destroyed, I that live after King Wen would not have participated in it. If heaven wills that this culture not be destroyed, what can those people in Kuang do to me?'" (p. 176).

116. *Mao shi*, 2c, 1:270.

117. Saussy also argues that the history to which the Great Preface refers is more ideal than real: "even if the Great Preface is unable to ground its interpretation in a prior history, it reorients interpretation toward an ongoing history, the history of exemplary reading." *The Problem of a Chinese Aesthetic*, p. 149.

Let us look at a few more examples from the *Book of Poetry* and see how traditional commentators frame their moral and political interpretations in a quasi-historical context, and what exactly such contextualization does in directing the reading of poems. The focus will be on the relationship between the actual language of a poem and the construct of a historical context in order to reveal the nature of the commentaries. Our first example is poem number 23 in the Mao text:

> There is a dead roe in the fields,
> With white rushes he wraps it up.
> There is a girl longing for spring,
> The fine young man entices her.
>
> There are shrubs in the woods,
> There is a dead deer in the fields,
> With white rushes he ties it up.
> There is a girl fair as jade.
>
> "Hey, slow down, and be gentle!
> Do not touch my kerchief.
> Do not make the dog bark!"[118]

Reading the poem without traditional commentaries, we may form a mental picture of a young hunter wrapping up the roe and the deer he has killed in the fields and bringing them as gifts to his beloved. When they meet, the beautiful young girl implores him to be quiet for fear that the family dog may bark and alarm everyone. In the traditional version of the *Book of Poetry*, to each poem is attached a prefatory note, known as a "minor preface." Each puts down guidelines for understanding in the light of which later commentators annotated each verse to interpret the whole text. The "minor preface" to poem 23 reads:

"There is a dead roe in the fields." This expresses aversion to the corruption of rites. When the world was in chaos, muscular bullies took advantage of people and licentiousness reigned everywhere. But those who had been under the good influence of King Wen would still feel aversion to the corruption of rites, even though living in a chaotic world.[119]

The poem itself, of course, says nothing about King Wen and the rites; the "aversion," on which so much emphasis falls in the commentary,

118. *Mao shi*, 24c–25a, 1:292–93.
119. Ibid., 24c, 1:292.

seems a most strange word for reading the last three lines. The young man may be making amorous advances, perhaps a little too eagerly, but the last lines spoken by the girl hardly suggest any strong feeling of dislike or repugnance. Indeed, it is not uncommon in love poems to find such mild chiding of lovers in half earnest. To take another example from the same Confucian classic: in poem 76, "Please, Zhongzi," we find a variation of this topos that goes some distance to explain why the young woman in the poem would ask her lover not to come too close:

> Please, Zhongzi,
> Do not climb into our backyard,
> Do not break our white willow.
> Not that I care about the willow,
> But I am afraid of my parents.
> In my heart I hold Zhongzi dear,
> But what my parents might say
> Is also what I fear.
>
> Please, Zhongzi,
> Do not climb over our wall,
> Do not break our mulberry tree.
> Not that I care about the mulberry,
> But I am afraid of my brothers.
> In my heart I hold Zhongzi dear,
> But what my brothers might say
> Is also what I fear.
>
> Please, Zhongzi,
> Do not climb into our garden,
> Do not break our hardwood tree.
> Not that I care about the hardwood,
> But I am afraid of people's gossip.
> In my heart I hold Zhongzi dear,
> But what people might gossip about
> Is also what I fear.[120]

The concern here is very much the same as in the poem quoted earlier, but while in the earlier poem the girl warns the young man not to "make the dog bark," in this one she explains that though she holds her lover dear at heart, she is afraid of her parents and brothers, also gossip among her neighbors. "Of the vicissitudes faced by lovers," as Malcolm Laws observes with reference to English ballads, "none is more familiar in balladry, more

---

120. Ibid., 69a–b, 1:337.

romantic, or inherently more believable than that of the lovers who face family opposition to their marriage."[121] That is exactly what we see in these songs from the *Book of Poetry*—facing family opposition to their love, the young woman speaks not so much to reject her lover as to implore him to be quiet and cautious, and to keep their love a secret affair.

According to traditional commentators, however, this is not at all what the poems are about. The theme of courtship is obvious enough in poem 23, in which there is a girl "longing for spring" (*huai chun*), a phrase that has ever since been invariably understood as "to be lovesick" or "to have sexual urges"; and there is this fine young man who brings gifts and "entices her." Zheng Xuan, however, and Kong Yingda following him, explain that "entice" (*you*) here really means "to lead," and that the two verses should be understood as just the opposite of enticement or a seduction scene. Zheng Xuan writes: "there is this chaste girl who is thinking of meeting her betrothed in mid-spring in conformity with the appropriate rites, and the fine gentleman sends a go-between to lead to the arrangement for marriage." The commentators thus purge away the danger of seduction and read the last stanza not as the woman's well-intended warning to tip off her lover, but as her aversion to improprieties. To make this interpretation seem plausible, they have to twist further the last stanza, saying that "slow down" and "be gentle" all refer to the slow procedures of marriage arrangement, and that the dog will bark if the young bully violates the proper rites in forcefully seeking sexual favors.[122] As Qian Zhongshu shows by citing many examples, the dog is a familiar presence in the secret rendezvous of lovers in both Chinese and European literatures.[123] To read the young woman's words whispered to her lover in private as a public announcement of moral indignation is only to misread them, but given the moralistic concerns of the Confucian commentators, there is no other choice for them but to give such a strong misreading in order to minimize the rather obvious elements of impropriety in the poem of a seduction scene.

For all their far-fetched moralistic readings, the commentators in this case at least acknowledge that the poem here has something to do with courtship and marriage. For poem 76 quoted above, however, the "historical context" built up in the commentaries differs so drastically from the literal sense of the text that it would be impossible for anyone to attain the same kind of understanding as one finds in the commentary without

121. Laws, Jr., *The British Literary Ballad*, pp. 43–44.
122. *Mao shi*, 24c-25a, 1:292–93.
123. See Qian Zhongshu, *Guan zhui bian*, 1:76.

the exegetical crutches provided by the commentators. That is to say, "historical contextualization" here not only serves to contain the meaning of the text, but also shapes the reader's understanding; and in this act of control we can see most clearly the ideological implications of the Confucian commentary tradition.

In our "naive" reading, we thought that in the poem "Please, Zhongzi," the speaker must be a young woman who holds her lover Zhongzi dear at heart, but urges him not to come to her house for fear of her parents, brothers, and neighborhood gossips. The "minor preface" to this poem, however, would have none of these:

> "Please, Zhongzi." This is a satire on Count Zhuang. He gave in to his mother and as a result harmed his younger brother. When his brother Shu lost the proper way, the Count did not stop him; when Zhai Zhong remonstrated with him about it, the Count did not listen to him. Unwilling to correct minor mistakes will lead to major disasters.[124]

What, one may ask, has this got anything to do with the poem we quoted earlier? This is, of course, a typical example of historical contextualization. The commentators use the story of Count Zhuang of Zheng and his mother, Lady Jiang, as an exegetical grid to interpret poem 76. The story is a famous one in *Zuo zhuan* and runs something like the following. In a difficult breech birth, Zhuang caused his mother Lady Jiang, the Countess of Zheng, a great deal of pain, and so she disliked him and favored his younger brother Shu Duan. She wanted Duan to be designated as the Count's heir apparent, but the Count refused. When Zhuang succeeded his father and became the Count of Zheng (743 B.C.E.), Lady Jiang persuaded him to give his younger brother Duan the land of Jing, where Duan built up his forces and began to take over more land. Zhai Zhong, a minister at the court, urged Count Zhuang to take action, but the Count hesitated because he did not want to offend his mother. Later, Duan gathered more force and was ready to attack Zheng, with Lady Jiang as his ally, secretly planning to open the city gate for his army. Only then did Zhuang send troops to defeat Duan at Yan and exiled his mother from the capital, swearing never to see her again until they would one day meet by the Yellow Spring, the river of the dead in the nether world. After some time, however, Count Zhuang regretted, and he ordered his men to dig down the earth until they found a spring underground; he then had them build a tunnel in which he met his mother and became reconciled with her.[125]

124. *Mao shi*, 69a, 1:337.
125. For the text of the story, see *Zuo zhuan*, 1st year of Duke Yin, 13c–14b, in *Shisan*

Put in the context of this intriguing story, poem 76 is completely purged of the theme of erotic love, because the speaker in the poem is now identified not as a young woman as we assumed, but the indecisive Count Zhuang talking to Zhai Zhong, his minister. Zhongzi is now Zhai Zhong, and the repeated pleas, "Do not climb into our backyard," "Do not climb into our garden," and so forth, all become metaphorical expressions (*yu*) for Count Zhuang to ask Zhai Zhong not to poke his nose into the Count's family business. Such historical contextualization thus completely changes the frame of reference and the way the text can be interpreted. Some may find such contextualization ingenious and even intriguing, but still, if one takes the historical context seriously, one may wonder who are Count Zhuang's "brothers" and "neighbors," and how could the powerful Count be afraid of them? If the poem is what the commentators say it is, why should it take a form that sounds so suspiciously like a lover's complaint?

One may argue in defense of the commentators and say that we should not take the historical context too seriously, that is, too literally, that the commentators did not mean to insist on an exact correspondence between every detail in the text and Count Zhuang's story, that the poem, though it superficially reads like a love song, was intended to be a satire on Count Zhuang, and therefore its real meaning is not about love, but about the Count and the moral lesson clearly formulated in the "minor preface"—"Unwilling to correct minor mistakes will lead to major disasters." Such a defense, however, would precisely characterize historical contextualization as allegoresis, because here contextualization emerges clearly as a hermeneutic move, an interpretive strategy that reads the poem as saying one thing but meaning another.[126] In any case, the discrepancies between the poem and its commentaries are too glaringly obvious to be ignored, and the exegetical grid and the literary text simply do not match closely.

In traditional commentaries on the *Book of Poetry*, to identify the speaker in the poem as a historical figure is often used as a discreet interpretive strategy, but it is never a simple statement of the poem's historicity. Let us quote an example to make this clear. The following one is poem 86, a short poem consisting of two stanzas:

---

jing zhushu, 2:1715–16.

126. For a reading of the Mao commentaries on the *Book of Poetry* as a "hermeneutic tool" to control the meaning of the text, see Martin Svensson, "Hermeneutica / Hermetica Serica: A Study of the Shijing and the Mao School of Confucian Hermeneutics," Ph.D. dissertation, Stockholm University, 1996.

O that crafty boy,
He does not talk with me.
All because of you,
It makes me unable to eat.

O that crafty boy,
He does not eat with me.
All because of you,
It makes me unable to rest.[127]

The commentators interpret this poem as a political satire on Count Zhao of Zheng, who had jeopardized the state by entrusting a notoriously perfidious minister with power, while ignoring the wise counsel of his loyal advisors. Again, the speaker in the poem is identified not as a young woman as we might have assumed, but a good and loyal minister remonstrating with his lord, calling the Count, rather strangely, "that crafty boy," and feeling miserable that the Count, because of his misplaced trust in the bad minister, becomes estranged from the good ones. Again, by using historical contextualization as an interpretive strategy, and especially by identifying the speaker in the poem with a historical figure or situation, the commentators aptly displaced a love triangle of pain and jealousy with a triangle of political power struggle.

In reading the Song of Songs, we have noted that the "two breasts" of the bride are identified in midrash as Moses and Aaron, and the theme of love is generally understood as the divine love between God and Israel. In Christian allegorization, this is interpreted as love between Christ and the Church. In traditional Chinese commentaries on the *Book of Poetry*, the speaker in a love poem is often identified with a historical figure and related to a historical situation, thus the reader's basic horizon of expectations is radically redefined. Such identification is crucial because it creates a historical or religious context within which the text can be read in a certain direction, in conformity with a certain ideological premise as the forestructure of understanding. The more precisely the commentator identifies the speaker in the poem, the more specific the reading of a poem will be. Such identification is also displacement, the essential interpretive strategy of allegoresis, because by identifying the speaker in a love poem with some hagiological or historical figure, the voice and tone of the poem are displaced and the meaning of the entire poem completely changed.

127. *Mao shi*, 74b, 1:342.

If reading normally begins with a generic assumption, namely, a determination as to what genre a given text belongs, then what the commentator does to the Song of Songs or the poems quoted above from the *Book of Poetry* is to modify that assumption, to displace the controversial textual elements with ideologically acceptable alternatives, and to change the genre of the text from a poem about love to a canonical text about moral virtue or spiritual truth. By superimposing a historical context on the love poems, therefore, the Confucian commentators do not merely give the poems specific referentiality, but try to eliminate any implication of erotic love, to turn the poem into either a praise (*mei*) of moral perfection under an ancient sage-king or a satire (*ci*) of moral defection during the reign of a wicked ruler. In so doing, they attach to poetry a significance that demonstrates the functions Confucius had defined for it in terms of ethical and political propriety. Traditional Chinese commentaries, as Burton Watson observes, "are designed, in almost all cases, to give the songs a political significance and, wherever possible, to relate them to some specific historical person or event."[128] Not to realize the ethico-political nature of traditional Chinese commentaries but to see them as pure historical contextualization will make it very difficult to understand what the commentaries are all about. Moreover, the historical context here is not, let me reiterate, a context of ordinary history as the mere past, but that of an ideal history as the bygone Golden Age, the reign of King Wen that provides a paradigm of moral perfection and political harmony.

The commentary tradition is not, however, a unified entity but has many changes, modifications, and revisions. If we carefully examine the various interpretations and reinterpretations, the demise of old commentaries and the birth of new ones in its long and complicated history, we may hope to have a better understanding of that commentary tradition and its internal dynamics. Indeed, the dynamic or tension between the text and interpretation, the literal and the figurative or allegorical, between language and its particular use in various ways and for different purposes, and above all the consequences of political overinterpretation, all need further exploration.

128. Watson, *Early Chinese Literature*, p. 208.

3

Interpretation and Ideology

It was a perfectly clear day in the eighth month of the year 207 B.C.E., at the court of the Second Emperor of Qin, the son of the famous Qin Shi Huangdi or the First Emperor of China. The Shi Huangdi had vanquished all the six rival states and, for the first time in Chinese history, put the vast land of China under the banner of one great empire in 221 B.C.E. He had wished that his progeny would rule over this great empire with the same iron-fist control for thousands of generations into eternity. But it is the relentless irony of history that the Qin dynasty hardly passed through two generations. The First Emperor's son, called *Er shi*, literally Emperor of the Second Generation, was an impressionable weakling completely manipulated by Zhao Gao, a treacherous eunuch. Using his influence over the emperor, Zhao Gao had just plotted the death of Li Si the prime minister and had taken that position himself. On that particular day at the court, in front of all the ministers, generals, and noblemen gathered before the emperor, and with secret ambitions and ulterior motives, Zhao Gao presented a stag to the emperor, saying, "This, your majesty, is a horse." "Are you not mistaken, prime minister?" said the young emperor with a laugh. "You just called a deer a horse."

The strange skirmish of the will to name caught everyone present totally unprepared when the young emperor asked those around him for confirmation. The entire court was struck dumb, and few had the courage to counter Zhao Gao's willful *mala fide* misnaming of the animal. Under the menacing gaze of the eunuch-turned-prime-minister, some timidly mumbled their forced consent—"Well, yes, it is—a horse"—while many were reduced to shameful silence. There were also one or two courtiers, guided either by common sense, good understanding, linguistic decency, moral sense of uprightness, loyalty, or misplaced trust in the emperor, who did correctly identify the animal as a stag. As the Grand Historian Sima Qian tells us, however, those who had called the animal by its right name were all purged and killed by the wicked eunuch, given that he used that incident to demonstrate his power, find out his potential enemies, and establish his supreme unchallenged position at the court.[1] In fact, soon after that incident, Zhao Gao sent his men to force the emperor himself to commit suicide. He then installed another young member of the royal family on the throne, who ruled only forty-six days when the Qin empire completely collapsed and was replaced in 206 B.C.E. by the next dynasty in Chinese history, the dynasty of Han.[2]

The story is so well-known that *zhi lu wei ma* or "to point at a stag and call it a horse" becomes a proverb in Chinese, a set phrase that indicates not so much a mistake in naming but bullying, coercion, and intimidation, a deliberate confusion or willful misinterpretation that knows itself to be wrong but is forced upon others as an authoritative reading on the basis of sheer power and domination. Whoever calls a stag a horse does so knowingly as an exercise of manipulation, a display of unchallengeable power, but the phrase also connotes arrogance and wickedness, and always carries a sense of condemnation. In Sima Qian's historical records, Zhao Gao's scheme to read one thing to mean another, his perverse capsule *allegoresis*, was intended to be "a test" in order to tell whether the court would resist his dominance, and who might be his potential opponents. Zhao Gao having his way at court in front of the emperor was scandalous, but it was so not because no one ever recognized the glaring misnomer, but because of the misnomer's significant political background. Here identification of the animal brought before the emperor and the political context for the identification offer a telling example of the important relations between text and the context, interpretation and politics or ideology. Such relations immensely complicate the apparently simple situation of calling a stag a stag and remind us of the presence of crucial extra-textual factors that have a definitive influence on how a particular text, an object, or an event is to be interpreted. This notorious episode is perhaps a particularly strange and unusual case where the control of meaning and interpretation is obviously

---

1. See Sima Qian (145?-90? B.C.E.), "Biography of the First Emperor of Qin," in *Shi ji*, 1:273. See also "Biography of Li Si," 8:2562.
2. See ibid., 1:274, 275.

heavy-handed, openly displayed, bordering on madness and the farcical. The lesson one can draw from it, however, is not that strange but has wide-ranging ramifications.

It is beyond doubt that Zhao Gao was calling the stag by another name, and indeed the whole point, both as Zhao Gao intended for the other courtiers in his action, and as Sima Qian intended for his readers in telling the story, depends on a clear sense of catachresis: of calling one thing by another thing's name. What the story shows is emphatically *not* how naming can be arbitrary, but how such arbitrariness implies the abuse of power in a time that is out of joint. In reading Sima Qian's narrative, the literal sense of *stag* as distinct from *horse*, the differentiation of the names of animals, provide readers the basis to see through and condemn Zhao Gao's willful misinterpretation and evil scheme, the basis for a sense of right and wrong, for moral judgment and political stance. Without that basis for the literal sense of words, there can be no ground for appropriate moral response and thus effective political action. The literal sense is of course conventional insofar as no natural or necessary relation exists between an animal with hoofs and antlers and the word stag, but once it is established in the linguistic community that the word stag signifies just such an animal, the relation between the word and its referent becomes a historical given, a relatively stable and fixed relation or agreement in the language as a social institution.[3] A breach of that agreement, a deliberate violation of that convention, as in Zhao Gao's case, is always something of an abnormality, something to be carefully examined for its motivation and significance. The stability of meaning, the proper sense of words as agreed upon by all speakers of the same language, constitute the linguistic normality to which Sima Qian appeals in exposing Zhao Gao's abuse of language as symptomatic of his abuse of political power. Considering that this episode is placed before the death of the Second Emperor and the final collapse of the empire of Qin, the sequence of events arranged in Sima Qian's historical narrative has a clearly moral significance, and the fact that a stag is confused with a horse already shows the confusion and corruption of the times.

---

3. In Chinese, however, both *lu* (deer, stag) and *ma* (horse), especially in their ancient written forms, are characters with strong pictographic elements that to some extent make these signs and their referents form a less arbitrary relation than that between the English words and their meanings. Nevertheless, most Chinese characters do not have the same degree of pictographic quality, nor are such qualities readily discernible in the modern forms of writing.

Despite its possible attractive implication for contemporary discussions of language that focus on the arbitrary nature of linguistic signs, the story in its Chinese context of historiography, as I have indicated above, is not about the arbitrariness of naming and signification but about political intrigue and coercion. The arbitrary use of one name for another is here propped up by political power, and the exposure of misnaming is not only a linguistic exercise, but above all a political action. It is therefore important to note that Sima Qian was able to return to linguistic normality and condemn Zhao Gao's misnaming because he was writing in a different time, under the rule of a different dynasty, for which the fate of the previous dynasty, the rise and fall of the empire of Qin, served as a mirror and a warning. For Sima Qian and his contemporaries in the Han, Zhao Gao no longer had any influence on the political scene, but only figured as a villain from an erroneous past, an alarming example of the danger of empowered eunuchs and treacherous schemers. It was the changed political structure of the times in addition to the literal, normative sense of words that has made it possible for the historian to correct Zhao Gao's deliberate error. That is to say, a misinterpretation, even an obviously absurd one like calling a stag a horse, stands or falls with the power that sustains its perpetration. To set a record straight often amounts to setting the whole political and ideological situation straight; the two enterprises of interpretation and ideology are thus closely interrelated and mutually dependent. This is an important insight that one may gain from reading Sima Qian's historical narrative and carry over to the reading of other histories, other narratives, and other texts.

The Complexity of the Literal

Traditional Chinese exegesis of the *Book of Poetry*, as we have seen, typically relates poetry to a historical situation and historical personages, but such contextualization is never purely historical, that is, it never merely tells us the story of the poem's putative origin in a specific time and place. Rather, the story about the poem's origin or historical context is often told by commentators in spite of what the poem actually says, and it is told in such a way as to shape the interpretation of the poem in moral and political terms and in conformity with the teachings of Confucianism. Such historical allegorism of poetry may remind us of the way the Targumist interprets the Song of Songs as an allegory of sacred history narrated in the Holy Scriptures, for in both the Targum and traditional Chinese commentaries, there is a great deal of effort to gloss words and phrases so that the letter of the text is not completely ignored but given ingenious and sometimes tortuous explanations.

In rabbinic interpretation, as Raphael Loewe points out, "the letter is not, as in Christian exegesis, the potentially jealous stepmother of allegory, but rather her willing handmaid or research assistant."[4] That is to say, the literal and the allegorical are not mutually exclusive here. James Kugel also notes that close attention paid to textual details characterizes rabbinic interpretations. In agreement with Loewe, Kugel observes that "Even in the most allegorical of rabbinic exegeses, those of the Song of Songs, the focus never shifts from the words of the text; if it is even proper to speak here of 'literal' and 'figurative' meanings at all, these words should be used in a way quite distinct from their normal application."[5] K. J. Woollcombe also remarks that in commenting on the Song of Songs, "the Rabbis used the *actual* text of the love-lyrics to describe the divine love. They did not discard the text, once they had found the undersense, as one discards the shell of a nut, having found the kernel." And that, he goes on to say, constitutes "the principal difference between the allegorism of Palestine and that of Alexandria."[6] All these biblical scholars acknowledge the importance of the literal sense in rabbinic interpretation and see this attention to the letter as the distinct feature of rabbinic exegesis as different from Christian hermeneutics. Loewe, Kugel, and Woollcombe, however, all consider rabbinic exegesis to be allegorical in one way or another, since the rabbis find in the biblical text a figurative sense that proves the divinity of the text.

In Chinese commentaries, much exegetical effort is likewise concentrated on individual words and textual details, but all the philological explications and textual maneuvers of the Confucian commentators never deviate from the one general purpose: the construction of a total meaning in conformity with an ethico-political interpretation of the *Book of Poetry*. The literal sense in both Jewish and Chinese commentaries thus forms a complicated relationship with the allegorical meaning these commentaries try to derive from the canonical texts.

Some scholars consider the textual orientation of rabbinic exegesis as qualitatively different from Christian allegorization, and they make the further claim that rabbinic interpretation is not allegorical at all. In a way reminiscent of the characterization of Chinese commentaries on the *Book of Poetry* as historical contextualization, Daniel Boyarin maintains that

---

4. Loewe, "Apologetic Motifs in the Targum to the Song of Songs," p. 159.

5. Kugel, *The Idea of Biblical Poetry*, p. 138.

6. Woollcombe, "The Biblical Origin and Patristic Development of Typology," p. 54.

Rabbi Aquiba's reading of the Song of Songs as the Holy of Holies does not involve any "translation" of the text into hidden meanings or abstract ideas, but "only a situating of the poem in a given historical or, more to the point, textual context." It is, in other words, intertextual connection, not allegorical interpretation. As Boyarin puts it, "reading on the highest level in midrash is intertextual reading, the connecting of texts to the ultimate Text [the Torah], and not allegory, the connecting of texts to abstract ideas."[7]

A too rigid distinction between intertextual and allegorical readings, however, is rather problematic. First, as we have seen in the previous chapter, allegory in Quintilian's classic definition does not require the translation of concrete signifiers into Platonic abstract ideas. Second, and more importantly, it would be naive and simplistic to read rabbinic exegetical works as entirely engaged in a self-contained, intertextual nexus of cross reference, or to understand the works of Chinese commentators as pure historical contextualization. We should not take both at face value as literalistic without looking into their textual manipulation, religious motivation, or ideological presumptions; otherwise, we would limit our understanding of the exegetical works to a narrowly textual dimension. If Christian allegoresis and typology were "translating" the biblical text into something else for ideological and political reasons, it would be naive and overhasty to conclude that the other exegetical traditions—the Jewish and the Chinese—were purely textual and free from such tendentious "translations."

Boyarin describes the hermeneutic move in midrash as "combining and recombining biblical verses into new texts, exposing the interpretive relations already in the text, as it were, as well as creating new ones by revealing linguistic connections hitherto unfelt."[8] It is true that the rabbis do read Scripture as hermeneutical as well as canonical and typically use the later books as tools for understanding the first five books of the Bible, but the connection of verses or intertextuality is not a mere game of combining and recombining words and phrases, and in the specific case of the Song of Songs, connecting its verses with those of Exodus can hardly be characterized as "exposing the interpretive relations already in the text." The same can be said of the Chinese commentaries that connect poetic texts with texts of the other Confucian classics, relating poetry with moral principles or historical narratives that embody such principles. Boyarin emphasizes that midrash operates "not by linking texts with their meanings but by linking texts with texts," not "relating signifier to signified—

---

7. Boyarin, "The Song of Songs: Lock or Key?" pp. 222, 226.
8. Ibid., p. 223.

but intertextual-relating signifier to signifier."[9] Such a clear-cut separation of text from its meaning, however, only makes one wonder whether the linking of signifiers is not already an act of meaning, that is, a hermeneutic act that tries to *make sense* of the scriptural texts in a given situation. The sense it makes is not so much the textual meaning per se as the relevance of those texts to a particular situation of present concerns. That is to say, the meaning of a text is not only textual but also always contextual. In connecting texts and linking signifiers, the rabbis are not merely engaged in language games without meaning; they are not reading the text with no particular purpose and addressing no real issues of social concerns. If midrash is *phronesis*, as Gerald Bruns suggests, then the connecting of signifiers does not just establish a textual or intertextual relation completely internal to the Bible, but it also finds the practical and political relevance of the Bible to the Jewish community. The Torah, says Bruns, "is a text that (whatever it speaks) speaks to the situation at hand."[10]

The point is that interpretation of a text, especially a canonical text, is never purely textual, never without making connections between the literal sense of the text and the reader's present concerns or the situation of a community in which the text has a meaningful presence. We may even say that interpretation is nothing but the effort to make the presence of a text meaningful to the reader and the community that receives it. Whenever the text seems unintelligible to the reader or incongruous with the beliefs and expectations of a certain community, whenever it challenges conventional values and ideas or fails to deliver an expected message, it is then the task of exegetes and interpreters to mediate between the text and the world, to make the text fit and able to "speak to the situation at hand."

In fulfilling such a task, the rabbis and the Chinese commentators try their best to seek support from the letter of the text, but that does not mean that the readings they produce are strictly literal, dictated, as it were, by the text, and thus essentially different from Christian allegorical interpretations. Since they all read their canonical texts from a perspective that already has some definite expectations, they are all trying to make the texts speak to the situation at hand. In fact, Boyarin also acknowledges that "it is indeed possible for midrashic-intertextual readings to be substantially the same thematically as allegorical readings, since the Torah-texts to which the Song of Songs was understood to refer describe the relationship of Israel to God. Thus the very same thematic material could be transposed, as it were, from the midrashic mode of the

---

9. Ibid., pp. 225, 226.
10. Bruns, *Hermeneutics Ancient and Modern*, p. 68.

earlier Rabbis to the allegorical mode of the later ones."[11] However much the letter is preserved in rabbinic interpretation, it is clear that the reading of the letter is always oriented toward the revelation of its sacred nature, because the midrashic exploration of linguistic polysemy is ultimately contained in a divine perspective. The meaning of Scripture is always larger than the literal sense of the text itself. Therefore, in the sense as Quintilian defined it, the letter and its meaning in midrash already form a potentially allegorical relationship.

It is important to note that even in Christian exegesis, the letter is not always regarded as the jealous stepmother of allegory. The Middle Ages certainly had an allegorical outlook that read everything as a sign of something else, and tended to translate things visible into something invisible with a deeper and spiritual meaning. Yet Umberto Eco argues emphatically that it is a modern bias to believe that the medieval time was utterly puritanical and metaphysical, obsessed with vague and abstract ideas and having no appreciation of beauty and the richness of the material world. Though the allegorist eventually finds his meaning beyond the letter, he nevertheless has to begin and work with the letter, and at times he pays more attention to the letter than we usually credit him for. As examples, Eco mentions Matthew of Vendôme laying down "rules for describing beautiful women in his *Ars Versificatoria*" and Ecclesiastics "writing on the *Canticle of Canticles*, discoursing on the beauty of the Spouse." Even though their aim was to find allegorical meanings in the canonical text, "ever so often we find them pontificating on the proper ideal of female beauty, and revealing in the process a quite spontaneous appreciation of women which is earthy enough for all its chastity."[12] That is to say, in Christian interpretations the literal level of meaning, which is closely related to the concrete and material world, is not always discarded for the sake of spiritual values, even in reading the most richly sensuous of all biblical texts, the Song of Songs.

According to Eco, the medieval mentality underwent a great change in the thirteenth century, which found its most eloquent articulation in the works of Thomas Aquinas. Instead of absorbing concrete reality into a symbolic universe of spiritual meanings, many in the thirteenth century came to conceive of nature as an ontological structure with its own formal reality of things. This shifted conception of nature and things had profound implications: "The symbolical vision turned into a naturalistic

11. Boyarin, "The Song of Songs: Lock or Key?" p. 226.
12. Eco, *Art and Beauty in the Middle Ages*, p. 11. Eco states that in this book he intends to overcome "a common objection, namely, that the Middle Ages did not have an aesthetics, indulging itself instead with metaphysical concepts, concepts at once vague and arid, and further confused by their entanglement with fable and allegory," p. 1.

vision, which aspired to study causal connections with critical acuity."[13] A new outlook and new hermeneutic theory were put forward in Aquinas's writings, which can best be understood in the context of this great shift from the symbolical to a naturalistic vision. In reading the scriptural text, Aquinas argues, the literal or historical sense is the first and most elementary way of understanding, and the multiplicity of senses originate not in the equivocation of words but in things themselves. As he put it in a famous passage of the *Summa theologica:*

> Thus in Holy Scripture no confusion results, for all the senses are founded on one—the literal—from which alone can any argument be drawn, and not from those intended allegorically, as Augustine says. Nevertheless, nothing of Holy Scripture perishes because of this, since nothing necessary to faith is contained under the spiritual sense which is not elsewhere put forward clearly by the Scripture in its literal sense.[14]

Eco explains that by putting the literal sense first as the basis for the spiritual sense, Aquinas invests Old Testament events and persons with "the value of a *sign*—that as well as their historical truth and reality they also have a symbolical reality."[15] Insofar as the spiritual sense or the symbolic reality of the sacred history narrated in the Old Testament consists in the prefiguration of the coming of Christ, Aquinas seems only to follow the tradition of Christian typological reading, but he differs from it in seeing the events and things in the Old Testament not as mere shadows of the reality of the New, but as historically true and real in themselves. Eco singles out two important claims Aquinas makes: first, the spiritual sense inhabits only the sacred history told in Scripture, not secular history or things in the natural world; and second, only the biblical text has a spiritual sense, not secular poetry. Once the spiritual sense is limited to the sacred texts, the allegorical outlook that reads nature as God's book, as mythical signs and letters filled with spiritual meanings in a symbolic universe, loses its foundation. "Mundane events are returned to their natural status," says Eco. "With Aquinas, we witness a kind of secularization of postbiblical history and the natural world."[16] In his approach to the biblical text, Aquinas may thus appear to stand closer to the school of Antioch than to that of Alexandria, but the point is not that he has

---

13. Eco, *The Aesthetics of Thomas Aquinas,* p. 141.
14. Aquinas, *Summa theologica,* 1a.1.10, in *Basic Writings of St. Thomas Aquinas,* ed. Anton Pagis, 1:17.
15. Eco, *The Aesthetics of Thomas Aquinas,* p. 151.
16. Ibid., p. 152.

rejected allegory—he clearly has not—but that he considers the literal sense as the only legitimate ground for allegorization.

If allegoresis means a mode of interpretation that builds up a total structure of meaning in contradistinction to the literal sense, but not to its exclusion, then, this Thomist notion of the allegorical can be said to offer a reasonably good characterization of traditional Chinese commentaries on the *Book of Poetry*. Of course, we must fully recognize the important difference between the ethico-political nature of Chinese commentaries and the religious nature of biblical exegesis, but the interpretive strategies employed in different commentary traditions, as John B. Henderson shows, have much in common. As commentators in different traditions all hold a similar set of assumptions that characterize their canonized scriptures as all-encompassing, coherent, self-consistent, profound, and fraught with moral and spiritual meanings, they adopt similar strategies to substantiate these claims or assumptions. Similarities beyond the specifics of textual sources thus become "a general rule," the necessary result of canonization. "The very act of canonization," says Henderson, "had systematic consequences that were in part independent of the peculiarities of the canonical text."[17] Though the specific canonical texts differ from one another, the canonicity of texts makes it necessary for commentators to develop a set of interpretive strategies that are remarkably similar in different textual traditions, either East or West.

Aquinas's insistence on the primacy of the literal sense, though definitely a significant shift in the medieval outlook, was not a complete and sudden change after all. The medieval fourfold sense of the Bible, as Karlfried Froehlich observes, was not a rigid scheme into which each biblical text could be pressed, nor did the literal and non-literal form a mutually exclusive dichotomy. "Moreover, no either / or was intended," says Froehlich. "The literal sense did not exclude the spiritual, or vice versa. Rather, the two were related in a dialectical movement from one to the other."[18] Aquinas's argument for the foundational value of the literal sense in understanding the Bible, his view that whatever Scripture contains under the spiritual sense is also clearly expressed elsewhere in the literal sense, reiterates an important point Augustine first made in his book, *On Christian Doctrine*.

In that early foundational work of Christian hermeneutics, Augustine takes a rhetorical approach to the Bible and argues that Scripture offers plain words to those who are hungry for clear understanding, but to those

17. Henderson, *Scripture, Canon, and Commentary*, p. 5.
18. Froehlich, "Problems of Lutheran Hermeneutics," in *Studies in Lutheran Hermeneutics*, ed. Reumann, p. 127.

who disdain plainness and seek rhetorical adornment, the obscure and figurative part of Scripture gives delight. "Thus the Holy Spirit," says Augustine, "has magnificently and wholesomely modulated the Holy Scriptures so that the more open places present themselves to hunger and the more obscure places may deter a disdainful attitude. Hardly anything may be found in these obscure places which is not found plainly said elsewhere."[19] The last sentence, which Aquinas adopted in the passage quoted above from the *Summa theologica*, turns Scripture into a self-explanatory text, a network of internal cross-reference, in which the plain, literal sense explains the obscure places and provides the textual basis for allegorical interpretation.

The gulf between the Bible and writings by human authors gradually shrank in the thirteenth century. Under the influence of Aquinas, there was a revival of interest in the literal sense of the Bible, and consequently the Hebraists could emphasize the importance of the original Hebrew texts and the inadequacy of translation. At the same time, the use of allegory in poetry of human as opposed to divine authorship also undermined the uniqueness of biblical texts in its predominance of the spiritual over the bodily sense. "Thus, if the Bible's uniqueness resided in its spiritual sense," as James Kugel remarks, "this uniqueness was under double attack, increasingly neglected and undermined by Hebraizing commentators, and in the meantime encroached upon at the other side by poets of secular and (still worse!) Divine intention."[20] For Luther, Calvin, and the other reformers, allegorization was of little use in dogmatic theology. Like Aquinas, Luther also sees the Bible as self-explanatory. What that means is that one does not, as Luther explains in his anti-Catholic polemic, need to go through the Church Fathers for adequate understanding of Scripture. Froehlich identifies three aspects in Lutheran hermeneutics that inherit late medieval, and specifically Thomist, presuppositions: the interest in the literal sense, in the clarity of Scripture, and in historical continuity of the exegetical tradition.[21] "Holy Scripture," in Luther's classic formulation, "is its own interpreter" (*scriptura sui ipsius interpres*).[22] "The Holy Spirit," says Luther, "is the simplest writer and speaker in heaven and on earth. This is why his words can have no more than the one simplest meaning which we call the written one, or the literal meaning of the tongue."[23] Here again, the letter and the spirit are not set up in a rigid opposition.

---

19. St. Augustine, *On Christian Doctrine*, II.vi.8, p. 38.
20. Kugel, *The Idea of Biblical Poetry*, pp. 218–19.
21. See Froehlich, "Problems of Lutheran Hermeneutics," pp. 133–35.
22. Ibid., p. 134.
23. Luther, *Works*, ed. Helmut T. Lehman, trans. Eric W. Gritsch and Ruth C. Gritsch

But what does Luther mean by the literal sense? Interest in the literal, which can be traced from Luther to Aquinas and back to Augustine, is not at all opposed to spiritual sense as such because the literal sense, for all these influential Christian theologians, as Gerald Bruns observes, "is not so much a *sensus litteralis* as the *sensus spiritualis;* . . . It is rather the spirit or fore-understanding in which the text is to be studied."[24] That is to say, from Augustine to Aquinas and Luther, the literal sense in Christian hermeneutics presupposes, and is contained by, a theological framework, the stipulation that whatever sense the biblical text may have, it is always about Christ and always in conformity with the Christian doctrine. Froehlich mentions that Luther, along with his emphasis on the one clear, simple, literal sense of the Bible, also maintains that "Scripture is everywhere about Christ, even in the Old Testament, and that this 'literal sense' is the essence of the true spiritual understanding of Scripture."[25] For Luther and his contemporaries, then, the literal sense is not truly or unconditionally literal, but the *sensus litteralis theologicus*, which is completely different from "mere words, a purely grammatical sense, the dead letter."[26]

Thus the literal sense in the tradition of Christian interpretation is to some extent already spiritually constituted, and to understand the literal sense adequately involves an effort to connect the surface of the text with a context that always goes beyond the purely linguistic and grammatical sense. "Scripture," says Luther, "does not tolerate the division of letter and Spirit."[27] In Christian exegesis, therefore, the literal sense is not opposed to the spiritual understanding of the Bible, but it provides spiritual understanding a solid foundation; it is not always ignored or disregarded, but is bound up with the Christian doctrine just as the spiritual meaning is. Interest in the literal sense, again as Froehlich remarks, "has become the hallmark of all respectable professional exegesis. To listen carefully to 'what the text says' is regarded as the main, if not the exclusive, task of the interpreter."[28] For Luther, a religious framework is prerequisite for adequate understanding of the literal sense, and "what the text says" is contained in a perspective that already anticipates, in one way or another, what the text has to say. The literal and the allegorical thus

---

(Philadelphia: Fortress Press, 1970), 39:178; quoted in Bruns, *Hermeneutics Ancient and Modern*, p. 143.
24. Bruns, p. 142.
25. Froehlich, "Problems of Lutheran Hermeneutics," p. 128.
26. Ibid., p. 133.
27. Luther, *Works*, vol. 39, p. 171; quoted in Bruns, p. 144.
28. Froehlich, "Problems of Lutheran Hermeneutics," p. 136.

form a complicated relation, and the line of demarcation between them is not absolutely clear-cut.

Does the spiritual perspective for understanding the literal sense suggest, then, that there is no difference between the two, or that the literal sense can be ignored or construed in any way one pleases? In a highly suggestive essay on the "literal reading" of biblical narrative, Hans Frei appropriates the theoretical argument of deconstruction to question the very idea of the literal and the interpretive enterprise of hermeneutics. The literal sense of the Bible, Frei argues, is a "consensus reading" in the Christian community, rather than any property of the linguistic sign as such. "The very notion of a true referent of the narrative texts of the New Testament—historical or ideal, accessible or not—and of the textual meaning as possible truth," he declares, "is an illusion."[29] Once the meaning of linguistic signs is thought to be illusory and contingent upon communal decisions, Frei continues, hermeneutics is deconstructed and becomes totally dysfunctional. "If 'meaning' implies absence and *difference* instead of centeredness or presence, then self-presence or 'understanding'—its indispensable polar correlate in the theory—is bound to be just as hollow."[30] Here Frei is making an important claim, but one may wonder whether meaning must be defined as either absolute presence or nothing at all (namely, *always already* an illusory absence), and whether such an "all or nothing" approach is helpful in understanding the very nature of understanding, the enterprise of hermeneutics. The erasure of the literal obviously does not transcend the either/or dichotomy but only subsumes one term under the other, and it has some serious consequences in theoretical as well as in practical terms.

The implications of such an erasure become rather clear when Kathryn Tanner applies Frei's ideas to a formulation of the relationship between Christian theology and the biblical text. What is called the literal or plain sense of the text, Tanner argues, cannot be identified with "what the text simply says," its "immanent sense," or anything of that sort. It is instead "a function of communal use: it is the obvious or direct sense of the text according to a *usus loquendi* established by the community in question."[31] That is to say, the *use* of the text *is* its meaning, the allegorical *is* the literal. Following Frei, Tanner speaks of the plain sense as "a consensus reading," as what the Christian community uses the text to mean, or what traditional

29. Frei, "The 'Literal Reading' of Biblical Narrative in the Christian Tradition: Does It Stretch or Will It Break?" in *The Bible and the Narrative Tradition*, ed. McConnell, p. 43.
30. Ibid., p. 58.
31. Tanner, "Theology and the Plain Sense," in *Scriptural Authority and Narrative Interpretation*, ed. Green, pp. 62–63.

interpretation has made it to mean. The plain sense is thus not differentiated from the allegorical or spiritual sense, but is identified with "the traditional sense of a text."[32] It is not "anything 'in self,' apart from an interpretive practice of using texts. As a result there is no longer any *absolute* distinction between the text's 'proper' sense and the contributions of an interpretive tradition." Finally, as a consequence of this nondifferentiation of the literal and the spiritual, the plain sense disappears altogether when Tanner declares, by paraphrasing Derrida, that "the literal [*propre*] meaning does not exist [strictly], its 'appearance' is a necessary function—and must be analyzed as such—in the system of differences."[33]

Tanner's formulation, however, turns the relationship between theology and Scripture into an obviously lopsided one, because theology gets all the weight, whereas the biblical text gets none. In doing away with the literal sense altogether, theology grows into something rather disturbingly hegemonic, since traditional exegeses and commentaries, the Church as embodiment of the Christian community, and Church fathers as its spokesmen become the sole frame of reference and the sole authority that decide what use or meaning the biblical text has. Theology, in other words, as Christian doctrine or the ideology of the Church, assumes total authority against which no one can raise questions or lodge protests by appealing to the literal sense of the biblical text. Communal consensus reigns supreme and no individual understanding is allowed to deviate from the collective "consensus reading." But to recognize the complexity of the literal is one thing, to eliminate the literal sense altogether is quite another. Tanner's argument may remind us of Jean Gerson's *De sensu literali sacrae Scripturae* of 1414, which maintains that the Church alone has the power to determine what the literal sense is. As Frank Kermode remarks, the implication of that pronouncement is rather serious. "Heretics claimed that their doctrines were founded on the literal sense of Scripture; but if the literal sense is by definition the 'literal sense of the Church,' and not anything more generally available, then merely to affirm a different sense from that of the Church was proof of heresy."[34] Evidently, elimination of the literal sense of the Bible only serves to make the authority of the Church and its leaders absolute and unanswerable.

It is only fair to note that Tanner is fully aware of these problems. In fact, in a typically self-deconstructive fashion, she raises some fairly pertinent questions about her own position.

---

32. Ibid., p. 63.
33. Ibid., p. 64; see Derrida, *Of Grammatology*, p. 89.
34. Kermode, "The Plain Sense of Things," *Midrash and Literature*, ed. Hartman and Budick, p. 188.

The approach itself assumes communal practices already set up and running; it does not go behind or beyond them to anything more basic from which they derive or to which they might be accountable. Without appeals to anything outside them, traditional practices seem to be granted a kind of inviolable givenness by our approach. Our holistic interpretive strategy might suggest, furthermore, a kind of built-in advocacy of conformity to established collective practices. Our initial functional definition of the plain sense in specific would seem only to highlight the self-enclosure of traditional practices according to our approach: what a text itself directly says becomes whatever the community makes of it. Since the plain sense of a text is already its traditional sense within some community of discourse, there seems to remain no sense of the text itself to which one might appeal against the prevailing opinion of a community's conventional reading. The text apparently becomes the captive of a sociocultural context whose interpretive habits enjoy an uncontested and potentially quite rigid monopoly over the determination of sense.[35]

Tanner promises to counter all these charges in her essay, but, Pilate-like, having raised those important questions above, she would not stay for an answer. Interpretation of the Bible in her formulation is not a response to the text but a communal decision about the use of the text, and all those questions she herself raised about text, meaning, and ideological control thus remain unanswered. As soon as we go beyond pure theorizing and move into the real world, however, the practical question of agency becomes extremely important. Notions like "community" or "consensus" are nothing but notions and words of abstract collectivity, which in political reality have the annoying tendency of turning into exactly the opposite of what they are supposed to signify; that is to say, they often become empty slogans that disguise the individual will and personal interest of powerful men who claim to represent consensus or the collective interest of the community. Tanner's formulation grants unchallengeable power to theologians or whoever represents, or claims to represent, the Christian interpretive community. If history is of any good in reminding us of the danger of such unchallengeable power, the potential alarming consequences of her argument should give us pause to take lightly the disappearance of the literal or "literal reading." In the meantime, it becomes clear that the concept of the literal is crucial for the resistance of willful misinterpretation and ideological manipulation, and no amount of obscurantist sophistry should cheat us out of the recognition of what the simple literal sense is. In fact, the strength of the literal lies in its very plainness and natural simplicity.

35. Tanner, "Theology and the Plain Sense," pp. 66–67.

Against the eloquence of the "consensus" argument, however, the text is not mute or completely passive. Although it may be bent and stretched to some extent, the literal sense of the text eventually places constraints on our reading and interpretations. The reading of a text is not, after all, a metaphorical picnic in which readers bring meanings to the author's words. To put it differently in analogy to the story of Zhao Gao's misnaming, a reader cannot simply declare that a stag (*lu*) means a horse (*ma*). Some do, of course, out of ignorance or bad faith, but they are to be exposed, as Zhao Gao was, for the abuse of language and the distortion of normative meaning. To the extent that language is one of the most basic social institutions in human society, the relatively stable meaning of words is precisely the one most basic "consensus of the community," and insofar as that community needs language for expression and communication, it must differentiate naming (to call a stag a stag) from misnaming (to call a stag a horse). The ancient Chinese knew that very well, for the rectification of names is one of the most important political and intellectual programs in Confucian philosophy. In contemporary theory, Umberto Eco develops a useful notion of the "intention of the text" (*intentio operis*) to guard against the excess of interpretation or what he calls overinterpretation. Eco maintains that the intention of the text is not something on the surface all by itself, severed from the reader's participation; rather, it is dialectically linked with the intention of the reader (*intention lectoris*). "One has to decide to 'see' it," says Eco. "Thus it is possible to speak of the text's intention only as the result of a conjecture on the part of the reader."[36] The point is, however, not that the reader decides what the text intends or means—though that is precisely so often argued in some irresponsible version of reader-response criticism—but that the reader's decision is constantly challenged by the text, that the reader's initial conjecture is continually adjusted and modified so that a more adequate understanding may arise in the process of reading.

The intention of the text, as Eco indicates, is the old idea of the literal sense and textual coherence that we find in the argument from Augustine to Aquinas: "any interpretation given of a certain portion of a text can be accepted if it is confirmed by, and must be rejected if it is challenged by, another portion of the same text. In this sense the internal textual coherence controls the otherwise uncontrollable drives of the reader."[37] The text's intention, in other words, is manifested as textual integrity, the

---

36. Eco with Richard Rorty, Jonathan Culler, and Christine Brooke-Rose, *Interpretation and Overinterpretation*, p. 64.

37. Ibid., p. 65.

coherence of meaning constructed out of words arranged in a particular sequence to form a specific text. To acknowledge the relevance of the text's intention is thus to attend to the literal or plain sense of the text. Even a word used in a metaphorical sense must be understood in this total structure of the text; and indeed it is only within this total structure that one can determine whether a word is used in a literal or a metaphorical sense.

Historically, close attention to the literal sense has yielded profound consequences in biblical hermeneutics. Once the importance of the letter was fully recognized, literary and stylistic studies of the Bible began to develop, and the greater appreciation of the biblical language in its own right made allegory less and less essential. In his lectures on biblical poetry (1753), Bishop Robert Lowth still understood the Song of Solomon as an allegory of love between Christ and the Church, but he termed it a "mystical allegory," an allegory "founded upon the basis of history," while his interest lay entirely in the imagery and the poetic excellence of the Canticle.[38] Lowth's Latin lectures were translated into English and published in the mid-nineteenth century with additional notes by several hands, which enable us to learn how scholars at the time responded to his work. A long note by John David Michaelis, a professor of philosophy at Göttingen, challenges the notion that the Song is an allegory, and argues instead that it is perfectly legitimate to read the Song in its plain sense. Against those "profound reasoners" who would read the Canticle allegorically, Michaelis contends that "the chaste and conjugal affections so carefully implanted by the Deity in the human heart, and upon which so great a portion of human happiness depends, are not unworthy of a muse fraught even with Divine inspiration."[39] When the poetic and stylistic features of biblical language become an object of study, and love and marriage as part of God's plan for human life are considered worthy theme of a divinely inspired poet, the Song of Songs hardly needs allegorical interpretation to prove its worthiness as part of the biblical canon.

The dismissal of allegory in Michaelis's note bears the distinct mark of romantic aesthetics in which the symbol was appreciated at the expense of allegory as a thin disguise of dogma. In *Truth and Method*, Gadamer offers a brief review of the history of the devaluation of allegory in the West since the eighteenth century, especially the negative reaction to Winckelmann's classicism in Germany and the rise of the symbol in romantic literary theory

38. Lowth, *Lectures on the Sacred Poetry of the Hebrews*, lecture 31, p. 339.
39. Ibid., p. 346.

as a counter-concept. He shows how Kant's concept of symbolic representation paved the way for an aesthetic evaluation of the symbolic, and how the word symbol, after Goethe, Schelling, Solger, and some other German thinkers of the late eighteenth and the nineteenth centuries, came to signify the inward unity of the idea and its appearance, whereas allegory was understood as indicating a mechanical relationship between the idea and its representation by means of something external and artificial. The romantic notion of art as a free and imaginative creation of genius finally discredited allegory, which was thought to be closely bound up with dogmatics, and "the moment art freed itself from all dogmatic bonds and could be defined as the unconscious production of genius," says Gadamer, "allegory inevitably became aesthetically suspect."[40] Symbol was seen as complicated with a disproportion of form and essence, which gave rise to that indeterminate quality, that undecidability, peculiar to all works of art and literature, while allegory was denigrated as simplistic, a shell that contained a meaning alien to its form.

That discredited concept of allegory in early German romanticism, however, is rather narrow and limited, serving a polemical purpose, but it continues to have a great influence in modern criticism. "Allegory," says Paul Ricoeur, "is a rhetorical procedure that can be eliminated once it has done its job. Having ascended the ladder, we can then descend it."[41] Northrop Frye calls such rhetorical procedure a "naive allegory," from which he distinguishes the more sophisticated "continuous allegory" such as *The Divine Comedy* or *The Faerie Queene*, which is "still a structure of images, not of disguised ideas, and commentary has to proceed with it exactly as it does with all other literature, trying to see what precepts and examples are suggested by the imagery as a whole."[42] In separating a literary work as "a structure of images" from allegory as a construct of "disguised ideas," Frye is in effect trying to save Dante's or Spenser's great allegorical works from the disrepute into which the term allegory has fallen in romantic aesthetics and modern criticism.

Many critics are likewise anxious to treat allegory as symbol, emphasizing its literal signification as ontologically meaningful. If allegory is to lay any claim to literary value at all, it must, under the pressure of this anxiety of the allegorical, have its own "structure of images." This is what C. S. Lewis argues in giving advice on how to read allegories: when the hidden meaning is discovered or when the reader has climbed up the allegorical

---

40. Gadamer, *Truth and Method*, p. 79.
41. Ricoeur, *Interpretation Theory: Discourse and the Surplus of Meaning*, p. 56.
42. Frye, *Anatomy of Criticism*, p. 90.

ladder, says Lewis in a way directly opposite to what Ricoeur asserts in the quotation above, the reader should not descend it: "Allegory, after all, is simile seen from the other end; and when we have seen the point of simile we do not throw it away."[43] Auerbach also warns against the suppression of the sensory occurrence when reading the Bible allegorically, especially in a typological framework. Such suppression implies "the danger that the visual element of the occurrences might succumb under the dense texture of meanings."[44] His discussion of *figura* as both historically true and capable of figuring forth something else to be realized in the future, his contrast of allegorical interpretation as abstractly spiritual with figurative interpretation as deeply historical, and his claim that in the West "the latter tendency was victorious," can all be understood as in some sense an effort to alleviate the anxiety of allegory in romantic aesthetics, to save allegory from its bad reputation.[45] Under the pressure of the critical legacy of romantic aesthetics, it is inevitable that many scholars tend to dissociate literature and literary interpretation from allegory and allegoresis. Given the modern skeptical tendency to question or reject any doctrinal authority, religious or secular, allegory as a rhetorical device is necessarily suspected of being a disguised preaching of dogmas; as such, it loses its respectability.

The ascendance of a literal reading of Scripture is also closely related to the increasing secularization of the modern world and the appreciation of aesthetic values of the biblical text. The most salient characteristic of modern scholarship on the Song of Songs, as Marvin Pope notes, is a general tendency to reject a simple allegory and to freely admit the application of the Song to human physical love. "Modern research," says Pope, "has tended to relate the origins and background of the Song to the sacral sexual rites of ancient Near Eastern fertility cults wherein the issues of life and death were the crucial concerns." Having worked through the text of the Song and reviewed the various interpretations, he is convinced that "the cultic interpretation, which has been vehemently resisted from its beginnings, is best able to account for the erotic imagery. Sexuality is a basic human interest and the affirmation that 'God is Love' includes all meanings of both words."[46] The outcome of the historical-critical approach has a tremendous impact. Archaeological findings, anthropological studies, and a renewed interest in the myths and folklore of the ancient Near East have put the Bible back in its historical and Palestinian context. Scholars have vigorously traced the possible contacts

43. Lewis, *The Allegory of Love*, p 125.
44. Auerbach, *Mimesis*, p. 48.
45. Auerbach, "Figura," in *Scenes from the Drama of European Literature*, p. 36.
46. Pope, *The Anchor Bible: Song of Songs*, p. 17.

between ancient India and Mesopotamia in King Solomon's time and have related the Canticle to the Indian sacred songs, in which erotic love often has a religious significance and symbolizes human longing for the divine. This is of course not to read the Song of Songs as really a celebration of erotic love and therefore not a definitive break from the older tradition of allegoresis, but it is an effort to put the Song in a different background in which the sacred and the sexual are not opposed to one another.

Today, even Christian exegetes, Catholic as well as Protestant, tend to take the plain sense of the Song as basis for any sacralization and regard the Song as about both secular and sacred love, Eros and Agape. As Helmut Gollwitzer remarks,

> If the Song is simply about human sexual love, then its inclusion in the Bible is itself a demand that the church and the Christians should finally establish an unabashed relation with sex and Eros, and it unabashedly commands us: *rejoice that there is such a thing.* Sexual desire [*diese Lust*], one of the most powerful and marvelous emotions, is a wonderful gift from our Creator.[47]

Only when we recall Origen and the traditional ascetic attitude toward secular love and sex, can we fully appreciate the tremendous change Gollwitzer articulates here. It may also be helpful to recall the story of the nightingale of Basle as Heinrich Heine told it in his brilliant satire of religious asceticism and its denial of natural human emotions. In May 1433, a group of clerics and monks attending the Ecumenical Council of Basle were walking in the woods near the city, discoursing and debating on the fine points of theological issues. Suddenly, they fell silent in front of a blossoming linden tree, in which a nightingale was pouring out the most enchanting notes of a sweet song. The tender melody seemed to penetrate the scholastic hearts of these pious and learned men and melt their numbed emotions from their torpid hibernation. At last, one of them remarked that the bird might be the devil himself trying to distract them away from their Christian discourse and to allure them into lust and sin, and he proceeded to exorcise the evil spirit, uttering the customary invocation: *Adjuro te per eum, qui venturus est, judicare vivas et mortuos,* etc. etc. "Yes, I am an evil spirit," the bird replied, and he flew away laughing. "This story," says our poet, "needs no commentary. It bears the dreadful impress of a time when all that was sweet and lovely was decried as the work of the devil."[48]

---

47. Gollwitzer, *Das hohe Lied der Liebe*, p. 21.
48. Heine, *Concerning the History of Religion and Philosophy in Germany*, in *Selected Works*, pp. 283–84.

For centuries, the denunciation of love and sex made it impossible to read the Song of Songs according to the plain, literal sense of the text, and allegorical interpretation was the only way to justify the Song as part of the biblical canon. It is only in modern time and in a much more secularized social context that Gollwitzer is finally able to announce the coming of a new age, of a completely new era of religious belief, when human beings do not have to apologize for their desire of love. He finds in the Canticle a free expression of the reunion of letter and spirit, the secular and divine love, a "Magna Charta of humanity"; and he reminds us with Karl Barth in regard to the Song of Songs that "We should not wish to take it out of the canon. We should not act as if it were not in the canon. Neither should we spiritualize it as if everything in the canon could only have spiritual meaning . . . The most profound interpretation here might well be none but the most natural one."[49] In recognizing the legitimacy of the plain sense of the biblical text and in acknowledging the significance of Eros in the Song of Songs, modern interpretation certainly does not reject the spiritual meaning, but reconciles it with the literal sense of the Holy Scriptures. Once the rigidity of dogma has lost its grip, once the letter and the spirit no longer form a mutually exclusive opposition, we then have the opportunity to strike a balance between what the text literally says and what it says as a canonical and sacred text. In the case of the Song of Songs, we can finally read the text for what it is in the healthy reunion of Eros and Agape, the human and the divine.

The Commentary Tradition and Its Discontents

If respect for the letter or the textual integrity of the Bible in the Christian tradition can be traced back to Luther, Aquinas, and Augustine, in China there were also some early efforts to read the Confucian classics according to the letter without what was perceived to be excessive exegetical impositions. To read the *Book of Poetry* literally as poetry without considering the moral and political meanings traditional commentators attributed to the text is often said to be a modern attitude in Chinese criticism. To be sure, such an attitude became predominant only in the twentieth century, but to call it "modern" is really stretching the word to its limits until it becomes seriously misleading, because this supposedly "modern" reading has its roots reaching back as early as the

---

49. Barth, *Kirchliche Dogmatik*, 3.2, pp. 354 f; quoted in Gollwitzer, *Das hohe Lied der Liebe*, p. 62.

Tang (618–907) and the Song dynasties (960–1279), when a number of poets and literati scholar-officials already started to voice their doubts about the heavily allegorical Han commentaries, and tried to read at least some of the poems in the Confucian classic as ancient rhymes for music and singing. Some of their skeptic views were later incorporated and assimilated into traditional understanding, and some were suppressed to form a subversive undercurrent in the commentary tradition. Therefore, when we speak of traditional interpretations of the *Book of Poetry* or the Chinese tradition of literary criticism in general, we are not speaking of a single, monolithic, and unified body of opinions and principles, but a variety of views, approaches, and dimensions. Commentaries on the first anthology of ancient Chinese poetry have a complicated history, and it is important to note that opinions in the commentary tradition differ from one another and change frequently, even though many of those old differences may have lost their urgency and relevance, and the divergent opinions may, from this side of a tremendous gap in time, appear to us now as rather similar.

The legend of Confucius selecting and compiling the *Book of Poetry* is nothing but a legend, and the fact that Confucius in the *Analects* refers to the anthology as the *Three Hundred Poems* suggests that a body of texts already existed in his time (5th century B.C.E.) in a relatively fixed form, fairly close to the anthology we now have with the three hundred and five poems. The *Book of Poetry* was probably compiled during the period of the Warring States (403–221 B.C.E.), and it was one of the works destroyed by the First Emperor of Qin in his draconian measures to control thinking, his infamous decree of book-burning (213 B.C.E.). The burning of books, however, did not stop the dissemination of ideas, and many pre-Qin works, including the *Book of Poetry*, survived the ordeal. These ancient books come to us in two versions, the so-called new texts (*jinwen*), which are texts circulated in the Western Han dynasty (206 B.C.E. to 25) and written in the form of characters current at the time, and the old texts (*guwen*) written in the old type of Chinese scripts and supposedly found hidden in the walls of some ancient buildings not consumed by the First Emperor's fire. The difference between the new and the old texts, however, concerns more than just the form or style of Chinese scripts, and the quarrelling and strife between the new text and the old text schools underlie much of the history of the study of Chinese classics.[50] Unlike some of the other books that have significant discrepancies

---

50. See Zhou Yutong, "The Study of Classics in the New Text and the Old Text," in *Jingxueshi lunzhu xuanji*, pp. 1–39.

between the new text and the old text versions, however, the *Book of Poetry* seems rather similar in the two versions, and it has been suggested that the textual integrity is probably due to the fact that the poems had already been widely popular before the burning of books, and that they were committed to memory and preserved through oral transmission rather than as written texts. In the case of the *Book of Poetry*, then, the frequent debates are largely concerned not with the text as such, but with its commentaries and interpretations.

In the early Han dynasty, there were three commentary traditions, known as Qi, Lu, and Han, all of which were officially sanctioned new text schools, and a special office, that of a Doctorate (*boshi*), was established in the second century B.C.E. for the study and teaching of each of these schools. An old text attributed to a certain Master Mao as redactor, known as the Mao text of the *Book of Poetry*, emerged later with a "preface" attached to each of the poems and began to contend for official recognition in the last few years of the first century B.C.E. Ever since the Han commentator Zheng Xuan (127–200) wrote his influential commentaries based on the Mao version, but also assimilating opinions of the three new text schools, the Mao text of the *Book of Poetry* gradually replaced the new text versions and has come down to us as the only surviving text today. By the fourth century, the three new text commentary traditions were already lost, and not only did the Mao version assume the authoritative position of a canon or classic, but its attendant commentaries also became quasi-canonical. The Mao and Zheng tradition, or the tradition of Han dynasty commentaries, was consolidated by Kong Yingda (574–648) in the Tang, with only infrequent and minor modifications. This tradition became an elaborate exegetical framework that firmly confined the interpretation of the poems within limits of Confucian moral and political philosophy and invariably related the poems to some quasi-historical figures, serving the useful social purposes of "praising" (*mei*), "satirizing" (*ci*), or "ironically remonstrating with" (*fengjian*) the rulers of states.

At the time when the Han commentaries were consolidated in the Tang as an orthodox tradition, however, the orthodoxy was also beginning to be challenged by some writers and scholars. In a famous piece, the great Tang poet Li Bai (701–762) ridiculed a "scholar from Lu," a textual scholar reminiscent of a Han commentator on the five classics, who had no idea of how to cope with the real world but "would die with hoary hairs, still studying his chapters and verses."[51] The Tang writer Han Yu

---

51. Li Bai, "Old Scholar from Lu: a Lampoon," in *Li Tai Bai quanji*, 3:1157.

(768–824) not only expressed his doubt in prose about the Mao preface to the *Book of Poetry*, but he also wrote in a poem:

> The three hundred poems of the Zhou,
> Elegance in gloss and counsel well ordered.
> As they had passed the sage's hand,
> Who dares to discuss them any further?[52]

In refusing to discuss the three hundred poems and participate in their exegeses, Han Yu seemed to have respectfully distanced himself from the entire commentary tradition. In the Song dynasty, the authority of the Mao and Zheng commentaries was seriously challenged by many writers and scholars, such as Ouyang Xiu (1007–72), Su Zhe (1039–1112), Zheng Qiao (1104–1162), and especially the influential Confucian scholar Zhu Xi (1130–1200). The Song dynasty commentaries thus took a different turn from the Han tradition and started a new trend that eventually led toward a literal reading of the poems without the exegetical framework of the "preface" or the Mao-Zheng commentaries.

Zhu Xi was by far the most influential Confucian scholar of his time, and his interpretation of the Four Books—the basic Confucian texts of the *Great Learning*, the *Analects*, the work of *Mencius*, and the *Doctrine of the Mean*—had profound significance for the institutionalization of Confucian teaching in later times. He was first and foremost a thinker and philosopher, not a literary critic. For him, poetry or literary writing is never really important in itself but only as an expression or emanation of the *tao*. Unlike Laozi's unnamable mystic *tao*, which was utterly unconcerned with the human world, this Confucian notion of *tao* is understood as the Way of Heaven, which gives man the ultimate origin and guiding principle of what is good and proper, as manifested in the cardinal Confucian virtues of humaneness, righteousness, propriety, wisdom, and truthfulness, and embodied in appropriate relationships in the family and in society at large. So the *tao* is both transcendent and immanent, very much in this world, everywhere visible and realizable as the essence, principle, reason or order (*li*) of things. Insomuch as literary writing manifests this *tao* in a suitable form, it has its purpose and legitimation. "*Tao* is the root

---

52. Han Yu, "Recommending a Scholar," in *Han Changli quanji*, p. 40. In the first line, Han Yu mentions the Zhou dynasty as the time in which the three hundred poems were composed. The second line is rather obscure and may have been corrupted; a different version has the word "bury" (*mai*) instead of "order" (*li*), and thus presents an even more critical view of the Han commentaries: "Elegance in gloss and counsel *buried*." The "sage's hand" in the third line alludes to Confucius who, according to the famous legend, had a hand in the compilation of the *Book of Poetry*.

and base of writing," says Zhu Xi, "and writing, the twigs and leaves of *tao*. Because it has such a root and base, whatever issues forth as writing is *tao*."[53] By writing Zhu Xi meant the appropriate kind of writing that embodied the moral ideas and teachings of Confucianism. Like the other Confucian philosophers of his time, Zhu Xi was sharply critical of poets and writers such as Han Yu or Su Shi, who valued writing for its own sake and had thus reversed the proper order of things by taking the twigs and leaves, so to speak, more seriously than the roots.

The ancient sages, Zhu Xi maintains, did not write to achieve rhetorical effects or to show off stylistic bravura, but to express as clearly as possible their intent that conforms to the *tao*. "The words of sages are clear and easy to understand, for they used words to make *tao* manifest so that later generations may seek it in their writing. If the sages wanted to make their words hard to understand, they surely would not have created any of the classics." In this understanding, the language of the Confucian classics is clear and easy, not difficult or obscure. The ancients, according to Zhu Xi, used a natural style of writing, accessible, rational, commonsensical, as if it "has a tone and accent that are born naturally."[54] In a way, Zhu Xi's emphasis on the clarity and self-explanatory nature of ancient classics may remind us of the important idea Luther inherited from Augustine and Aquinas, namely, that "Holy Scripture is its own interpreter" (*scriptura sui ipsius interpres*). Indeed, as in the case of Luther, Zhu Xi's emphasis on the natural style of writing and the clarity of meaning also aimed to promote an effective means for expressing doctrinal ideas and teachings, and his belief in the accessibility of the classics led to an attitude that paid more attention to the plain sense of the canonical text than to its commentaries. As a result, Zhu Xi shook up the tradition of classical studies with a radical revision that promoted a more literal reading of the canon.

Compared with many other Confucian thinkers of the Song and the Ming period, Zhu Xi had a much greater talent in literary writing and was more appreciative of the value of literary form as such. The heavily moralistic bias and political concerns of Neo-Confucianism never completely stifled his personal love of a good poem, an elegant piece of prose, a graceful style of writing. Richard Lynn argues that though both Zhu Xi and Zhou Dunyi (1017–1073) advocated the idea that writing should

---

53. Zhu Xi, *Zhuzi yulei, juan* 139, 8:3319. Hereafter abbreviated as *Yulei*. The metaphor of roots and twigs may remind us of Liu Xie's similar arboreal metaphor: "The use of writing is indeed that of the branches and twigs of the classics." *Wenxin diaolong*, p. 534.

54. Zhu Xi, ibid., 8:3318, 3322. The relation between writing and *tao* again recalls Liu Xie's similar formulation: "*Tao* shows the pattern by way of the sages, and the sages make *tao* manifest in their writing." *Wenxin diaolong*, p. 2.

serve as vehicle for carrying the *tao*, "they do not disparage the aesthetic aspects of writing but regard them merely as subsidiary to the pragmatic / didactic function." And in this, Lynn remarks, they "differ sharply" from the more austere Neo-Confucian philosophers Cheng Yi (1033–1107) and Cheng Hao (1032–1085), who "regarded all *wen* (literature as a fine art) as detrimental to the Way."[55] According to Luo Genze, Zhu Xi not only differs from the Cheng brothers, but he also sets a greater value on literature than does Zhou Dunyi. If Zhu Xi calls *tao* "the root and base of writing" and writing the "twigs and leaves of *tao*," the metaphors definitely evoke the image of a great tree as an organic whole that implicitly points out the essential connection between *tao* and writing in that the two differ only as "different parts, but form the same body." Since he maintains that writing "issues forth" from the *tao*, writing and *tao* are thus continuous: they are unified, not opposed. "In this," Luo Genze observes, "Zhu Xi surely differs from Han Yu and Ouyang Xiu as writers of literary prose, but he differs even more from Zhou Dunyi and the Cheng brothers as *daoxue* philosophers."[56]

In spite of his critique of writers from a philosopher's point of view, Zhu Xi does often praise Han Yu, Su Shi, and others for their literary talent, their artfulness, and the formal beauty of their writings. He was himself the author of some poems and prose works of considerable literary merits; and he edited the writings of Han Yu and compiled an annotated edition of the southern style of poetry in the state of Chu, the famous *Chu ci* by Qu Yuan (340?–277? B.C.E.) and others. Such literary sensibilities and sympathies naturally led to his appreciation of the value of the canonical text and the integrity of its form. His acclaimed *Shi jizhuan* [*The Book of Poetry with Collected Commentaries*] was truly unprecedented in rejecting much of the Han commentaries in order to read the classic as a plain and self-explanatory text. Zhu Xi's approach to the *Book of Poetry*, as Qian Mu observes in a critical study, treats this canonical work as literature and tries to understand the meaning of poetry not through the so-called "minor prefaces" and commentaries, but through repeated reading, reciting, and self-rumination. Such an approach makes it possible, Qian observes, "to gain independent understanding in studying it as literature and to be free from the shackles of scholasticism in classical studies."[57] Zhu Xi's love of literature thus also contributed to a way of reading that

---

55. Lynn, "Chu Hsi as Literary Theorist and Critic," in *Chu Hsi and Neo-Confucianism,* ed. Wing-tsit Chan, p. 337.
56. Luo Genze, *Zhongguo wenxue piping shi,* 3:191.
57. Qian Mu, *Zhuzi xin xue'an,* 2:1271–72.

was attentive to the formal features of the poetic text, the stimulating effect (*xing*) of poetry, and the literal sense of what the poem actually says.

In many of his conversations as noted down by his students and followers, Zhu Xi made it very clear that he respected the textual integrity of the poems, rather than the Mao "prefaces" or the Zheng commentaries. These recorded sayings (*yü lu*) in a rather modern-sounding vernacular provide a wealth of the great Confucian thinker's ideas about a variety of important subjects in his own words. "Nowadays people do not explain the poems by the poems, but interpret them by the 'prefaces,'" we catch Zhu Xi complaining. "They force the text by tortuous means to comply with the preface and even willingly sacrifice the poet's original intention with no scruples. That is the great damage the preface brings about!" It is clear from these words that Zhu Xi made a distinction between the text of the classic and the Mao-Zheng "prefaces," and he dismissed conventional readings at his time that ignored the integrity of the canonical text and its literal sense. His own way of reading was radically different from such blind compliance with the Mao-Zheng tradition. "When I interpret the poems, I mostly do not follow the prefaces," he declares. "Even if I failed to give a good interpretation, I would have at most wronged the author of the prefaces, but if I interpreted the poems solely according to the prefaces without considering the meaning of the poems in their own context, then I would have wronged the sages themselves."[58] In attacking the Han commentary tradition, Zhu Xi evidently followed the footsteps of earlier critics like Ouyang Xiu and Zheng Qiao. He recalls how he came to reject the Mao "preface":

> The prefaces to the poems are really not trustworthy. I once read Zheng Qiao's *Refutation of the Absurdities on the Book of Poetry* that spares no blows in attacking the prefaces. Sometimes his words seemed excessive, as he claimed that the prefaces were all written by some crazy country bumpkin. At first, I also doubted his words, but later I carefully examined several prefaces and checked them up with *Records of the Grand Historian* and the *Conversations of the States,* and then I realized that the prefaces are indeed unreliable.[59]

Zhu Xi did more, however, than just reiterating the skeptical views that Zheng Qiao and others had adumbrated. In the preface to his own edition of the *Book of Poetry*, he defines poetry as "the excess of language in which the mind formulates what the heart feels when affected by things. Since

58. Zhu Xi, *Yulei, juan* 80, 6:2077, 2092.
59. Ibid., 6:2076.

what the heart feels may be correct or deviant, its formulation in language can be virtuous or vicious." When Confucius compiled the classic, Zhu Xi argues, the sage included both kinds of poetry "so that one may study it to examine the gain and the loss, to follow the good and remedy the evil."[60] He boldly declares that Confucius's famous summary comment on the *Book of Poetry* does not apply to all the poems: "Only the line 'Not deviating from the good path' is good; this is not to say that the entire book is 'Not deviating from the good path.'"[61] To acknowledge that not every poem in the classic imparts a moral meaning makes a truly radical move and presents the Confucian classic in a very different light from that of the Han commentaries. With the claim that the great classic contains both virtuous and deviant ancient songs, Zhu Xi laid the ground for reading the poems in their plain sense without relating each and every one of them to the moralistic framework set up by the Han commentators.

In the first part of the *Book of Poetry* known as "Airs of the States," Zhu Xi recognizes the poems as folksongs and divides them into virtuous and deviant ones that reflect different times and mores.

> What is called the "Airs" in the *Book of Poetry* are mostly folksongs and ballads which originate from the streets and lanes, songs that men and women sing to one another to express their affections. Only the *Zhou nan* and the *Shao nan* are virtuous because of the direct influence of King Wen, and because people at the time could all be correct in their affection and disposition, and consequently what they expressed in words was not excessive, but joy without licentiousness and sorrow without self-inflicted harm. Thus only these two pieces set up the correct norm of poems in the "Airs" section. Beginning with "Airs from the State of Bei," however, as

60. Zhu Xi, *Shi jizhuan*, preface, p. 1. This preface was written much earlier than the completion of *Shi jizhuan*, when Zhu Xi was at the age of forty and still under the influence of the Han commentaries. His views changed further in later years, as he told his students when he was about sixty: "I once wrote some interpretations of the *Book of Poetry* and used the 'minor prefaces,' and I made far-fetched circumlocutions when the interpretation did not make sense. Later I felt uneasy. When I tried the second time, though I still kept the 'minor prefaces,' I occasionally argued against and broke away from them. Eventually, however, I did not quite get the poet's original meaning. It was only later that I realized that I need only to discard the 'minor prefaces' and the poems would make sense of themselves. So I completely got rid of old interpretations; only then the meaning of the *Book of Poetry* came out alive," *Yulei, juan* 80, 6:2085.

61. Zhu Xi, *Yulei, juan* 80, 6:2065. "Not deviating from the good path," a line from poem 297 describing horses, has the same three characters as the comment Confucius made on the *Book of Poetry*, which can be understood as to mean "herein there is no evil" (see Confucius, *Lunyu*, ii.2, p. 21). Zhu Xi insists that Confucius was thinking of this particular line from the *Book of Poetry* rather than the entire classic when he made that comment, and therefore the Confucian classic may contain poems that are indeed "deviating from the good path," licentious, even vicious.

the conditions of government in the various states were different, some stable and some chaotic, and as the people also differed, some good and some wicked, their expressions of feelings likewise differed, some correct and some deviant, some virtuous and some vicious, and thus what was known as Airs under the former kings were altered at that point.[62]

Insofar as he views the poems in the classic as corresponding to historical conditions for which the moral influence of King Wen played a definitive role, Zhu Xi seems still to walk in the shadow of the Mao "prefaces." In fact, the ideas all hark back to the Great Preface of the Mao text: that poetry reflects the moral condition of the times, that from King Wen to the later kings history took a steady fall from moral perfection and political harmony to decadence, and that poetry in reflection of this fall changed from "correct Airs" to "altered" ones. In the Great Preface, however, though an "altered" poem may reflect the decadent and corrupt moral condition of the time, the poet's intention is said to "satirize" or "remonstrate with" the current king, thus to express implicitly a longing for the correct norm and a better time under ancient sage kings. The poets, as we read in the Great Preface, "understood the change of affairs and recalled the old customs nostalgically. Thus the altered Airs start out from the condition of the people but remain within limits of rites and propriety."[63] Here the Great Preface, as Saussy argues, presents the "altered Airs" not as a reflection of decadence but its implicit critique; it turns poetic mimesis into "ironic mimesis," and adds to its "mirroring function" a "critical one," the function of social commentary.[64]

But that is precisely what Zhu Xi saw as problematic and heavy-handed, for the "prefaces" shout out ironic "praises" and "blames" over a muted text and usurp the authority of a classic that should have been allowed to speak for itself without such overriding noises. If Zhu Xi saw the origin of poetry as the natural expression of human emotions, it would then appear unnatural and unnecessary for commentators to add a layer of "ironic mimesis" on top of the self-explanatory text. As he puts it,

When the ancients composed poems, it was mostly just like people today writing poetry. Among these are also poems that they sang to articulate their emotions and natural dispositions when they were moved by things. How could they mean each and every time to blame and satirize others? Only because the author of the prefaces made it a rule that each of the poems should be interpreted either as praise or as blame, the poets' meanings are all

62. Zhu Xi, *Shi jizhuan*, preface, p. 2.
63. *Mao shi*, 4a, in *Shisan jing zhushu*, ed. Ruan Yuan, 1:272.
64. Saussy, *The Problem of a Chinese Aesthetic*, p. 107.

ruined through farfetched interpretations! If catching a glimpse of a person doing something, a man today would immediately write a poem to praise or to blame that person, wouldn't that strike you as absurd?[65]

In the Han commentary tradition, the assumed implicit nostalgia and criticism, the ironic "praise" and "blame," are all crucial for the legitimation of "altered Airs," those problematic, erotic or improper poems presumably created in a time of decadence. Once Zhu Xi had detached poetry from that commentary tradition, he was able to read the poetic text in its plain sense and let it stand on its own, unconcealed—but also unprotected—by the layer of legitimizing moralistic exegesis. An inevitable consequence, and a truly unprecedented one, is that he realized perforce that some of the "altered Airs" are in fact "licentious poems," far from what moralistic commentaries had made them out to be. "In a bold step that no one dared take before," as Wing-tsit Chan remarks, "[Zhu Xi] identified twenty-four of the 305 poems in the *Book of Odes* as strictly love songs instead of moral lessons."[66] This was truly scandalous for his time, but also something new in the interpretation of the *Book of Poetry*. As Zhou Yutong observes, Zhu Xi not only followed earlier critics in doubting and rejecting the "prefaces," but "he shines out in the history of the study of the *Book of Poetry* in boldly proposing new interpretations, that is, identifying the allegedly 'licentious poems.'"[67] In other words, Zhu Xi was ready to acknowledge that not every text in the *Book of Poetry* enjoyed the status of canonicity.

To gauge the distance between the Han commentators and Zhu Xi, we need only to compare earlier commentaries on poem 42, "*Jing nü*" [A Graceful Girl], with Zhu Xi's notes to the same poem. The text reads:

> A graceful girl most beautiful
> Was to meet me at the corner of the town.
> I loved her but couldn't find her,
> Scratching my head, I paced up and down.

> A graceful girl most amicable
> Gave a nice red tube to me.
> The red tube has a lovely shine,
> It makes me admire her beauty.

> From the fields she brought me

65. Zhu Xi, *Yulei, juan* 80, 6:2076.
66. Wing-Tsit Chan, *Chu Hsi: Life and Thought*, p. 41.
67. Zhou Yutong, *Zhu Xi*, in *Jingxueshi lunzhu xuanji*, p. 158.

A pretty and rare shoot of reed.
It is not you that are so pretty,
But a pretty girl gave it to me.[68]

The "graceful girl" appears to be the love the speaker in the poem praises for both her beauty and her generosity. He is anxiously waiting for her at the corner of the town, perhaps for a secret rendezvous, but she fails to show up, and in thinking of her, he remembers the few things she has given him as gifts, and declares that the value of whatever present she gave resides not so much in the thing itself as in the fact that it comes from her precious hand.

Despite the obvious expression of a man's love for his beloved and his impatience of waiting to see her, the "minor preface" in the Mao text states that this poem "satirizes the times. The ruler of Wei deviated from the Way, and his Lady had no virtue." According to Zheng Xuan, because the ruler and the Lady of Wei were not virtuous, the poem speaks about a graceful girl who "has so much virtue that she could replace the Lady to become the royal consort."[69] In the Mao-Zheng commentaries, then, the whole poem is turned around and becomes an allegory of the search for virtue or a virtuous lady, a satire on the vicious ones without directly naming them. Zhu Xi, however, rejected such a convoluted and disingenuous explanation. Taking the words of the text literally, he bluntly declares that "this is a poem of lust and elopement and the rendezvous of lovers."[70] In Zheng Xuan's strained explanation, the "red tube" mentioned in the second stanza is said to symbolize some elaborate "ancient rules," but Zhu Xi honestly acknowledges that "it is not clear what this object is, but it is given as a token of affection."[71] Such an honest attitude evinces his confidence in the self-explanatory nature of the canonical text, for he would sooner admit his own uncertainty or ignorance than to impose an improbable interpretation on the classic. The mistake Zhu Xi saw in the "prefaces" is precisely a dishonest covering up of the commentator's ignorance. He argues that if the author of the "minor prefaces" had followed the text closely, readers of later generations would have sooner excused him of his mistakes and would have greater respect for his commentaries even if he failed to explain everything.

---

68. *Mao shi*, 42c–43a, in *Shisan jing zhushu*, 1:310–11.
69. Ibid., p. 310.
70. Zhu Xi, *Shi jizhuan*, p. 26.
71. Ibid. The meaning of the "red tube" and a number of other things in this apparently simple poem prove to be rather difficult to ascertain. They become the subject of a spirited debate for Gu Jiegang and other modern scholars. See *Gu shi bian*, 3:510–73.

In Zhu Xi's sensible reading, then, the historical contextualization used in the Han commentaries only conceals the commentator's embarrassment and ignorance and distorts the meaning of the text. For many of the "altered Airs," Zhu Xi's interpretation resolutely rejects the "prefaces" and boldly acknowledges that the *Book of Poetry*, though highly revered as a Confucian classic, contains a number of erotic and "licentious" poems. For poem 76, "Please, Zhongzi" (discussed in the last chapter), the Han commentators constructed an exegetical grid that connects the poem with the story of Count Zhuang and his advisor Zhai Zhong, and thus glossed over the erotic connotations of the text. Zhu Xi totally discards such a farfetched contextualization and declares that the poem represents, quite simply, the "words of an eloper." He identifies the speaker in the poem as a woman imploring her lover not to climb into her backyard and break the trees for fear that her family and neighbors might know of their secret affair.[72]

Another poem, "Crafty Boy" (poem 86), also discussed in the last chapter, clearly sounds like a lover's complaint when we read:

> O that crafty boy,
> He does not talk with me.
> All because of you,
> It makes me unable to eat.

The "preface" in the Mao text interprets it as a political satire on the Count Zhao of Zheng, named Hu, who "could not rule and make plans with the help of his good advisors, but let an ambitious councillor arrogate all powers to himself."[73] The speaker in the poem, according to the Han commentators, is a good minister complaining about his lord who mistakenly trusted Zhai Zhong, the ambitious councillor mentioned in the "minor preface." Zhu Xi argues forcefully against such an improbable reading and points out its absurdities. All those poems said to satirize Hu, he remarks, "have nothing corresponding to reality when checked with the biography of Hu. He is even called a 'crafty boy,' how can that express the poet's love of his lord? Moreover, it was precisely owing to his frailty and carelessness that Hu lost his state, when was he ever 'crafty'?" Zhu Xi goes on to say, "Poor Hu of Zheng was really made the most miserable, as all the vicious poems in the 'Airs of the State of Zheng' were said to satirize him. . . . But Hu was never really 'crafty'; if he was, he would have sought assistance from the state of Qi to control the likes of Zhai Zhong

---

72. Zhu Xi, *Shi jizhuan*, p. 48.
73. *Mao shi*, 74b, in *Shisan jing zhushu*, 1:342.

tightly, and would not have lost his power over the state."[74] By staying close to the plain sense of the text, Zhu Xi offers a much more sensible and probable reading of this poem: "These are also words of a wanton woman teasing her lover who is leaving her. She says to him: 'Many are trying to woo me; though you are leaving me, you are not going to make me unable to eat.'"[75] Zhu Xi's literal readings not only make better sense of the poems, but they also constitute a radical and significant revision of the Han commentary tradition and start forming a remarkably "modern" attitude toward the canonical text. The legacy of Zhu Xi's revision in reading the *Book of Poetry* becomes increasingly influential. It definitely marks an important turning point in the commentary tradition and exerts a profound impact on twentieth-century scholars in their iconoclastic rethinking of the entire heritage of traditional culture and literature.

The dismantling of farfetched interpretations of the *Book of Poetry*, the rejection of the moral and political allegoresis in the Han commentary tradition, became part of the New Culture Movement following the famous May Fourth students' demonstration in 1919. May Fourth marked the advent of a new period in Chinese history, a period of national crisis, of war and revolution, in which the Chinese felt acutely the burden and anxiety of a cultural tradition vis-à-vis the challenge of modernity and the Western-derived ideas of science and democracy. The study of classics and the critical reexamination of the entire cultural tradition by native Chinese scholars in the modern period cannot be understood apart from the social and historical conditions at the time. The Revolution of 1911 put an end to the last dynasty of imperial China, and some years before that, abolition of the traditional examination system and the establishment of new schools with Western style curricula had already deprived the Confucian classics of their sacred status. Suffering from Japanese imperialist invasion and the threat of Western colonialism, fragmented and overrun by ruthless war-lords and despots, many Chinese, and especially Chinese intellectuals, who were modern-day literati scholars and who maintained the traditional sense of social responsibility, felt that China at the time was on the brink of total collapse and extinction. The crisis of survival of the Chinese nation forced them to take an extremely hard look at traditional Chinese culture and society in order to understand the course of history and see what had gone wrong.

The forerunners of the New Culture attempted to shake the bedrock of Confucian doctrine and to redefine their own relations with tradition.

---

74. Zhu Xi, *Yulei, juan* 80, 6:2075, 2091.
75. Zhu Xi, *Shi jizhuan*, p. 53.

Time-honored views and traditional values were questioned; the language spoken by the common people became an entirely new medium for literary expression, and literature began to claim its freedom from the traditional notion that it served as a vehicle for carrying the Confucian Way. Without the constraints of one particular intellectual orthodoxy, a variety of responses to the crisis arose: while some radical intellectuals advocated total Westernization as a means to modernize China, conservative traditionalists put up a last-ditch resistance, and many scholars took the middle road of a critical reexamination of traditional culture in order to salvage whatever was still relevant to the contemporary situation and viable for building a strong China in modern times. In the effort to sift the viable from the moribund in traditional culture, Hu Shih (1891–1962) provided leadership in the intellectual movement known as "sorting out the nation's traditional culture" (*zhengli guogu*), and the historian Gu Jiegang (1893–1980) made a tremendous and enduring impact on modern Chinese scholarship in the study of ancient history and classics mainly through the publication of iconoclastic papers under his general editorship—the seven volumes of *Gu shi bian* [*Discriminations of Ancient History*, 1926–1941]. The contribution of Gu Jiegang, as Yu Ying-shih argues, was "the first systematic embodiment of the modern concept of historiography," which was, insofar as the study of Chinese history is concerned, nothing less than the creation of a new "Kuhnian paradigm."[76]

In attacking traditional commentaries as the embodiment of a moribund culture, as well as an outmoded notion of history, Gu Jiegang gives full credit to Zhu Xi and the legacy of Song dynasty critical scholarship. In the preface to the third volume of *Gu shi bian*, which contains essays, letters, and critical notes by different authors on the *Book of Changes* and the *Book of Poetry*, Gu fully acknowledges the iconoclastic, destructive nature of their scholarly work, but sees it as absolutely necessary for the construction and "restoration" of Chinese culture. The materials in that volume, says Gu, are at once destructive and constructive:

> For the *Book of Changes*, we destroy its status as the sacred scripture of Fu Xi and Shen Nong and construct its status as a book of divination. For the *Book of Poetry*, we destroy its status as the sacred scripture of King Wen, King Wu, and the Duke of Zhou and construct its status as a book of musical songs. I implore readers not to mistake what I call construction here for

76. Yu Ying-shih, "Gu Jiegang, Hong Ye and the Modern Chinese Historiography," in *Shixue yu chuantong*, p. 274. For a study in English of Gu Jiegang and modern Chinese historiography, see Laurence A. Schneider, *Ku Chieh-kang and China's New History: Nationalism and the Quest for Alternative Traditions*.

our own invention. The *Book of Changes* was originally divination, and the *Book of Poetry* was originally musical songs, and what we do is nothing but to wash and rinse their true faces out. Thus by construction we only mean "restoration," and the so-called destruction is only equal to sweeping clean the blurring dust and dirt. All such views have their origin in the Song dynasty and often find expression in Zhu Xi's writings and recorded conversations. Once we add to them our modern knowledge and extend their implications, we find in them a great deal of new meanings.[77]

The legacy of Song dynasty scholarship, and that of Zhu Xi, in particular, give modern scholars a critical genealogy and a sense of continuity in their effort to examine critically the Chinese cultural tradition. At the same time, however, the effort at rethinking and reexamination is unmistakably modern, informed by "modern knowledge" and filled with "new meanings" that are available only in the twentieth century, after the demise of the last imperial dynasty and China's entrance into a global relationship with the outside world. To the extent that Zhu Xi's revisionist critique of Han commentary tradition still represents a sort of internal conflict between the Han and the Song scholarship within the Confucian tradition, it quickly becomes the very sign of modernity, a necessary consequence of the modern way of thinking informed by notions of evolution and progress, that the twentieth-century critique of traditional culture must transcend Zhu Xi and the Song dynasty scholarship as well. It is therefore not surprising that in his critical survey of traditional commentaries and their divergences and debates, Zheng Zhenduo finds Zhu Xi not much different from the Han commentators after all. Despite Zhu Xi's effort to step out of the shadow of the Han commentary tradition, what left Zheng Zhenduo unsatisfied with Zhu Xi's *Shi jizhuan* is the fact that it still "copies too much of the Mao prefaces." Zheng Zhenduo continues,

> Zhu Xi was widely acknowledged to be the most vehement attacker of the Mao prefaces and the first to have the courage to separate them from the *Book of Poetry*, but except for reading the "Airs of the States" as folksongs and identifying the "Airs of the State of Zheng" as licentious poems, which greatly contradict the prefaces, the rest of his opinions are in fact still confined within limits set up by the Mao preface.[78]

Zheng Zhenduo and the other twentieth-century critics are neither the first nor the only ones to push the radical critique started by Zhu Xi toward its logical conclusion, because the potential consequences of Zhu

77. Gu Jiegang, preface to *Gu shi bian*, 3:1.
78. Zheng Zhenduo, "Reading the Mao Preface to the *Book of Poetry*," ibid., 3:386.

Xi's reinterpretation of the classics were already seen in his own time, in the works of his follower Wang Bo (1197–1274). Wang developed further the insight of *Shi jizhuan* in a radical, egregious and yet logical direction. Once Zhu Xi established that there were "licentious poems" in the canonical *Book of Poetry*, Wang started to argue for purging or "banishing" those poems from the great Confucian classic. Wang's *Shi yi* [*Doubts about the Book of Poetry*] draws audacious conclusions from the literal reading of canonical texts that Zhu Xi first proposed, but the very effort to remove the so-called "licentious poems" from the Confucian classic shows the bias of Confucian moralism. Gu Jiegang printed a modern edition of Wang Bo's work and pointed out in the editor's introduction where modern scholarship differs from, and improves upon, the works of Song dynasty scholars. The presence of erotic poems in the *Book of Poetry* tends to contradict the canonicity of this work allegedly compiled by Confucius himself and thus poses a basic hermeneutic problem for traditional commentators. The Han commentators, as exemplified by the minor "prefaces," tried to solve the problem through tortuous interpretations that made "many of the erotic poems into words that supposedly house the idea of 'thinking of the virtuous ones.'"[79] The contradiction was thus transferred to the tension between the plain sense of the canonical text and its allegorical, sometimes farfetched, interpretations. Although Zhu Xi and the other Song critics abandoned the most tortuous arguments in the Han commentaries, they did not discard all of them, nor did they doubt the legend of Confucius's compilation of the *Book of Poetry*. Trying to challenge the Han commentaries without discarding their basic presumptions, however, the Song critics only caused that old contradiction to resurface as an interpretive problem.

Under these circumstances, it is only logical as well as courageous of Wang Bo to propose as solution to rid the canonical text of all the "licentious poems," a solution that would acknowledge the integrity and the plain sense of the text while insist on the propriety and canonicity of the Confucian classic as a whole. Wang Bo, as Gu Jiegang observes, "would read the *Book of Poetry* only because it was a sacred classic; now that he found in it so many licentious poems that would taint the classic, he naturally proposed to exclude them in order to defend its propriety."[80] This may remind us of those detractors of the Song of Songs in the Christian tradition who would deny its canonicity precisely because they were able to recognize it as a love

---

79. Gu Jiegang, "Introduction to the Reprinted Edition of *Doubts about the Book of Poetry*," ibid., 3:408.

80. Ibid., 3:407.

song. It is only from a completely different perspective and a different understanding of the nature of canon that the possibility arises to listen to the canonical text for what it literally says without denying its canonicity, and that possibility marks the distinction of a modern attitude in both biblical and Chinese hermeneutics from traditional commentaries. Being a doctrinal purist, Wang Bo, like those Christian detractors who wanted to take the Song of Songs out of the Holy Bible, actually posed a threat to the very existence of the canonical collection of ancient poetry in his relentless pursuit of purity and moral propriety.

Ironically, therefore, it is through distortion and farfetched allegorization that those poems could have survived as part of the Confucian canon. From this we may learn, says Gu Jiegang, "that one can break up idols only when the idea of history has been fully developed, or otherwise many important historical materials would be lost." That is to say, when traditional assumptions for scholarship were not in doubt, when the *Book of Poetry* depended on its canonical status as a Confucian classic for survival and preservation, moral and political allegorization served to protect those "licentious poems" in its very distortion of textual meanings. "On this point," says Gu, "we must not forget the merits of the Han commentators in preserving the *Book of Poetry!*"[81] Once the canonicity of the *Book of Poetry* is no longer tied to Confucian moral teachings, however, the imposition of farfetched interpretations is no longer justifiable, and so modern critical scholarship becomes mostly concerned with recovering the plain sense of the text from underneath the distortion of traditional commentaries. In fact, canonicity itself becomes a moot question, since the *Book of Poetry*, similar to other Confucian classics, no longer enjoys the sacred status in modern times that it used to have in traditional pedagogy and the imperial examination system; similarly, old interpretive strategies that ensured the canonicity of the *Book of Poetry* in conformity to Confucian moral and political teachings have quickly lost their usefulness and legitimacy.

Gu Jiegang used a powerful metaphor to formulate the task of modern scholarship in recuperating the plain sense of the *Book of Poetry* from traditional moral and political allegorizations. He compares the text of the classic to "a high stele that has stood in the field for so long that it is completely covered by tall grass and clutching tendrils." To learn the truth about this valuable stone tablet and its ancient inscription, one must cut out the grass and tendrils until "the true face of the stele appears."[82]

81. Ibid., 3:411, 412.
82. Gu Jiegang, "The Place of the *Book of Poetry* during the Period of the Spring and Autumn and the Warring States," ibid., 3:309, 310.

Canonicity in Confucian terms thus comes to be seen as a burden or, as Zheng Zhenduo puts it, a misfortune. "While the status of the *Book of Poetry* was enhanced through canonization, its true nature and value were obscured by the Confucian scholars of the Han dynasty with nonsensical distortions. This is exactly like the Song of Solomon which, being unfortunately included in the Bible, lost its true nature and value for thousands of years!"[83] To be sure, it would be easy for us to criticize Zheng for putting canonicity and the aesthetic value of a literary work in a rigid opposition and for believing, perhaps overconfidently, that modern scholars are now in a position to grasp the "true nature" of texts. Given the burden of traditional interpretations, however, Zheng's rejection of canonicity in moral, political, and religious terms is not at all difficult to understand. Umberto Eco also relates canonicity with farfetched overinterpretation when he says, "As soon as a text becomes 'sacred' for a certain culture, it becomes subject to the process of suspicious reading and therefore to what is undoubtedly an excess of interpretation."[84] Zheng Zhenduo used a metaphor to describe the canon and its exegesis, which recalls Gu Jiegang's own metaphor of a stele smothered in grass and tendrils. Like the other important ancient classics, says Zheng, the *Book of Poetry* "has long been buried by layer upon layer of exegetical debris," from which it is the task of the modern scholar to rescue the poetic text and bring it to the light of new literary studies.[85]

The metaphor of recovery or discovery is not so unusual when we consider that disappearance of primary texts among a thicket of commentaries is in fact a common phenomenon found in different traditions. As Lee Patterson observes, commentaries tend to put into question the power of the very original that they are meant to explain and serve. Medieval commentaries on patristic texts often became quasi-canonical and generated a whole set of commentaries on themselves. "As for the patrological originals that served to initiate the project," says Patterson, "they were submerged within the welter of their own offspring to the point of disappearing entirely—patriarchal authority undone by its own potency." There is even a physical "submergence" of the original in the medieval manuscripts, "where only a few lines of text—sometimes only a single line—appear on a page entirely surrounded by commentary."[86]

83. Zheng Zhenduo, *Chatu ben Zhongguo wenxue shi,* 1:37.

84. Eco, *Interpretation and Overinterpretation,* p. 52.

85. Zheng Zhenduo, "Reading the Mao Preface to the *Book of Poetry,*" in *Gu shi bian,* 3:383.

86. Patterson, "Introduction" to the special issue on "Commentary as Cultural Artifact," *South Atlantic Quarterly* 91 (Fall 1992): 789.

That is certainly true also of the physical form of many classical Chinese texts, in which lines of the canonical text are buried in interlinear notes, commentaries, and marginal annotations. The physical dominance of such ponderous commentaries on the page signals the control of meaning as well as its illumination, the strategic deployment of philological and interpretive skills to make the text align with the needs and demands of the times. When the social and historical conditions have changed and readers come to the canonical text with a different attitude and new ideas, commentaries from the past may become irrelevant or erroneous, obstacles to be removed for a new way of reading and interpretation.

Gu Jiegang, Zheng Zhenduo, and many other scholars in modern China were very conscious of the change of times and its implications for the study of ancient classics. They were convinced that once the "exegetical debris" was swept away, scholarship would at long last be able to make significant progress. And indeed, their works are exemplary of modern scholarship that takes a very different direction from traditional classical studies. The seminal essays written in the nineteen thirties and forties by the poet and scholar Wen Yiduo provide brilliant examples of mythological and archetypal criticism in which archaeology, anthropology, folklore, and the study of literature are brought together to shed new light on ancient songs and poems. In his essay on the archetypal image of fish, for instance, Wen Yiduo argues that fish, fishing, and the cooking and eating of fish, so often found in Chinese poems ranging from the ancient *Book of Poetry* to modern folksongs, are very likely euphemistic expressions for sexual desire or sexual act because fish is recognized, from fairly early on, as "a species most capable of multiplication."[87] Such a new direction in literary study obviously runs counter to the traditional mode of interpretation and cultivates a moral sensibility that makes traditional allegorization appear completely dull and insensitive to the aesthetic value of eroticism in literary expressions. Once Confucianism ceases to dominate social and cultural life in modern society and the *Book of Poetry* no longer needs to be regarded as a Confucian classic to be fully appreciated, the kind of allegorical interpretation in traditional commentaries becomes obsolete and tends to lose all credibility.

From the survey and comparison of biblical exegeses of the Song of Songs and traditional Chinese commentaries on the *Book of Poetry*, we may now draw some inferences bearing on the nature of allegoresis and its relation with ideology. "Allegories are the natural mirrors of ideology," says Angus Fletcher as he concludes his thorough study of allegory as a mode

---

87. Wen Yiduo, "Of Fish," in *Shenhua yu shi*, p. 135.

of symbolic representation.[88] If this is true of allegory as a literary text that consciously structures its language and imagery in ways that implicitly invite and guide an allegorical reading, it is even truer of allegoresis as a mode of interpretation that works to bring a text in line with certain ideological presumptions. When texts like the Homeric epics, the Song of Solomon, and the *Book of Poetry* are canonized for religious, moral, political or other purposes, the community that holds such a text as canonical would naturally expect of it a certain meaning or social function, but a meaning or function the text may not necessarily impart or endorse in its plain sense. Allegorical interpretation is then called upon to attribute such meaning or function to the canonized text. "As soon as a text becomes 'sacred' for a certain culture," to quote Umberto Eco's words again, "it becomes subject to the process of suspicious reading and therefore to what is undoubtedly an excess of interpretation. It had happened, with classical allegory, in the case of Homeric texts, and it could not but have happened in the patristic and scholastic periods with the Scriptures, as in Jewish culture with the interpretation of the Torah."[89] So it had also happened, we may add, in Chinese culture with the interpretation of the *Book of Poetry*. Here again, a clear notion of the literal sense is very helpful as it serves to lay bare, so to speak, the ideological presumptions of interpretive strategies and to reveal the often obscured fact that the moral, political, or religious meaning one finds in allegorical interpretation is defined not so much by the text per se as by the function expected of the text when it is canonized and becomes "sacred." Canonization, as we have seen, is often closely related to allegorical interpretation.

Augustine's interesting discussion of how to solve textual problems in reading Scripture may provide us with a revealing example of the close relationship between interpretation and ideology. His approach to Scripture is based on an impressive early formulation of semiotic theory attached to theological concerns. All signs, including signs in the biblical text, says Augustine, are either literal or figurative:

> They are called literal when they are used to designate those things on account of which they were instituted; thus we say *bos* [ox] when we mean an animal of a herd because all men using the Latin language call it by that name just as we do. Figurative signs occur when that thing which we designate by a literal sign is used to signify something else; thus we say "ox" and by that syllable understand the animal which is ordinarily designated by that word, but again by that animal we understand an evangelist, as is

88. Fletcher, *Allegory*, p. 368.
89. Eco, *Interpretation and Overinterpretation*, p. 52.

signified in the Scripture, according to the interpretation of the Apostle, when it says, "Thou shalt not muzzle the ox that treadeth out the corn."[90]

For Augustine, it is crucial to understand correctly a particular sign in the biblical text either in its literal or its figurative sense. When the reader faces semantic or syntactic ambiguities, or ambiguities in punctuation, pronunciation and so on, the hermeneutic principle that guides him, says Augustine, must first of all be the rule of faith, and then the context of the parts that precede and follow the ambiguous passages. The second half of this principle is philological, dealing with matters of a technical nature, whereas the first is obviously ideological, providing the real foundation of interpretation and the authority to which the reader must ultimately appeal in case of doubt. Augustine warns the reader not to mistake figurative expressions as literal, nor to take literal ones as though they were figurative. "Therefore a method of determining whether a locution is literal or figurative must be established. And generally this method consists in this: that whatever appears in the divine Word that does not literally pertain to virtuous behavior or to the truth of faith you must take to be figurative."[91] In other words, it is the truth of faith that determines when and where a textual problem arises: even before the ideological presumptions of Christian faith enable the reader to find correct solution to a hermeneutic problem, they enable him to identify where the problem lies in the first place. What the reader may understand the biblical text to mean thus depends in significant ways on what the rule of faith stipulates; and that is in turn determined by the establishment of the Church. As Augustine puts it, "the rule of faith should be consulted as it is found in the more open places of the Scriptures and in the authority of the Church."[92] Here we see clearly that interpretive or hermeneutic decisions are closely bound up with the particular ideology of the Church, with its overbearing authority.

From this we can see that what may lose validity and become questionable for later generations of readers, who hold different views or articles of faith, is not allegoresis as such, but the ideological presumptions that inform a particular allegorization. We resent traditional moral and political interpretations of the *Book of Poetry* not just because they are allegorical readings, not even because they so violently distort what the poems mean in their literal sense, but because they read poems in such a way as to make

90. Augustine, *On Christian Doctrine*, II.x.15, p. 43.
91. Ibid., III.x.14, pp. 87–88.
92. Ibid., III.ii.2, p. 79.

them nothing but disguised propaganda for ideologies we now reject. However, we may find Wen Yiduo's reading of fish and fishing as sexual symbols extremely interesting, even though such a modern reading also interprets the text as meaning something different from its literal sense.

Indeed, whenever we try to understand a text and describe "what it means," we begin to interpret the text as something more or other than its literal sense, since to understand is not just to know what the text literally says but to relate what it says to us in our present situation. In a broad sense, this may be seen as allegorical, but as I argued in the previous chapter, to see all texts and all interpretation as allegorical only renders the allegorical quite useless as a concept and a critical term. I would propose instead to understand allegorical interpretation in a narrower sense as a strongly ideological interpretation, one that makes strenuous efforts to make the text fit in with a certain religious doctrine, a particular philosophical outlook, a moral teaching, an intellectual or political orthodoxy, over the resistance of the plain sense of the text. Of course, there is no clear demarcation line between allegorical interpretation thus defined and an interpretation that is less strongly ideological, just as there is no rigid line between a canonical text and one that is not or not yet canonical. The distinction here is a matter of degree, not of kind, but such a distinction exists nonetheless and serves the useful purpose of separating the significantly ideological from the less significantly so.

Understanding and interpretation thus closely relate to a certain ideological basis. When a powerful system of ideology like Christianity in the West or Confucianism in China exerts a predominant influence on a community in a certain period of time, a corresponding system of allegorical exegesis inevitably arises to form the frame of reference in the transmission of culture. Such exegeses and commentaries often assume a quasi-canonical status themselves, and to challenge the authoritative exegesis is then nothing less than challenging the whole system of ideological orthodoxy. The ecclesiastical history of the West is full of revealing examples and, as Froehlich shows, it takes "nothing less than dogmatic *condemnation*" at ecumenical councils to suppress literal interpretations of the Bible.[93] In the Chinese tradition, interpretation of the *Book of Poetry* was confined within the Confucian framework for many centuries, and the authority of its orthodox commentaries was not successfully challenged until the twentieth century.

---

93. Froehlich, "'Always to Keep the Literal Sense in Holy Scripture Means to Kill One's Soul': The State of Biblical Hermeneutics at the Beginning of the Fifteenth Century," *Literary Uses of Typology*, ed. Miner, p. 28ff.

When we look back at the long history of what seems to us mistaken allegoresis, what becomes interesting is the way in which commentaries shaped not only the reading of canonical texts but also, owing to the prestige of the canon, the writing of other texts that were consciously modeled on allegorically interpreted texts of the canon. One important lesson we may learn from the long history of farfetched and distorted interpretations is how important it is to respect the integrity of the text, the plain and literal sense of the original language, and how we may appreciate a well-crafted piece of writing for its aesthetic value. There always seems to be a correlation between the emancipation from dogma and the acknowledgment of the literal sense for the validity of understanding. It is on the grounds of such respect for textual integrity and the literal sense that we are justified in rejecting the narrowly allegorical readings of the Song of Songs or the love poems in the *Book of Poetry*. The famous legitimation of allegoresis in the Christian tradition is the often evoked Pauline dichotomy that "the letter killeth, but the spirit giveth life" (2 Cor. 3:6). That dichotomy, however, is a false one, for the letter and the spirit cannot and need not exclude one another. If the suppression of the letter has been characteristic of centuries of misreading and overinterpretation, if it has fundamentally misunderstood how the text and the reader interact, then the future of a more constructive way of interpretation lies in the true catholicity of hermeneutic principles, the healthy reunion of the letter and the spirit.

Poetry and Political Interpretation

Given the deeply skeptical attitude in contemporary critical theory toward any claim to truth or to correct understanding based on a solid grasp of the literal sense, it may sound naive and even suspiciously self-complacent to speak of centuries of traditional commentaries as gross misreading and misinterpretation. If we follow the relativist and skeptical line of argument, we are not supposed to pass judgment on a cultural system of a different time or place—the past or the Other—but to be aware, above all, of the assumptions and biases, ideological and otherwise, that underlie our own stance or point of view. That is fine as far as self-consciousness goes, but, having acknowledged our own historicity and blindness, which are perhaps inseparable from our insight, dare we yet judge and evaluate, dare we say that there *are*, after all, misreadings and misinterpretations? Should realization of our own limitations in knowledge completely paralyze our sense of right and wrong, our ability to distinguish a reasonably valid reading from a glaringly mistaken or willfully distorted one? When we recall Zhao

Gao's misnaming of *stag* as *horse*, briefly discussed at the beginning of this chapter, are we justified to call it a willful and deliberate abuse of language, a clear symptom of the corruption of social order and abuse of political power? What position should we take in facing such strong misreading and misinterpretations?

As I have argued earlier, a notion of the literal sense and of linguistic normality is crucial here, though what constitutes the literal is by no means simple. The complexity of the literal, however, does not mean that we must give up all our critical responsibility and declare that there is no ground for rejecting distortions of textual meaning; it only means that the literal ground for valid interpretation needs to be negotiated and carefully examined each time *in situ*. Moreover, certainly not every figurative or allegorical reading beyond the literal is unwarranted and forced upon the text, and there is no simple rule of thumb that would help distinguish a valid from an invalid reading in each and every case. Therefore, a better way to discuss the validity in interpretation and to understand the relationship between interpretation and ideology lies in the scrutiny of concrete examples, rather than setting up abstract principles and self-evident axioms. It is again the actual text with its literal sense that will provide us with the measurement for judging the validity in interpretation. In the Chinese tradition, Confucian ideas as embodied in the Han commentaries on the *Book of Poetry* have a pervasive influence on literature and criticism in later times, giving them a heavily moral and political emphasis. The usability of a literary text in promoting moral values defined in Confucian terms becomes an important criterion of value judgment, measured by which works that do not explicitly impart such values are likely to be depreciated, even though they may have a perfect form and appear to be artistically refined. For example, Li Bai and Du Fu of the Tang dynasty are generally acknowledged to be the two most accomplished poets in classical Chinese literature, but there has always been a tendency in traditional criticism to put Du Fu above Li Bai on the grounds of greater moral propriety and political relevance. Wang Anshi (1021–1086), a famous political reformist in the Song dynasty and himself a fine poet, once compared the works of four famous poets and ranked Du Fu the first, Ouyang Xiu the next, Han Yu lower still, and Li Bai at the bottom. "Many expressed doubts about his ranking, but he replied, 'Bai's poems verge on the vulgar and that is why they so easily please. He has a low and foul mind, so of his poems nine out of ten speak of women and wine. Yet his talent is great and compelling, and that is also something worthwhile.'"[94] In the eyes of Wang Anshi, then,

---

94. Cai Zhengsun, *Shilin guangji*, p. 55.

not only was Li Bai unable to reach the excellence of Du Fu, but he could not even stand equal with Ouyang Xiu and Han Yu, who would usually rank not as high as Li Bai in most critical evaluations. To be sure, "many expressed doubts" about Wang Anshi's ranking, which may prove to be one of his idiosyncrasies rather than a generally accepted opinion, while the more widely held view would regard Li Bai and Du Fu as the two greatest figures with the highest achievement in classical Chinese poetry.

Ever since the Tang, however, many critics have debated on the relative merits of Li and Du, and the battle is won more often by those in favor of Du than those who hold Li in greater esteem. For instance, in his inscription on Du Fu's tomb, the Tang poet Yuan Zhen (779–831) brought up the comparison only to dismiss Li Bai as "unable to reach [Du Fu'] doorsteps, not to mention entering the deep recesses of his hall."[95] Holding both Li and Du in high esteem, Han Yu considered such comparisons silly and pointless, and he called those who engaged in such insipid comparisons "foolish." Later critics, however, tend mostly to agree with Yuan Zhen rather than Han Yu. Ge Lifang (?-1164) of the Song dynasty, for example, remarked that "Du Fu and Li Bai are equal in their reputation for accomplishment in poetry, and it seems difficult to rank them when we hear Han Yu saying: 'Li and Du have left us with their literary writings / That shine with beams of fiery splendor.'" Nevertheless, Ge went on precisely to rank them and declared Du Fu's poetry as "the wonder that one man alone could have achieved ever since the Tang; how could Li Bai possibly hope to reach it?"[96]

Another critic in the Song dynasty, Huang Che (fl. 1140), who commented on poetry from a heavily moral and political perspective and often erred, as Guo Shaoyu notes, "in his rigidity of understanding and his failure to get the poet's meaning," consistently praised Du Fu at Li Bai's expense.[97] Huang laid out the principles of his evaluation in the preface to *Gongxi shihua* [*Gongxi's Remarks on Poetry*] and stated clearly that poetry should express "devotion to one's king and parents, kindness to one's brothers and friends, and concerns about the well-being of the people; it should serve as indirect advice to the prince and aid moral teaching."[98] Putting Li Bai to a rigorous test by applying these principles,

---

95. Yuan Zhen, "Tomb Inscription for Mr. Du, the Late Tang Assistant Secretary of the Ministry of Works," in *Zhongguo lidai wenlun xuan*, ed. Guo Shaoyu and Wang Wensheng, 2:66.

96. Ge Lifang, *Yunyu yangqiu* [*The Spring and Autumn of Rhymed Language*], *juan* 1, in *Lidai shihua*, ed. He Wenhuan, 2:486.

97. Guo Shaoyu, *Song shihua kao*, p. 66.

98. Huang Che, *Gongxi shihua* [*Gongxi's Remarks on Poetry*], in *Lidai shihua xubian*, ed. Ding Fubao, 1:345.

Huang Che found his poetry lacking. Although the Tang Emperor Xuan-zong seemed to have appreciated Li Bai's talent, what the emperor really wanted, Huang sneered, was only some poetic extravaganza in order "to please his women with some elaborate pieces of sensuous language." And that, he went on to say, was exactly what Li Bai supplied in his poetry, for "reading through all his works, how rarely does one find expressions like Du Fu's that reveal a heart loving his country and caring about the people!"[99] That is to say, Huang dismissed Li Bai because the poet, in comparison with Du Fu, never professed the same degree of loyalty to the country or displayed the same kind of concerns about the people suffering from the calamities of war. We should notice, of course, that Huang Che was writing in the Song, not the Tang, and therefore he could criticize the Tang emperor Xuanzong who once patronized Li Bai. In the history of Chinese literature, both Li and Du are respected as great poets, and sometimes the beauty of Li Bai's effortless and free style, his individual spirit, his bold imagination, and passionate expressions are better appreciated, but by and large, as Qian Zhongshu points out, "Du Fu has been revered since the mid-Tang by almost all as the greatest poet." A number of critics considered Du Fu to be "the king of poets" (*shi wang*), or "the sage among poets" (*shi sheng*), obviously in analogy to Confucius as "the supreme sage among philosophers," and regarded Du's works as a kind of "Confucian classic" in verse. Even though they might acknowledge the greatness of both Li and Du, "it is rather like the literati scholars paying homage to both Confucius and Mencius, of whom one is the 'supreme sage' and the other 'sage in the second place,' so Du Fu would still turn out to be superior."[100]

Here I am not concerned with the relative ranking of Li Bai and Du Fu, or whether the usual traditional ranking is justifiable. Such judgments are inevitably variable and diverse in accordance with personal tastes and dispositions, and thus impossible to gauge by a uniform criterion. We can, however, discuss the underlying assumptions for such ranking and value judgment. When Wang Anshi remarked that "nine out of ten" of Li Bai's poems spoke of "women and wine," he meant to criticize Li for lack of serious, significant themes; Li has nothing like Du Fu's frequently expressed loyalty to the emperor and sympathy with the common people. Li Bai thus failed to satisfy the moral and political expectations of a Confucian critic. If *Wein, Weib, und Gesang* have always constituted a central

---

99. Ibid., 1:351.
100. Qian Zhongshu, "Chinese Poetry and Chinese Painting," in *Qi zhui ji*, pp. 18, 19–20.

theme in much of Western literature, the counterpart to the Anacreontics in Chinese literature is hardly ever granted more than a light-hearted connivance in much of traditional criticism.

Another comparison of Li and Du would make the point very clear. In a poem about a small town in high mountains in Sichuan, Du Fu describes how dangerous it is for soldiers to climb the high cliffs for a safe pass. How much easier it would be, the poet imagined, if the mountains were removed to clear a path for the royal army. So he exclaims: "I shall indict the True Master, / And would level the wavy cliffs!"[101] In terms of rhetorical efficacy, these lines are similar to Li Bai's hyperbolic expressions in two different poems: "I shall smash for you the Yellow Crane Tower," says the poet; "Better to raze the Jun Mountain / And let the River Xiang run flat."[102] Huang Che quoted all these lines that contain the striking images of smashing mountains, but he found them of very different values. Du Fu's poem laments the relentless and gory strife among local warlords who destroyed a unified country by occupying strategically important locations buttressed by natural obstacles like high mountains and big rivers, and the hyperbolic poetic expression articulates the poet's desire to remove those wavy cliffs that protect disloyal and separatist forces. The meaning of Du Fu's poem, Huang argues, "is about the elimination of treacherous rebels and reverence for the royal house, and it is thus animated with the spirit of loyalty and righteousness, while [Li Bai's] words like 'smash' and 'raze' only sound self-indulgently coarse and bombastic. Thus when the ancients commented on literary writings, they looked at meaning above everything else."[103]

What Huang Che calls meaning here refers not just to the decorum of poetry but specifically the proper moral virtue and political significance in conformity with the teachings of Confucianism. Du Fu's poem is judged superior because the hyperbole used in the poem is not a mere figure of speech, but serves the praiseworthy purpose of promoting "the spirit of loyalty and righteousness," whereas Li Bai's similar expressions, unsustained by claims to moral virtue or proper political objectives, are nothing but meaningless drunken bluff. That is to say, no matter how splendid a picture the poet depicts with bold metaphors and memorable images, and no matter how impressive the turn of a phrase, a poem may be judged insignificant, if not harmful, when it does not measure up to the Confucian notions of virtue and proprieties. Although such moralistic

---

101. Du Fu, "The Pass at Jian Ge," in *Du shi xiangzhu*, ed. Qiu Zhao'ao, 2:721.
102. Li Bai, *Li Taibai quanji*, 2:584, 952.
103. Huang Che, *Gongxi shihua*, in *Lidai shihua xubian*, 1:347.

comments do not represent all traditional criticism, they do fill up many pages of critical works and occupy a central place in the critical evaluation of literature.

Confucius himself has commented on the *Book of Poetry*, saying that "Of the three hundred poems one can sum up the substance in one phrase: herein there is no evil."[104] The comment was obviously made from a moral and political point of view, and indeed the three hundred poems were turned into canonical texts only through the moral and political allegorization by Confucian commentators during the Han dynasty. Confucius already saw this anthology as a primer for ethical and rhetorical education, and the ultimate purpose of studying poetry, he claims, is first of all "to serve one's father at home and to serve one's king abroad," and then "to learn the many names of birds, animals, herbs, and trees."[105] Because of the tremendous influence of Confucianism in the Chinese tradition, the utilitarian concept of poetry and the moral and political concerns Confucius expressed in the *Analects* became core ideas of much of traditional criticism. Even in a major critical work such as Liu Xie's *Literary Mind or the Carving of Dragons*, the idea of writing is first of all "the writing of *tao*," of which the Confucian classics provide the perfect model in both form and content. That is what Liu Xie meant by saying that "*tao* shows the pattern (*wen*) by way of the sages, and the sages make *tao* manifest in their writing (*wen*)," and by defining "the use of writing" as "that of the branches and twigs of the classics."[106] In other words, influenced by the teachings of Confucian ethics and politics, Liu Xie took as his point of departure the concept of writing as a useful tool for the illumination of *tao* or the Confucian Way. It is only when he goes into detailed discussion of many literary genres that Liu offers insightful comments and observations relevant to the appreciation of classical Chinese literature. Thus in Liu Xie's *Literary Mind* and in many other critical works, comments and remarks, we can see how politics and poetics are inextricably mingled in traditional Chinese criticism.

The emphasis on moral and political content in poems leads to considerations of the poet or the poet's intention in ethical and political terms. Mencius gave his famous expression to such an intentionalist hermeneutics by arguing that the critic should endeavor to "trace back to the original intention with sympathetic understanding."[107] In order to reconstruct the authorial intention that had informed poetry from the ancient past,

104. Confucius, *Lunyu*, ii.2, p. 21.
105. Ibid., xvii.9, p. 374.
106. Liu Xie, *wenxin diaolong*, pp. 2, 534.
107. *Mencius*, ix.4, p. 377.

the reader should "study the age in which the poet lived," and try to "make friends with the ancients."[108] The hermeneutic task, as Mencius envisioned for the interpreter of poetry, is thus to achieve total understanding through historical sympathy, an effort that puts understanding of the poetic text on the basis of full comprehension of the poet as a living person. In Mencius, the effort to understand a poem with reference to the poet's lived experience did not directly result in a simplistic equation of the poetic text with the reconstructed intention or the poet's life as context, for he cautioned the interpreter of a poem not to let the words obscure the text, nor to let the text obscure the intention. That is to say, Mencius tried to balance the text and the context, the literal sense and figurative reading.

In later development, however, the equation of text with intention and the confusion of poetry with lived experience became increasingly aggravated, and many critics did read poems as a sort of footnote to the poet's life and personality, and construct, rather than simply reconstruct, the authorial intention as a moral or political intervention. Traditional criticism does not, however, simply equate a Chinese poem with the poet's lived experience or reality; it does not read a poem as though it were a literal recording of what the poet actually saw or felt. On the contrary, moral and political interpretation treats poems as allegories that "present one thing in words but another in meaning." As we have seen, that is how traditional commentators read the poems in the *Book of Poetry*, especially when the "words" of the canonical text pose certain problems to the expectations of moral and political proprieties, thus calling for the establishment of a proper "meaning" beyond the literal sense. In many cases, as we have seen, such a proper "meaning" needs to be erected in spite of the literal sense of the text.

The allegorical way of reading the *Book of Poetry* has a tremendous influence on how other poems are read in the tradition, and sometimes we find there the same kind of farfetched interpretations that force a moral and political meaning upon the poem hardly compatible with its literal sense. To interpret a poem in political terms and to construct the authorial intention as a cryptic and seditious message may have serious, and sometimes dangerous, consequences: that is what we have seen in the so-called "Crow Terrace Poetry Case" in which Su Shi was framed and accused of treason. The reading of a famous poem by Wang Wei (699–761) may provide another example. Of all Chinese poets, Wang Wei is famous for his artistic blending of the elegance of an exquisite

---

108. Ibid., x.8, p. 428.

scroll of landscape painting, a literary understanding of Chan Buddhism, and a highly suggestive verbal picture of beautiful scenery. He is a great poet, a superb painter, a musician with consummate skills, and a philosophical mind capable of detecting intimations of Taoist and Chan Buddhist ideas in the beauty of nature. "The Zhongnan Mountain" is one of Wang Wei's representative works:

> Mount Taiyi is close against the heavenly palace,
> With ranges reaching out to the end of the sea.
> Looking back, white clouds are merging together,
> Stepping in, the ethereal blue disappears before the eye.
> Different regions divide by the middle cliff,
> And light and darkness diverse fall o'er all valleys.
> Intent on finding a lodging for the night,
> I ask the woodcutter, across the small river.[109]

This poem not only depicts a mountain scene as beautiful as in a refined Chinese painting of ink and brush, but it also conveys the atmosphere of the environment and the kinetic sense of animated movement. Following the poetic voice, we can experience the movement, the journey to the Zhongnan Mountain, also known as Taiyi. The speaker in the poem first views the mountain from afar, admiring the ranges of the great Zhongnan for its incredible height and for reaching out as far as the sea. From a distance, the damp mountain air seems to glisten with a greenish-blue luster, but when the speaker steps in it up close, it becomes transparent and disappears into nothingness (*wu*, which is the same character used in Chinese to translate the Buddhist concept of *abhava* or non-existence). As he looks back while climbing up, white clouds seem to close in on all sides; having scaled to the very top, he now enjoys a panoramic view of the great mountain with its different areas in light or shade, divided by the high peak in the middle. And finally, when he comes down in the dusk, thinking of finding a shelter for the night, he is led by the sound of an ax to a woodcutter on the yonder bank of a river, to whom he shouts his inquiry in the otherwise quiet woods. The original poem with its simple form of five-character lines, its striking contrast of colors, shapes, and of light and darkness, its effortless, natural flow of poetic language with graceful rhythm and harmonious rhyme, and the final implications of sound echoing beyond the limits of the text, both the sound of the woodcutter's ax and the human voice inquiring about a lodging, suggest the blending of the human and the natural in a most peaceful relationship.

109. Wang Dajin, ed., *Wang Wei Meng Haoran xuanji*, p. 47.

Here we have a wonderful example of the seamless combination of human feelings (*qing*) and natural scenery (*jing*), the infusion of things and the poetic subjectivity, which is characteristic of classical landscape poetry, and of the works of Wang Wei, in particular, a combination or infusion highly valued in classical Chinese literature.

According to Ji Yougong (fl. 1126), however, this poem was understood by some politically minded literati-scholars not as depicting natural beauty at all but presenting a political "satire," containing a cryptic message that expressed the poet's anxiety over the corruption at the court, the usurpation of power by Li Linfu, the cunning prime minister at the time, and Yang Guozhong, brother to the Emperor Xuanzong's favorite consort, the legendary beauty, Lady Yang Guifei. In such a political reading, Wang Wei's poem only superficially speaks of the Zhongnan Mountain, whereas its real meaning is something quite different: it contains a cryptic message, an expression of the poet's secret desire to avoid imminent danger by hiding himself away in seclusion. On top of the literal sense of the text that seems to speak of nature, then, the poem is understood as containing a hidden political message. So we read in the *Records of Tang Poetry:*

> Some say that this poem was written with reference to current affairs. "Mount Taiyi is close against the heavenly palace, / With ranges reaching out to the end of the sea," this speaks of the evil influence that prevails at court as well as in the country. "Looking back, white clouds are merging together, / Stepping in, the ethereal blue disappears before the eye," this implies that the evil forces are only strong in appearance but have no substance. "Different regions divide by the middle cliff, / And light and darkness diverse fall o'er all valleys," this implies that the Emperor is biased in granting his favors. "Intent on finding a lodging for the night, / I ask the woodcutter, across the small river," this indicates the profound anxiety of the poet over impending danger.[110]

The interpretation above obviously constructs another layer of hidden meaning on top of the literal level of the plain sense, and thereby allegorizes the whole poem and changes it from a brilliant description of the natural beauty of the Zhongnan Mountain into a totally different poem about the political intrigues at court in the capital city Chang'an. The problem with such an allegorical reading is that the alleged hidden meaning does not fit in nicely with the whole of Wang Wei's poem. Not only is this hidden meaning hardly suggested by anything in the text, but it also

---

110. Ji Yougong, *Tang shi jishi*, 1:237.

becomes patently self-contradictory when we test it against the various images in different lines. If indeed the evil forces are symbolized by the great mountain and its many ranges, why are they also said to be "only strong in appearance but have no substance," likened to the insubstantial white clouds and the evaporating blue air? If the great Zhongnan Mountain indeed stands for the evil forces, why would the poet, who supposedly has great fear and "profound anxiety over impending danger," want to find lodging and spend the night there? In the reading quoted above, the Zhongnan Mountain seems to be taken literally as a quiet place in which the poet wants to take refuge from political troubles, but at the same time, it is also taken allegorically as the image of evil forces from which the poet wants to escape. In other words, the Zhongnan Mountain is interpreted as, on the one hand, evil and, on the other hand, a safe haven that protects the poet from evil. The literal sense and the allegorical meaning are thus opposed to each other, and their conflict renders such a reading incoherent and unintelligible. An incoherent and self-contradictory interpretation is often the symptom of a forced moral, political, or religious allegoresis.

The point is not that landscape poetry cannot intimate a secret message in the form of a political allegory, but that a persuasive allegorical reading must build on the basis of the literal sense and respect the poem's textual integrity. As Eco argues in reiterating the old Augustinian principle: "any interpretation given of a certain portion of a text can be accepted if it is confirmed by, and must be rejected if it is challenged by, another portion of the same text."[111] Using such a principle in textual criticism, the allegorical reading of the Wang Wei poem can hardly sustain its claims. An overinterpretation, such as the one offered here, fails to convince because it is detached from the text: it does not put all the textual elements together as mutually supportive parts, nor does it account for all the parts in the frame of a coherent whole. In fact, the totality of meaning and textual integrity are normally assumed in traditional Chinese criticism, and therefore it is not surprising that even a traditional scholar like He Wenhuan (1732–1809), when commenting on the various remarks on poetry he had collected into a compendious anthology, would single out this farfetched interpretation of the Wang Wei poem and call it "truly abominable."[112] In such a political misreading, poetry is turned into something of an encrypted message, a confession of dangerous thoughts of a political nature, which often has dangerous consequences

111. Eco, *Interpretation and Overinterpretation*, p. 65.
112. *Lidai shihua*, 2: 810.

for the poet in a society where the autonomy of literary creation is not granted and the innocence of the accused not assumed.

The weakness of such an overinterpretation of the Wang Wei poem, like the weakness of many Han commentaries on the *Book of Poetry*, lies in the discrepancy between the literal sense and the allegorical meaning, the forced identification of poetic imagery with some metatextual referents that do not fit in with the totality of the text and meaning. To identify Zhongnan Mountain with forces of evil that surround the emperor at the court—similar to identifying the speakers in the love poems of the *Book of Poetry* with quasi-historical personages in antiquity—constitutes a displacement of poetry by moral and political commentary. A reading of the poem according to the literal sense is thus preempted by an intrusive allegoresis, and the interpretation of literature is turned into the decoding of a cryptic moral and political message. The displacement of poetic imagery is crucial for such forced allegoresis. For example, in the tendentious reading of Su Shi's poem on two juniper trees, as we have seen at the end of the introductory chapter, the core of contention is the question of how to identify the various poetic images: the tall and unbending juniper trees, and especially the sleeping dragon under ground. It is identification of these poetic images that determines not only how to understand the Su Shi poem, but also what consequences that understanding might have in real life for the poet. Whatever motivation Emperor Shenzong might have for his reading of the poem, it was fortunate for Su Shi that the emperor cleared him of the charge of treason brought up by the prime minister in an overtly political interpretation. There are numerous cases throughout Chinese history, however, in which poets and writers are not so fortunate, and political allegoresis is turned into a means of fabricating groundless charges and accusations, a dangerous game that often proves to be an effective scheme of ruthless persecution.

It is important to realize that such dangerous political interpretations are not just unfortunate cases from an erroneous bygone age, but very much part of the reality of our own time. I shall have occasion later to examine the politics of allegorical reading in some detail, but from the above examples of the tendentious reading of Wang Wei, Su Shi, and canonical texts from the *Book of Poetry*, we may already see clearly that allegoresis, the reading of literature beyond the literal sense, may have serious consequences that are not just a matter of taste and aesthetic judgment. Literature is of course related to ethics and politics, and it does not differ drastically in purpose from the purposes of ethics and politics insofar as they all purport to contribute to the quality of life and the moral and spiritual well-being of humankind. Literature takes materials from life in all its aspects for artistic representation, and these surely include moral and political subjects. Therefore, political interpretation is not by definition alien to literary criticism, but what we must guard against is the displacement of literary criticism by moral and political considerations, the forced reading of a literary text that disregards the literal sense in the interest of a ulterior motive or hidden agenda, the heavy-handed impositions of ideological and political interpretations.

4

The Utopian Vision, East and West

If there is one literary genre that is inherently political in nature, it is utopia—a form of writing that gives literary form to the imagination of an ideal society. Utopia may be a social fantasy, but as Dominic Baker-Smith observes, it is a "political fantasy."[1] It is also inherently allegorical because its story of a socially organized way of life is always meant to expound a political idea, the ideal and principles of a good society. In our discussion of utopia in this chapter, our emphasis will shift slightly from allegoresis as interpretation to allegory as articulation of the utopian vision. Indeed, if allegory breaks the bounds of texts and promises emancipation through the augmentation of meaning, this possibility of expression beyond textual constraints offers something intriguingly valuable for writers of utopia who want to convey the vision of an alternative human condition, the desire for a better life or an ideal society beyond the constraints of reality. Thus allegory has a natural affinity with utopia, and insofar as the proposal of an alternative human condition already implies some degree of discontent with the *status quo* and therefore suggests a critique, the utopian vision invariably presents itself as a social commentary, an allegory of the desire for change and transformation.

Such a desire seems to be deeply ingrained in the very nature of the human condition, as no one in any society is unwilling, if not actively trying, to make life better and to achieve the optimum out of our limited

1. Baker-Smith, *More's Utopia*, p. 75.

resources and capabilities. The desire for utopia is thus everywhere. As Oscar Wilde puts it eloquently with his typical wit and elegance,

> A map of the world that does not include Utopia is not worth even glancing at, for it leaves out the one country at which Humanity is always landing. And when Humanity lands there, it looks out, and, seeing a better country, sets sail. Progress is the realisation of Utopias.[2]

The desire for utopia is not only universal but also perennial, as the prospect of a better society lies always ahead, at the end of an ever-receding future in front of us, the end of a new millennium. From the biblical Garden of Eden, Plato's *Republic*, to the long list of literary utopias, there is a rich tradition of imagining the best commonwealth in Western philosophy, literature, and political theory. But just as we faced the question of translatability in terms of allegory and allegoresis, we also face similar questions with regard to utopia. Is utopia accessible through conceptual as well as linguistic translatability? Is utopia translatable across the gap of cultural differences? Does the utopian vision manifest itself in the East, for example, in Chinese philosophy and literature? Are there expressions of the desire for an alternative and better society in Chinese texts? In answering these questions, there seems no general agreement.

"In the strictest sense of the word, utopia came into being at the beginning of the sixteenth century"; thus Roland Schaer begins his introductory essay in an important recent publication on utopia. He emphasizes the historical significance of Thomas More's work and asserts that "the history of utopia necessarily begins with Thomas More."[3] In the same volume, however, Lyman Tower Sargent understands utopia in a much broader sense and traces the theme of utopianism throughout history. "Not every culture appears to have utopias brought about through human effort that predate knowledge of More's *Utopia*," says Sargent, "but such utopias do exist in China, India, and various Buddhist and Islamic cultures."[4] Whether utopia is a sixteenth-century European invention or something much larger in scope that can be found much earlier in different cultural traditions is the question I am concerned with here—and again it is a question of translatability. Before trying to answer the question from the perspective of East-West studies, however, let us first consider utopia in the West. Where is that utopian country at which

---

2. Wilde, *The Soul of Man under Socialism*, in *Plays, Prose: Writings and Poems*, p. 28.
3. Schaer, "Utopia, Space, Time, History," in *Utopia: The Search for the Ideal Society in the Western World*, ed. Schaer, trans. Nadia Benabid, p. 3.
4. Sargent, "Utopian Traditions: Themes and Variations," in *Utopia: The Search*, p. 8.

Wilde saw humanity always landing and always setting sail to? In what context did it arise, and what does it look like? We must first search for utopia and find its most salient features before we can argue with any degree of assurance whether its core concept transcends the specific boundaries of languages and cultural traditions.

Utopia and Secularism

"Utopia expresses and explores what is desired," says Ruth Levitas in concluding her study of the various definitions and approaches in utopian studies. "The essential element in utopia is not hope, but desire—the desire for a better way of being."[5] Levitas surveys many works on utopia and argues that definitions on the basis of content, form, or function all tend to be too restrictive, while the broad definition she offers purports to accommodate all the different kinds of utopias. Her attempt at a broad and inclusive definition seems encouraging, and yet her concept of utopia is not without restrictions, for she seems reluctant to ground her concept in anything that might be suspect of being "essentialist" or "universalist"—such as human nature. Instead, Levitas emphasizes the constructedness of the concept. Although the "desire for a better way of being" may sound universal, utopia, she argues, "is a social construct which arises not from a 'natural' impulse subject to social mediation, but as a socially constructed response to an *equally* socially constructed gap between the needs and wants by a particular society and the satisfactions available to and distributed by it."[6] Without positing some basic impulse in the human psyche or human nature, however, the very idea or metaphor of a social construction may seem empty or rootless; and one may wonder why there is so much "desire for a better way of being" in so many different cultures and societies in the first place? What is the basis for any kind of social construction, utopian or otherwise? In fact, the idea of human nature and that of constructedness need not be mutually exclusive, for it is precisely on the notion of some basic characteristics of human nature that utopia or the idea of "a better way of being" is constructed.

In one of the most comprehensive and engaging discussions of utopia, Krishan Kumar relates the concept of utopia first with the changed meaning of human nature in the Renaissance. The Genesis story of the

5. Levitas, *The Concept of Utopia*, p. 191.
6. Ibid., pp. 181–82.

fall of man supplies the basic text for reflection on human nature in the West, and the early Christians and their Jewish predecessors, as Elaine Pagels points out, first understood Adam's disobedience and its terrible consequences as a story about choice and human freedom. Although Jews and early Christians all accepted the idea that Adam's sin brought suffering and death upon mankind, Pagels observes that they "would also have agreed that Adam left each of his offspring free to make his or her own choice of good or evil. The whole point of the story of Adam, most Christians assumed, was to warn everyone who heard it not to misuse that divinely given capacity for free choice."[7] But on a very different social and historical background, when Christianity became a state religion in place of a persecuted clandestine sect, St. Augustine radically altered earlier interpretations of the Genesis story and offered an analysis of human nature that became "for better and worse, the heritage of all subsequent generations of western Christians and the major influence on their psychological and political thinking."[8]

Augustine, and the medieval Church that he influenced, saw human nature as essentially bad, because it was irrevocably corrupted by original sin, which Adam committed in eating of the forbidden tree. If John Chrysostom emphasized moral choice and individual responsibility in arguing that the example of Adam served as a warning for each individual to take responsibility for his own deeds, Augustine would see Adam not as an individual but as a corporate personality, the symbol of all humanity. "In the first man," says Augustine, "there existed the whole human nature, which was to be transmitted by the woman to posterity, when that conjugal union received the divine sentence of its own condemnation; and what man was made, not when created, but when he sinned and was punished, this he propagated, so far as the origin of sin and death are concerned."[9] Pagels argues that Augustine's reading turns the story about free choice into a story of human bondage, for he insisted that "every human being is in bondage not only from birth but indeed from the moment of conception."[10] Nothing free can arise, according to Augustine, from human nature "as from a corrupt root," contaminated by original sin.[11] In such a view, then, human beings cannot possibly save themselves but can only hope to be redeemed by Jesus Christ, to have their souls received by God in Heaven after death. What Augustine called

7. Pagels, *Adam, Eve, and the Serpent,* p. 108.
8. Ibid., p. xxvi.
9. St. Augustine, *The City of God,* xiii.3, p. 414.
10. Pagels, *Adam, Eve, and the Serpent,* p. 109.
11. St. Augustine, *The City of God,* xiii.14, p. 423.

the City of God was thus conceived in direct opposition to the City of Man. The two cities, as Augustine put it, "have been formed by two loves: the earthly by the love of self, even to the contempt of God; the heavenly by the love of God, even to the contempt of self. The former, in a word, glories in itself, the latter in the Lord. For the one seeks glory from men; but the greatest glory of the other is God, the witness of conscience."[12] Augustine's City of God was obviously the opposite of any human commonwealth; its nature was spiritual rather than material, and its realization in Heaven, not on earth.

That is where utopia as a concept differs fundamentally from the ideology of the medieval Church, because utopia is an ideal society built by human beings in this life on earth, not a vision of God's paradise in Heaven. Kumar argues persuasively that there is "a fundamental contradiction between religion and utopia," because "religion typically has an other-worldly concern; utopia's interest is in this world."[13] To be sure, there is the story of paradise in the Bible, but the point of that story, as we have seen in Augustine's interpretation, is to tell us about the origin of sin and death. As Alain Touraine remarks, "the history of utopia began only when society abandoned the image of paradise. Utopia is one of the products of secularization."[14] In any case, the biblical paradise is forever lost because of man's first disobedience, and it would be nothing but incredible arrogance and blasphemy, from a religious point of view, to entertain the possibility that human beings could build a paradise on earth unaided by divine power. What Augustine tried to do in *The City of God*, says Kumar, is to warn against "too much absorption in the affairs of the earthly city, as leading to an alienation from the heavenly city of God." If sin and corruption dominate the world, and if human beings are all sinners, what could the ideal of a utopia be except a manifestation of human pride and arrogance? And that, as Kumar observes, "seems to have been the general attitude towards utopianism during the Christian Middle Ages, when Augustine's influence was paramount in orthodox theological circles. The *comtemptus mundi* was profoundly discouraging to utopian speculation; as a result, the Middle Ages are a conspicuously barren period in the history of utopian thought."[15]

To be sure, there are utopian elements in Christian doctrine, such as the richly imagined Garden of Eden, the meliorist belief in man's capacity to improve, and the idea of the millennium. All these ideas already existed

12. Ibid., xiv.28, p. 477.
13. Kumar, *Utopia and Anti-Utopia in Modern Times*, p. 10.
14. Touraine, "Society as Utopia," trans. Susan Emanuel, in *Utopia: The Search*, p. 29.
15. Kumar, *Utopia and Anti-Utopia in Modern Times*, p. 11.

in Judaism, and some of the Jewish concepts, particularly the apocalypse and messianic prophecies, were further developed in Christianity and articulated in a potent mystical form in the Revelation. For Jews the prophets spoke about the coming of a Messiah at the end of time, in the apocalyptic vision of the "end of the days," but for Christians, Jesus was the Messiah who had come and died, and whose Second Coming would deliver all the good souls to the hand of God in Heaven. "And I saw a new heaven and a new earth," proclaims St. John, "the holy city, new Jerusalem, coming down from God out of heaven, prepared as a bride adorned for her husband. . . . And God shall wipe away all tears from their eyes; and there shall be no more death, neither sorrow, nor crying, neither shall there be any more pain: for the former things are passed away" (Rev. 21:1–4). In its expectation of a perfectly happy condition of things cleansed of suffering and miseries in this world, the millennium is thus very close to the utopian vision, and the various millenarian sects in the medieval and early modern times constituted a most serious challenge to Augustinian orthodoxy. The millennium, as Kumar observes, "holds out the prospect of 'heaven on earth,' of a 'new earth' which in its paradisiac perfection harks back to the Paradise before the Fall and anticipates the heavenly Paradise of the life to come." It is here, therefore, "that religion and utopia overlapped one another. The normal religious devaluation of the world—and hence of utopia—when set against the promise of other-worldly fulfillment, was here radically qualified."[16] Though deeply religious, the concept of the millennium with its expectations of a "new earth" and "heaven on earth" has thus contributed to the idea of utopia.

And yet, the millennium is not utopia as such because, according to Kumar, utopia is a uniquely modern concept emerged in specific historical conditions. The core of the utopian vision is a fundamental secularism, defined against the medieval and Augustinian idea of original sin; and its prerequisite, the idea of an essentially good human nature, or at least the perfectibility of human nature. That is to say, Renaissance humanism provides one of the basic preconditions for the birth of *Utopia*, a name derived from Thomas More's famous book published in 1516. Several years before he wrote *Utopia*, More had given a series of public lectures on Augustine's *City of God*, and in a way More's *Utopia* can be read as a response to Augustine's religious concept of the best way of life. Gerard Wegemer has shown that More used Augustine's *City of God* mainly for contrast: "Utopia is 'not merely the best but the only [political order] which can rightly claim the name of a commonwealth' (237.38–9);

16. Ibid., p. 17.

the *City of God* denies that a truly just commonwealth is possible anywhere or at any time here on earth (xix.20–21)."[17] But as More envisioned it, utopia was precisely the good commonwealth here on earth, thus directly opposed to Augustine's City of God as a spiritual presence beyond this world. Despite More's religious piety and commitment, therefore, "in his *Utopia* it is his humanism which is clearly uppermost. Over and above the specifically Christian influences, such as monasticism, it is More's veneration for Plato and his delight in the Roman satirists that most strongly shine through."[18] The utopians as More described them are not Christians but pagans, and they hold a fairly open attitude of tolerance toward different religious beliefs.

Barely within a year after the publication of More's *Utopia*, Martin Luther nailed his ninety-five Theses on the door of the church at Wittenburg (1517) and initiated a period of intense religious conflict between the Catholic Church and the Protestant Reformation. The bitter strife and religious wars left Europe deeply divided, but also led to radical secularization when people no longer sought solution to social problems through the mediation of the church and the dictate of Christian doctrine. The decline of the medieval religious world-view, says Kumar, was "a necessary condition for the emergence of utopia." Yet another historic event at the time, the discovery of the New World, led to the vogue of travelogue literature, to which More's *Utopia* owes much of its literary form. The customs and social institutions of distant countries, whether real or imagined, had always fed the craze for better conditions of being. "These travellers' tales were," as Kumar points out, "the raw material of utopias—almost incipient utopias."[19] Therefore we may say that the discovery of the New World provided yet another condition for the birth of utopia.

Since it can be so specifically defined in the historical context of the Renaissance, the Reformation, and the discovery of the American continent, Kumar argues that "utopia is *not* universal. It appears only in societies with the classical and Christian heritage, that is, only in the West. Other societies have, in relative abundance, paradises, primitivist myths of a Golden Age of justice and equality, Cokaygne-type fantasies, even messianic beliefs; they do not have utopia." Intriguingly, however, Kumar makes China the only possible exception when he remarks that "of all non-western civilizations, China does indeed come closest to developing

17. Wegemer, *"The City of God* in Thomas More's *Utopia,"* *Renascence* 44 (Winter 1992): 118.

18. Kumar, *Utopia and Anti-Utopia*, p. 22.

19. Ibid., pp. 22,23.

some concept of utopia." But based on an article by Jean Chesneaux concerning the possibility of a Chinese utopia, Kumar finally comes to the conclusion that, after all, of all the ideas Chesneaux emphasized, *datong* (Great Unity), *taiping* (Great Equality), etc., "none of these 'utopian' elements cohered into a true utopia as they did in the West, with its similar utopian religious and mythical 'pre-history.' Nothing like a utopian *tradition* of writing was ever established in China."[20] In a more recent book, Kumar offers some further discussion of the idea of a Chinese utopia, but unfortunately his discussion is still limited by Chesneaux's article published in the 1960's, which has a rather different purpose than Kumar's concerns. By tracing back to traditional egalitarian ideas like *datong, taiping, pingjun* (equalization), and *juntian* (equal distribution of land), Chesneaux tried to explain why socialism was so successful in China. He meant to set up a cultural and historical context in which the political situation of contemporary China would seem to make better sense. "Even if implanted in the East by an external process, socialism has shown itself," Chesneaux argues, "capable of carrying out and realising the confused dreams that had been entertained by men for generations. In this sense it is not as 'foreign' to the East as one might sometimes think."[21] The ideas he discussed are mostly Taoist and Buddhist, and mostly religious and political, though he also mentioned a few literary texts, including Tao Yuanming's (365–427) famous story of the *Peach Blossom Spring* and Li Ruzhen's (1763–1828) novel *Romance of Flowers in the Mirror*, in which we find a depiction of a state governed by women, what Chesneaux called a "feminist Utopia."[22]

For a discussion of utopia, however, Chesneaux's article falls short of a complete guide because it does not go very far in tracing the main source of utopian thought in Chinese tradition, and it largely ignores the social and political philosophy of Confucianism. Under the influence of that article, therefore, Kumar could not provide a full view of the Chinese utopian vision and came to the dubious conclusion that all the Chinese utopian elements put together are still "a far cry from genuine utopianism." In the Chinese version, he goes on to say, the idea of utopia "is almost always coupled with messianic and millenarian expectations associated with the Buddhist *Maitreya* or *Mi-Lo-Fu*." Religious beliefs, according to Kumar, make utopia quite impossible in non-Western cultures. "One reason why it is difficult to find utopia in non-Western societies," he argues, "is that they have

---

20. Ibid., pp. 19, 428 n. 29.

21. Chesneaux, "Egalitarian and Utopian Traditions in the East," trans. Simon Pleasance, *Diogenes* 62 (Summer 1968): 78.

22. Ibid., pp. 82–84.

mostly been dominated by religious systems of thought."[23] This is, as I shall try to demonstrate, not a true picture of the Chinese situation. However, the point I want to emphasize is not that Kumar is wrong and ill informed (after all, he is not a Sinologist mainly concerned with the idea of a Chinese utopia); rather, I want to emphasize his persuasive argument about the nature of utopia and its close relationship to secular thinking. In fact, building on that argument, we may clearly see the existence of utopian thinking precisely in China. For Kumar, secularism is the necessary condition for utopia, and he finds it missing in the East. We may argue, however, that under the influence of Confucianism, Chinese society is traditionally not dominated by any religious system of thought, and that secularism is a remarkably salient feature of Chinese culture in general. With that preliminary assumption, let us now turn to investigate the possibility of utopia in the Chinese tradition and see whether utopia as a concept is translatable across the gaps of cultural differences between the East and the West: whether the utopian desire finds articulation in the Chinese tradition.

Utopian Tendencies in Confucianism

If secularism is a prerequisite for utopia, then the Chinese tradition and Confucianism, in particular, may provide a model of secular culture quite different from that of medieval Europe. Confucius as we find him in the *Analects* is a thinker largely concerned with the reality of this life rather than the afterlife. We may have a glimpse of his rationalism when we read in the *Analects* that "the Master did not talk about uncanny things, violence, disorder, or deities."[24] He was rather ambivalent about gods and spirits, for he held that in attending religious rituals, one should "sacrifice as if ancestors were present, and sacrifice to the gods as if the gods were present."[25] This skeptical attitude is also evident from another passage, in which his disciple Ji Lu inquired about how to serve gods and the spirits properly. Confucius quickly dismissed the whole question when he asked, rather bluntly, "How can you serve the spirits, when you are not even able to serve human beings?" Ji Lu went on to ask about death, but the Master replied, "How can you know anything about death, when you don't even understand life?"[26] The question of death is surely a central concern in most religions, but Confucius was

23. Kumar, *Utopianism*, pp. 34, 35.
24. Confucius, *Lunyu*, vii.21, p. 146.
25. Ibid., iii.12, p. 53.
26. Ibid., xi.12, p. 243.

more concerned with the here and now than whatever was going on in heaven or the underworld.

Many scholars have commented on Confucius's secular and rational attitude with regard to such matters. In a discussion of the religious and philosophical thinking in Confucius's time, Feng Youlan argues that "Confucius already held a skeptical attitude toward the existence of ghosts and spirits."[27] Zhou Yutong also points out that Confucius, who doubted the existence of gods and ghosts but did not discard rituals completely, intended to use religious rituals "as auxiliaries to his moral philosophy. Thus the ancestor worship and ritual offerings to heaven and earth performed by Confucius and the later Confucians were all outer forms meant to induce inner respect for antiquity and former kings, and to bring individual and social ethics to perfection. Thus Confucius's remarks on rituals had gone beyond old beliefs in ghosts and become a skilful application of the psychology of religion."[28] Many Sinologists also note the secular orientation of Confucianism. According to Raymond Dawson, "the central concern of Confucius was the moral guidance of mankind, and the chief virtue for Confucius was humaneness. If his purpose was to restore a paradise on this earth, there was little room for religion."[29] The "paradise" here certainly does not refer to the biblical Garden of Eden, but to the ancient human kingdom of Zhou under the reign of King Wen, which Confucius idealized and considered to be the perfect model for moral conduct and kingly rule. "I transmit but do not innovate," Confucius described himself in great humility. "I trust and devote myself to the study of the ancients."[30] He particularly admired the ancient dynasty of Zhou under the rule of King Wen, and this nostalgia for a wonderful time in antiquity, the adoration for the benevolence of ancient sage kings, constitute in the Chinese tradition something almost parallel to the lost paradise of Eden. The essential difference is, however, that this is a paradise lost through no original sin and with no religious ramifications.

For Confucius, the way back to ancient perfection is not through faith or divine intervention, not by waiting for the apocalypse or the Second Coming, but by a vigorous human effort in this world at the present, by means of the individual striving of each moral being (*junzi*), to revive the culture of that lost golden age. The ultimate purpose of reviving the culture of the past is for perfection to be achieved in the future. In Confucianism, therefore, the exemplary past is not just a golden age to wistfully

27. Feng Youlan, *Zhongguo zhexue shi,* 1:49.
28. Zhou Yutong, *Confucius,* in *Zhou Yutong jingxue shi lunzhu xuanji,* p. 385.
29. Dawson, *Confucius,* p. 44.
30. Confucius, *Lunyu,* vii.1, p. 134.

look back upon and admire, a past one can never hope to recuperate. On the contrary, that ideal past has an important presence in social life, it can, and indeed often does, serve as a measure against which the present is judged and criticized. That is to say, the discourse of ancient perfection has an invariably critical function, because it offers a social allegory as an ideal that also serves as a yardstick to measure the quality of life, or the lack thereof, in the real world.

In this context we can understand the sense of urgency so often attached to the teaching of Confucius, as evident in some of the conversations between the teacher and his disciples. When his favorite student Yan Yuan asked him what one should do to achieve benevolence, the supreme virtue in Confucius's teaching, the Master replied:

> Restraining one's self and reviving the observance of the rites would lead to benevolence. The day one restrains one's self and revives the observance of the rites, all under Heaven will call it benevolence. It is on one's self that one depends for achieving benevolence. Does it need to rely on others?[31]

In the Confucian program of education, then, it is the individual effort at self-discipline and following the ancient rites that will lead to the socially good; and more importantly, it is a human effort unsustained by divine intervention and oriented toward future perfection. This is perhaps where the Confucian vision differs from the Western yearning for paradise or the Greek nostalgia for an ancient Golden Age. Of course, Confucius often mentioned heaven or heaven's mandate, which indicates the presence of religious and transcendental ideas in Confucianism, but by and large the Confucian tradition is definitely more concerned with social and ethical issues in the human world than the realm of the divine. Under the influence of that tradition, Chinese culture is open and tolerant toward different religious beliefs and may be seen as uniquely secular in many ways, particularly when compared with many other cultures in the world.[32]

"Whatever else the classical utopias might say or fail to say," Kumar observes, "all were attacks on the radical theory of the original sin. Utopia is always a measure of the moral heights man can attain using only his natural powers 'purely by the natural light.'"[33] That may well apply to Confucius's idea of a virtuous man who relies on himself for achieving benevolence,

31. Ibid., xii.1, p. 262.

32. I have discussed the relationship between secular tendencies and religious toleration in China. See Zhang Longxi, "Toleration, Accommodation, and the East-West Dialogue," in Laursen (ed.), *Religious Toleration: "The Variety of Rites" from Cyrus to Defoe*, pp. 37–57.

33. Kumar, *Utopia and Anti-Utopia*, p. 28.

"using only his natural powers." Here the underlying idea—the core of the social allegory—is the confidence in man's own nature, his moral strength and perfectibility. And that, of course, is an entrenched idea in the Confucian tradition. In his remark that "people are close to one another in nature, but their customs and habits set them apart,"[34] Confucius did not clearly state whether the nature of man is good or bad, but he did acknowledge that our nature is malleable. By and large, he did not concern himself so much with human nature as with human life in its practical, social dimensions. His student Zigong observed that "What we get to know is the Master's teachings about ancient writings, but what we don't get to know is his ideas about human nature and the *tao* of heaven."[35]

Many traditional commentators, however, insisted that Confucius had already believed in the goodness of human nature and that there was no discrepancy between the two great thinkers in the tradition, Confucius and Mencius, even though they lived more than a hundred years apart. In commenting on Zigong's remark quoted above, Liu Baonan maintains that "the idea of good human nature was first articulated by Confucius. When he said that people are 'close to one another in nature,' he meant that people with their different nature are all close to the good."[36] Liu even quoted Mencius in his commentary on Confucius, maintaining that "because Gaozi and others at the time put forward various specious arguments, Mencius felt it necessary to affirm definitely that human nature is good. Confucius, on the other hand, only remarked that people are close to one another in nature, for his intention was to call people's attention to their customs and habits, not to make a comment on human nature, and so he did not need to put it directly that human nature is good."[37] In a modern discussion of ancient Chinese views on human nature, Xu Fuguan also argues that the "nature" in Confucius's phrase "close to one another in nature" must have been good rather than bad, and that "Confucius was actually speaking of nature as being good when he said that people all have a similar nature."[38] All such readings and interpretations may not have succeeded in proving that Confucius actually believed in a good human nature, but they have had a great impact on the way Confucius's remarks are understood in China.

In the Confucian tradition, it is Mencius who gave us the classic expression of the idea of an inherently good human nature. This idea emerged, as Liu Baonan noted, in a debate between Mencius and another

34. Confucius, *Lunyu*, xvii.2, p. 367.
35. Ibid., v.13, p. 98.
36. Ibid., p. 99.
37. Ibid., xvii.2, p. 367.
38. Xu Fuguan, *Zhongguo renxinglun shi: Xian Qin pian*, p. 89.

philosopher, Gaozi, who maintained that human nature is neither good nor bad, just as water is not predisposed to run in any particular direction on the ground. Depending on the geographical condition, Gaozi observes, water can be channeled to flow either to the east or the west. Taking up Gaozi's hydraulic metaphor, however, Mencius ingeniously changed the horizontal view to a vertical one and pointed out that the nature of water is such that it always runs downward. "Human nature is as necessarily good as water necessarily comes down," Mencius goes on to say. "There is no man who is not good, just as there is no water that does not run downward."[39] Of course there is evil in the human world, but that, he insists, is the work of harsh environment and circumstances rather than something bad in human nature as such. Just as water can be forced to go up by mechanic means against its nature, so can human beings be misled to crime and evil. According to Mencius, human beings all possess the "four beginnings" or four innate potentialities to be compassionate, to feel shame, to behave in modesty and courtesy, and to know the right and the wrong.[40] In other words, human beings have the roots of goodness in their nature which, when fully developed, will make them perfect. Unlike the sinners in the medieval Christian view, for Mencius "all men can become sages like Yao and Shun."[41] When we recall Augustine's view of human nature as "a corrupt root," we may appreciate the fundamental difference between such an optimistic Confucian humanism and the stern view of the original sin in the medieval Christian church.

For utopia, however, what is important is not so much the idea of a good human nature or perfectibility, but the social and political theories coming out of it. Mencius advocated a "humane government" ultimately based on the idea of a good human nature. What he imagined as an ideal society has the definite mark of a classical utopia where people dress in silk and have meat for their meals, and where the young are well schooled and the elderly do not need to overwork.[42] In the actuality of the time—the period of the Warring States—such a simple life of rural utopia would still seem far beyond reach. What Mencius saw around him was a miserable picture: "There is fat meat in the royal kitchen and well-fed horses in the royal stable, but people look hungry and haggard, and corpses dead from starvation lie in the fields. This is as though to lead animals to devour people alive."[43] This last metaphor sounds very much like the critique in

39. *Mencius*, vi.a.2, pp. 433–34.
40. Ibid., ii.a.6, p. 139.
41. Ibid., vi.b.2, p. 477.
42. See ibid., i.a.3, pp. 33–35.
43. Ibid., i.a.4, p. 37.

More's *Utopia* where the "enclosure" of cultivated land for pasture in the expansion of wool trade in England is portrayed by a vivid image: "Your sheep," says Raphael Hythloday (the narrator of Utopia), "that commonly are so meek and eat so little; now, as I hear, they become so greedy and fierce that they devour human beings themselves."[44] In both we find the image of animals devouring human beings as a sharp contrast to the idealized picture of a utopian society of peace and harmony, and in both the utopian vision thus serves more as a device of social critique than a blueprint for reality. Utopia as social allegory is presented as a measure against which reality is judged and found lacking.

Mencius's "humane government" remained an ideal, even a fantasy about a just and good society; and so did Confucius's desire to turn his moral and political ideas into reality. He had dozens of fine disciples who could, one might hope, when perfectly trained in the rigorous program of a Confucian education, serve as counselors to kings or emperors and achieve moral perfection and political harmony everywhere in China. In a way, such a hope is not unlike the famous Platonic idea of philosopher-king, but just as Plato was clearly aware of the unrealistic nature of his notion, Confucius also knew that he was going against the grain of the times. The idea that either philosophers should be kings or kings should take to the pursuit of philosophy, Plato admits, may very well be "likened to the greatest wave of paradox," one that is "likely to wash us away on billows of laughter and scorn."[45] In the case of Confucius, the Master traveled from one kingdom to another, trying to convince the rulers of the value of his political ideas, but he never quite succeeded. In the words of a gatekeeper who left us with a famous character sketch, Confucius was "a fellow who does what he knows to be impossible to accomplish."[46] Through repeated disappointment and frustration, even a saint might feel that his patience was beginning to wear thin. Thus even Confucius sometimes complained. The failure to have his moral and political ideas realized in his time, the difficulties he faced and the frustration he suffered must all have given rise, at least at some particularly vexing moments, to flights of fancies, unreal hopes, and sudden desires for an imagined place: a strange, faraway place where the prospect of a better society according to Confucius would not seem so utterly implausible.

That is exactly what we find in the *Analects* where Confucius says with a sigh, "If the *tao* should fail to prevail, I would get on a raft and sail out to

44. More, *Utopia*, p. 63.
45. Plato, *Republic* 5.473c, *The Collected Dialogues*, p. 712.
46. Confucius, *Lunyu*, xiv.38, p. 325.

sea."[47] Confucius himself did not specify where he would want to go, but in elaborate traditional commentaries, many interpreters are quick to suggest that the destination of Confucius's voyage might be somewhere to the east, in the Korean peninsula, the home of "eastern barbarians." Those commentators claim that "unlike those from the other three directions, the eastern barbarians have a pliable nature." Confucius "would ride on a raft to reach the eastern barbarians because their country had yielded to the moral influence of ancient sages and so the *tao* could prevail there."[48] That is to say, the Koreans, unlike the primitive tribes that inhabited the other corners of the earth, had a pliable nature that rendered them susceptible to Confucius's moral influence.

On a similar remark in the *Analects* that "the Master wanted to dwell among the nine barbarian clans," Liu Baonan maintains that these words, "like the remark of sailing to sea on a raft, all refer to Korea. Since the Master's teaching was not adopted in China, he wanted to let his *tao* prevail in a foreign land, for in that country there was influence of the benevolent and the good."[49] The commentator wants to make sure that the reader understand Confucius's desire to "sail out to sea" as clearly distinct from the escapist idea of "avoiding the world in dark seclusion," an all-too-familiar desire among the Chinese literati who often wished to live like a recluse released from social responsibilities, while comfortably enjoying the beauty of nature. Even though Confucius said that he would sail out to sea and dwell among the simple barbarians to the east, the Master was hoping, so the commentator tells us, that "the *tao* should prevail," if not in China, at least in some far off land beyond the sea.[50]

Such commentaries are perhaps little more than fanciful speculations, but they are intriguing speculations nonetheless. Korea in Confucius's time was certainly an exotic "foreign land," a fertile ground for constructing imaginary communities not unlike the Utopia as More envisioned or the New Atlantis in Francis Bacon's scientific and literary imagination. The natives there were barbaric and primitive, and yet pure and innocent in their pristine natural condition. Given the right kind of influence and education, they could become agents for implementing the philosopher's social and political ideas. In describing the history of Utopia, More says that the ruler Utopus, having conquered the land, "brought its rude, uncouth inhabitants to such a high level of culture and humanity that

47. Ibid., v.7, p. 90.
48. Ibid., p. 91.
49. Ibid., ix.14, p. 185.
50. Ibid., v.7, p. 91.

they now surpass almost every other people."[51] This is certainly very close to the imaginary picture of the "eastern barbarians" that we find in traditional commentaries on the Confucian *Analects*. It is true that Confucius or Mencius never depicted a complete picture of a literary utopia, but there are moments in their teachings that have an unmistakably utopian character. In passages such as Confucius desiring to sail out to sea on a raft or to dwell among barbarian tribes far from China, and in the commentator's emphasis on the moral and political meaning of those passages, we already have all the basic ingredients for making utopias: an imaginary sea voyage, a mysterious foreign land yet to be discovered and explored, and some innocently naive and barbaric natives like noble savages, whose nature and condition are infinitely malleable so that the ideal of a good society can yet be realized on earth. All it takes now is a literary imagination to put these ingredients together as some sort of a narrative or description, and to draw the picture of a perfect, ideal society.

Literary Variations

In Chinese literature, the poem "Big Rat" (*Shuo shu*) in the *Book of Poetry* is perhaps the earliest poetic expression of the desire for a happy land or an ideal society. It may not be truly utopian for the lack of an elaborate description of the happy land, but if we agree with Ruth Levitas that the essential element of utopia is the basic "desire for a better way of being," then this little ancient poem definitely articulates such a desire.[52] The first stanza of the poem reads:

> Big rat, big rat,
> Don't eat my grains.
> I've fed you three years,
> And nothing I've gained.
> I'll leave you and go
> To a land of happiness.
> Oh that happy, happy land
> Is where I long to rest.[53]

The poem has the form of a typical folk-song of several stanzas, with many lines of repetition with slight variation in each stanza. Although it does

51. More, *Utopia*, p. 111.
52. Levitas, *The Concept of Utopia*, p. 191.
53. *Maoshi*, in *Shisan jing zhushu*, 1:359.

not describe what the "land of happiness" looks like, this simple poem does give voice to the dissatisfaction with the present and, reminiscent of Confucius's wish to sail out to sea and dwell among the nine barbarian clans, it articulates the desire to seek a better society elsewhere, away from the here and now. According to traditional commentators, the poem is a political satire against a ruler's "greed" and his "heavy taxes," but also the expression of a desire "to abandon the king for another land of happiness and virtue."[54] In other words, the poem has traditionally been read as a social satire, a sort of political allegory, as an expression of the desire for a better way of living in a happy land beyond the immediately available reality. Because the *Book of Poetry* is an important Confucian canon, this little poem should occupy a significant place in the Chinese utopian literary imagination.

From the ancient folk song, we now move to Cao Cao (155–220), a famous statesman and poet in the period of the Three Kingdoms, who depicted in one of his "Drinking Songs" an unmistakably utopian vision that drew on Mencius and a number of other ancient sources. He imagined a community in "a time of peace, when no official would knock on the door"; when all those in power are "good and wise," and "no feud or strife" are reported to magistrates. Barns are stuffed with grains, the elderly need not overwork, and people all treat each other as kinsfolk. "No valuables will be lost even dropped on the road"; there are no prisoners, nor executions. And the poem ends on an optimistic note that extends benevolence beyond even the human realm, as "The dew of grace covers all plants, animals and insects."[55] Cao's lived experience, however, was quite different from the utopian society he imagined, for he had led many military expeditions, gone through countless battles and wars, and laid the foundation for the Kingdom of Wei with sword and fire. We may appreciate even more the utopian vision he presented in the poem discussed above when we contrast that vision to the horrific battle scenes portrayed in his other poems. In one of his elegiac poems, he described the powerful ministers and generals at the Han emperor's court as "Apes dressed up in caps and robes, / With little knowledge for their ambitious plan."[56] In another poem, he wrote about the strife for gains among different rival forces and the devastating effect of war:

> Men's armors are infested with lice;
> Tens of thousands fell dead.
> White bones are exposed in wilderness,
> And no cock crows for a thousand miles.

54. Ibid.
55. Cao, "Drinking Song," in *San Cao shixuan*, ed. Yu Guanying, pp. 4–5.
56. Cao, "Song of Dew Drops in Wilderness," in ibid., p. 4.

> My heart broke when I thought that one
> Out of a hundred may only survive.[57]

The utopian vision was evidently born out of a desperate need to find peace and happiness away from the brutal reality of war, as a sort of imaginary relief of the horror of devastation he experienced in the real world. Crucial to the utopian allegory is therefore the discrepancy between the ideal and the real: the discontent of social reality and at the same time the desire for a better way of being.

In classical Chinese literature, the most famous literary utopia with some concrete description is undoubtedly Tao Yuanming's (365–427) elegant narration in *Peach Blossom Spring*, a work some two hundred years later than Cao's poems. In Tao Yuanming's work, the poet lets us have a glimpse of a community in peace and harmony quite out of this world. The hidden community is discovered by a fisherman, a native of Wuling, who has to go, as in so many other utopian narratives, through a narrow path from his mundane reality to reach a secluded and totally different world. In an elegant passage, Tao describes the fisherman's discovery of the Peach Blossom Spring, which has ever since become a classic image of an ideal society in the Chinese literary tradition.

> He was gliding along a small river, quite oblivious of how far he had gone, when suddenly he came upon a stretch of peach trees in blossom. For a couple of hundred feet along the banks on both sides, there were no shrubs mixed among the peach trees, and he saw many fragrant plants and a lush green strewn with the petals of fallen blossoms. Quite amazed, the fisherman rowed on, curious to find the end of this grove. It ended at the source of the river, and there he found a mountain with a small cave in front, from which some light seemed to come through. So he abandoned his boat and entered the opening. At first, the cave was so narrow that it allowed only one person to get through. Further down a few dozen steps, however, it suddenly opened up and led to an expanse of level land with rows and rows of houses. There were fertile farm fields, clear ponds, mulberry trees, bamboo groves and the like. Roads and thoroughfares crossed one another, and one could hear cocks crowing and dogs barking in the neighborhood. Men and women moving around or working in the fields all dressed the same way as people outside. The elderly and the young enjoyed themselves alike in leisure and contentment.[58]

---

57. Cao, "Song of the Valley of the Dead," ibid.
58. Tao Yuanming, "Narration and a Poem on the Peach Blossom Spring," in *Tao Yuanming ji*, p. 165.

Like More's Utopia, this community in Peach Blossom Spring was isolated from the rest of the world by water, mountains, and dense forests, discovered by a fisherman after going through a narrow passage. Once there, he found a self-sufficient and self-governed community that formed a sharp contrast to the world outside. People there told the fisherman that "their ancestors found this inaccessible place when they took their wives, children, and relatives in flight from the tyrannical rule of the Emperor of Qin, and since then they had never gone out. So they had been separated from people outside. They asked what dynasty it was now, and had no idea that there had been Han, let alone Wei and Jin."[59] The sense of timelessness is important for all utopias as they are conceived to be a good society that stays unchanged, a perfect social condition that allows neither decline nor the need for improvement. As a stranger from the outside, the fisherman represents an element of connection with the reality of the outside and the present: he is a man from the world of changes and finitude that contrasts with the timeless world of the utopian community. As an outsider he got a lot of attention and was invited to every household for meals and wine, while he told his hosts stories about the outside world with its wars, sufferings, and dynastic changes.

The fisherman took leave after a couple of days and was told not to mention this place to anyone outside this hidden paradise. When he came out and found his boat, however, he marked the route carefully and reported it to the magistrate in the area. This is not just a breach of the agreement to which the fisherman has committed himself, but it also represents a threat of the reality of time and change to the eternal and perfect condition of utopia. To preserve the utopian vision, the story has to end in a mysterious manner: several men were dispatched with the fisherman to find the secluded community, but for all their effort Peach Blossom Spring simply vanished without a trace and could never be found again. It has since remained an intriguing dream and illusion in the Chinese literary imagination, an archetype of an ideal society outside the known world.

In his famous *Ranking of Poetry*, Zhong Rong (459–518) characterized Tao Yuanming as "the paragon of all hermit poets, past and present."[60] In *Peach Blossom Spring*, however, Tao Yuanming did not write the usual "hermit poetry," the kind of individual fantasies about spirits and immortals. Rather, what he described is unmistakably a farming village, a community of simple, earthy, and kind-hearted people. He wrote in the poem:

59. Ibid., p. 166.
60. Zhong Rong, *Shipin zhu*, p. 41.

> Together they engaged in farming the land,
> And retired to rest when the sun had set. . . .
> Spring silkworms produced long threads,
> And no king's tax was levied on autumn crops.[61]

For a fourth-century Chinese poet, the picture of a peaceful society that paid no tax to the king's coffers was, to say the least, rather bold imagination. Many poets in later time felt inspired by Tao Yuanming and wrote their own variations on the Peach Blossom Spring, but most of these sequels and variations missed the crucial point in Tao Yuanming's original poem because they turned the theme precisely into the sort of "hermit poetry" that Tao Yuanming did not write. They made their Peach Blossom Spring a fairyland with superhuman immortals as inhabitants. For example, this is how the famous Tang poet, Wang Wei, described the residents in his "Ballad of Peach Blossom Spring": "First they left the human world to escape from troubled spots, / They were said to have become immortals and never returned." When the fisherman went back to the old route and tried to find the hidden place again, Wang Wei wrote: "In spring, Peach Blossom waters were everywhere, / But the abode of immortals was nowhere to be found."[62] In Wang's poem, then, the fisherman represents a thinly disguised Taoist adept in search of immortality, and the elusive Peach Blossom Spring becomes the fairyland where, for a brief moment, the fisherman encountered the mythical immortals.

Another Tang poet, Meng Haoran (689–740), wrote a poem about Wuling, the place where Tao Yuanming's fisherman supposedly found the mysterious Peach Blossom Spring. Here again, the emphasis is on the land of the immortals beyond the world of mundane reality:

> Wuling has narrow waterways, and the oar
> Guides the boat into a blooming forest;
> No one knows how deep the immortals reside
> In the shaded place whence the river flows.[63]

In yet another variation on the theme of the Peach Blossom Spring, Liu Yuxi (772–842) changed Tao Yuanming's simple villagers into immortals, and the fisherman's discovery was portrayed with more dramatic mystery.

---

61. Tao Yuanming, *Tao Yuanming ji*, p. 167.
62. Wang Wei, "Ballad of the Peach Blossom Spring," in *Wang Youcheng ji jianzhu*, pp. 98–99.
63. Meng Haoran, "On a Boat in Wuling," in *Meng Haoran ji jiaozhu*, p. 152.

The cave was dark with foggy gloom,
But yielded to an ethereal light after some steps.
The fairies were startled to find a mortal man,
And asked how did he find his way hither?
Soon all tension melted, and with smile
They inquired about the world of mortals.

At the end of the poem, Liu Yuxi developed the idea of a contrast between the fairyland of a pure and ethereal quality and the muddy world of human trivialities.

Covered with peach blossoms, the water shone like mirrors;
Sadly the heart of dust could not be washed clean.
The immortals' abode vanished without a trace;
Now only the river and mountains yet remain.[64]

Water shining like "mirrors" and "the heart of dust" are all familiar Buddhist metaphors, which effectively and fundamentally change Tao Yuanming's original Peach Blossom Spring from a recognizably human community into a fairyland beyond the human world. In Liu Yuxi's poem, then, we find a locale quite different in spirit and intent from Tao Yuanming's simple agrarian utopia.

It is the great poet Su Shi in the Song dynasty that pointed out the distortion of Tao Yuanming's original theme in later variations. "Most of the legends about Peach Blossom Spring that circulate widely," he observes, "exaggerate the story beyond credibility. A careful examination of what Yuanming described will show that he only said that the ancestors of those people had come to the place in flight from the tyrannical rule of the Emperor of Qin. Therefore those the fisherman saw were their descendents, not immortals from the time of Qin."[65] In this comment, Su Shi made the crucial point that the Peach Blossom Spring is a human community, not the land of mythical and immortal beings. Wang Anshi (1021–1086), the well-known poet and political reformer and Su Shi's contemporary, is one of the few in the Chinese literary tradition to have truly developed the utopian theme in Tao Yuanming's work. His "Ballad of Peach Blossom Spring" is a worthy sequel to Tao Yuanming's own poem— only sharper in its contrast between the ideal of a peaceful community and the reality of war and tyranny throughout history. The poem begins with a description of the tyranny of Qin: "Half of Qin population

64. Liu Yuxi, "Ballad of the Peach Blossom Spring," in *Liu Yuxi ji*, p. 346.
65. Quoted in Cai Zhengsun, *Shilin guangji*, p. 10.

perished under the great wall. / Not only the old men of Shangshan but also farmers / In Peach Blossom Spring tried to escape it all." The building of the great wall is here evoked as a testimony to the tyrannical rule of the First Emperor of Qin, because it was a project executed through forced labor and at the cost of thousands of lives. Following Tao Yuanming, Wang Anshi made it clear that the ancestors of those farmers, like the hermits known as the four White-headed Men of Shangshan, found a secret place to hide when they fled from unbearable tyranny. He then describes how those people lived in seclusion:

> For generations they planted peach trees,
> Gathered flowers, ate fruit, made fire with twigs.
> Their descendants grew in separation from the world,
> Knowing fathers and sons, but not king and subjects.

In Tao Yuanming's poem, farmers in Peach Blossom Spring do not pay taxes on their crops, while in Wang Anshi's poem, the imaginary community is organized on an even more radical principle as people recognize only kinship relations, not the hierarchy of ruler and the ruled, king and the subjects. The separation between Peach Blossom Spring and the outside world is reinforced in a sharp contrast of memory and knowledge: people outside hardly remembered the terrible past of Qin, while the inhabitants in Peach Blossom Spring knew nothing about the fisherman's time.

> Who in the world could remember the Qin of old?
> While those in the mountain knew not the Jin today.
> Hearing that Chang'an was covered by the dust of war,
> They looked outward and shed tears in the spring wind.

Chang'an was the capital of Han and Western Jin, and it serves here as a synecdoche to represent China in general. Those happy residents of the Peach Blossom Spring have no knowledge of the outside world and its endless suffering, but their kindness is shown in the tears they shed over the misery of people outside, under the shadow of "the dust of war." The political intent of the poem becomes even clearer at the end when the poet pronounces the relentless truth that much of history is suffering under tyrannical rulers like the Emperor of Qin, while ancient sage kings like Shun remain a legend, an illusory hope and wishful impossibility.[66] It is true that the Peach Blossom Spring in Tao Yuanming's and Wang Anshi's texts is very much an agrarian society, quite different from the

---

66. Wang Anshi, *Wang Anshi shixuan*, p. 68.

typical urban utopias we find in the West. After all, Tao Yuanming lived 1,200 years before Thomas More, and the different social conditions of their times inevitably had an impact on their respective utopian visions. What makes Tao Yuanming's *Peach Blossom Spring* and Wang Anshi's variation definitely utopian, however, is the human and secular character of this secluded place: it is an imaginary community of human beings, not a fairyland of immortals.

Despite its fictive nature, utopia has a particularly realistic character that makes the genre more important as the articulation of a social and political idea rather than the manifestation of artistic ingenuity. Wilde points out this realistic character when he says, "Progress is the realisation of Utopias."[67] When it was first conceived as the model of a good society in Thomas More, Francis Bacon, and others, utopia indeed formed part of the idea of progress, a major concept in the imaginary social constructions of modernity. As Roland Schaer argues, utopia brings literature and politics together in an especially close relationship: "On the one hand, utopia is an imaginary projection onto a fictitious space created by the text of the narrative; on the other hand, the project it sets forth assumes implementation and as such it veers toward the side of history while simultaneously drawing its sustenance from fiction."[68] Utopia is essentially the concept of a secular paradise, the imaginary model and allegory of a social theory. It is perhaps this transformability of art into life that Wilde might have seen as essential for his understanding of socialism. In the Chinese tradition, the fictitious idea of a Peach Blossom Spring is closely related with the political idea of an equal and just society, a society that has all the marks of a utopian vision. Therefore, it is not just in literary works like Tao Yuanming's, but also in traditional imaginary constructs of social structures that we need to look for utopian ideas and expressions.

Great Unity as a Social Vision

Other than Tao Yuanming's famous *Peach-Blossom Spring*, the quintessential notion of an ideal society in the Chinese tradition finds expression in very early texts of the Confucian classics. Indeed, utopia in the Chinese tradition is not so much a literary representation as a philosophical vision, and it is not only in literature but also in moral and

---

67. Wilde, *The Soul of Man under Socialism*, in *Plays, Prose: Writings and Poems*, p. 28.
68. Schaer, "Utopia, Space, Time, History," in *Utopia: The Search*, p. 5.

political philosophy that we may look for utopian constructions. If the poem "Big Rat" in the *Book of Poetry* gives an early indication of what one may call the utopian desire for a "happy land" far away from reality, then a significant passage describing the idea of Great Unity (*datong*) in *Li ji* or the *Records of Rites* provides yet another well-known example of the utopian vision in Chinese antiquity, a simple but unmistakably utopian portrayal of an ideal social condition. Like Great Equality (*taiping*) and several other similar ideas in ancient China, Great Unity articulates a social vision that has often inspired egalitarian aspirations in traditional Chinese thought, in which rebels and revolutionaries often sought legitimacy for their radical political agendas and actions. As the articulation of an important utopian ideal in traditional Chinese thinking, the passage about *datong* in the *Records of Rites* deserves to be quoted in full:

> When the great *tao* ran its course, all under heaven were for the public good; they elected those who were virtuous and competent for various offices, and people kept to their words and cultivated amicable relationships. As a result, people were kind not just to their kin, and they cared not just for their own children; so the elderly could enjoy old age, the mature ones made good use of their strength, and the young all grew up well and fine. Those who had lost their husbands or wives and had no one to support them were all taken good care of, and so were those who suffered from handicap or illness. Men all had suitable jobs, and women all found good families through marriage. They hated to see goods discarded on the ground, but they kept those goods not for their own use; and they hated to see efforts made not by themselves, but they made efforts not in their own interests. Thus no plot or conspiracy would arise; no thieves, robbers, or troublemakers would emerge, so much so that the outer gates to houses were never closed, and that was indeed the condition of having achieved Great Unity.[69]

The natural course of the great *tao* gives the social vision presented here its ultimate metaphysical basis, and at the same time, the harmonious condition of social relationships portrayed here can be seen as a manifestation of the smooth running of the great *tao* itself. The social condition in which "all under heaven were for the public good" and individuals held no goods of their own seem to suggest a simple notion of public ownership, while the election of the virtuous and competent for office can be interpreted as a sort of simple form of social contract. The spirit of the public or communal good stands out in this social vision, and

69. *Li ji zhengyi*, in Ruan Yuan, *Shisan jing zhushu*, 2:1414.

in its emphasis on the public good rather than individual interest, the idea of *datong* or Great Unity does resonate with the utopian vision as we find in Thomas More and others.

In the original context, this famous description of Great Unity is ascribed to Confucius in a conversation, and it is made clear that the whole condition of having achieved Great Unity is a lost perfection, something that had happened in the remote past but had already vanished even at the time when Confucius described it to his interlocutor. Such a perfect condition, as Ge Zhaoguang remarks, represents an idealized world picture created by the ancients when they imagined what the past was like in even more ancient times. In that picture, they "often took the remote antiquity as the era to entrust their own ideals and added to it a bit too much of an idealistic hue in their imagination."[70] The picture of a society in Great Unity was, in this case, self-consciously imaginary as Confucius contrasted it with the condition of "Small Prosperity" (*xiaokang*), which was presumably a social condition achievable in his time, a condition not of unity but of social division and inequality when "the great *tao* has become invisible, and all under heaven are for their own families."[71]

Although supposedly articulated by Confucius, the idea that "the great *tao* ran its course" with the spirit of natural benevolence is strongly reminiscent of the emphasis on natural equality and justice in the Taoist classic, the *Laozi*. "The *tao* of heaven diminishes the superfluous to complement the deficient," says Laozi. "The *tao* of man is different: it diminishes the deficient to add extra to the superfluous."[72] The contrast here is between the condition of natural equilibrium and that of social inequality as a result of human activity and intervention—a contrast between nature and culture, if you like. Since Confucianism had a tremendous influence in social and political life in traditional society and established itself as norm and orthodoxy, many of the unorthodox egalitarian ideas in Chinese history, such as "Great Equality," took on a Taoist coloring of naturalism vis-à-vis the Confucian emphasis on ethics and politics, on rules, regulations, on state authority and intervention.

In a Taoist book, *Taiping jing* or the *Classic of Great Equality*, for example, the very concept of *taiping* is defined in terms of natural equilibrium of heaven and earth: "*Tai* means 'Great,' that is, accumulating things toward the greatness of heaven, for whatever is great cannot be greater than heaven. *Ping* means 'Equal' in governing, that is, handling things in

---

70. Ge Zhaoguang, *Qi shiji qian Zhongguo de zhishi, sixiang yu xinyang shijie: Zhongguo sixiang shi, di yi juan*, pp. 74–75.
71. *Li ji zhengyi*, in Ruan Yuan, *Shisan jing zhushu*, 2:1414.
72. *Laozi*, chapt. 77, p. 45.

accordance with their reasons so that there is no secret dealings in favor of one side; so to be equal is to keep things in balance, as equal as the level ground of the earth."[73] However, the ideological background of the *Classic of Great Equality* is a mixed bag, of which the Taoist understanding of natural equilibrium constitutes only a small part, and the book as a whole does not reject but totally accepts the hierarchical social structure of the ruler and the ruled. The equality it advocates thus mainly serves the practical purpose of promoting fair treatment of the subjects below by those in power above, particularly the king and his ministers. Therefore, as a Chinese scholar comments, the society called for in the *Classic of Great Equality* "is not an equal society without the hierarchy of ranks or distinction of the high and the low, but merely a hierarchical feudal society with a sagely prince and responsible officials." It is not, he goes on to say, a society based on "the egalitarian principle of equality for all."[74]

Of course, a utopia does not have to be completely free of social hierarchy, as More's Utopia is ruled by a king and many officials, but the *Classic of Great Equality* does not describe any ideal society in imaginary details in the typical form of a utopia. The idea of Great Equality has inspired radicals and rebels to rise against repression and injustice in several peasant rebellions in Chinese history, notably the second-century Yellow Turban Rebellion in the Eastern Han dynasty and the nineteenth-century Taiping Rebellion in the Qing. Although it serves as a measure of the inequality in real life and a stimulant to opposition, it hardly articulates a truly utopian vision for a good society.

Throughout Chinese history, there are a number of brief descriptions of an ideal society that allow us glimpses of a more or less recognizably utopian vision. Ruan Ji (210–263), a famous poet of the Wei-Jin period, had his own imagination of a peaceful "primordial society" of naïveté and innocence. "In antiquity when heaven and earth were laid open and all things started to grow together, the large ones had a quiet nature and the small ones had simple forms," he wrote. Here again, heaven and earth provide a model of natural equilibrium for Ruan Ji's "primordial society" tinted with an unmistakably Taoist color, which was typical of the intellectual trends of his time. It is a society where people "need not avoid any danger, nor strive for any gains. Things left unattended would not be lost, nor would anything taken in overfull to the brim." The most prominent feature of such a way of life is its uncalculated, natural quality: "There were no premature deaths, nor exceedingly long lives; happiness came

73. Wang Ming, ed., *Taiping jing hejiao*, 1:148.
74. Wang Ping, *Taiping jing yanjiu*, p. 48.

not on account of anyone's effort, nor misfortune fell because of anyone's fault. They all followed the course of their destinies and lived in moderation." What is unusual and radical in Ruan Ji's imaginary society is the total absence of social hierarchy, for it ran of its own accord without the intervention of a government: "They had no prince and yet everything was in order; they had no officials and yet all events were managed well. They all kept their bodies fit and cultivated their nature without ever violating any rules. Precisely because things were so, they could last for a long time."[75] But again, such a peaceful and innocent "primordial society" was imagined more as a contrast to reality at the time than the full description of an ideal society for the future.

This is also the case of Ji Kang (224–263), Ruan Ji's close friend and another famous poet of the Wei-Jin period, whose imaginary society is also striking in diminishing the function of government and the distinction of social ranks. "The prince had no patterns above, and the people had no competition below," Ji Kang wrote. "Things were all complete in themselves according to their own nature, and no one was discontented with oneself. People went to sleep when they were full; and they went to eat when they felt hungry. Satisfied and well fed, they had no idea that theirs was the world of supreme virtue. In such a condition, how could they care about the beginning of benevolence and righteousness, or the elaborate rites and rituals?"[76] Taoist notions of non-action and following the natural course of things stand out in sharp contrast to the Confucian emphasis on rules, regulations, on human actions of moral and political propriety. Therefore, the ideal way of life, described by Ruan Ji and Ji Kang, tends to be "primordial" or primitive, and presents a lost perfection that existed presumably in remote antiquity; moreover, the Taoist sages they imagined often appear to be close to superhuman immortals rather than the average people we find in a typical utopian narrative. Nevertheless, though the ideal society they depicted is very sketchy, rendered with just a few strokes and sparse coloring, it does express a basic desire for a better way of being, that is, it expresses a basic utopian desire or vision.

It is more than a hundred years after the death of Ruan Ji and Ji Kang that the poet Tao Yuanming created the most famous literary utopia in China, but that utopian work, *Peach Blossom Spring*, as I have discussed earlier, was in some sense unique to its time; it was not fully understood

---

75. Ruan Ji, "Biography of Mr. Great Man," in *Ruan Ji ji jiaozhu*, pp. 169–70.
76. Ji Kang, "Refutation of the Claim that Men Are Naturally Inclined to Learn," in *Ji Kang ji zhu*, pp. 265–66.

by contemporaries or by later generations of poets and readers, even for quite a long time. In the Northern Song dynasty, however, even before Su Shi made Tao Yuanming truly famous, the poet and writer Wang Yucheng (954–1001) already wrote a curious piece that bore some noticeable resemblance to Tao's tale of the community in Peach Blossom Spring. Wang's work is a short text in the form of a recorded letter supposedly written by a seafarer from a barbarian tribe, and, just as in Tao's story, that letter refers to the tyrannical reign of the First Emperor of Qin as its historical background, or more precisely, to the notorious expedition led by Xu Fu, a Taoist adept, in quest for the island of immortals. According to historical records, Xu Fu had presented to the First Emperor a memorial in which he made the claim that there were three magic mountains out in the sea where some immortals dwelled and held the secret of longevity. Curious as he was about Taoist magic and anxious to acquire the elixir of everlasting life, the First Emperor sent Xu Fu on a voyage in search of the fairyland and those immortals. He also sent several thousand young children before puberty to go along with Xu Fu as his entourage of pure souls. Not surprisingly, none of them was ever heard of again. Using that legend as a background, Wang Yucheng had his barbarian seafarer giving an account of his unusual adventure and discovery. "My family has lived by the sea for generations," wrote the seafarer in the letter supposedly meant for the emperor of China. He told the story of a sudden storm that swept his boat far away from the shore, and that when the strong wind finally died down and the sea became calm again, he found himself near an island in unknown waters. The fictitious letter continues:

Upon my arrival, I found the place inhabited by a hundred or so families, all living in small houses with fences and walls, and also some tilled land. Some people were lying on the ground with their backs exposed, basking in the sunshine, some were sitting by the river, washing their feet; some men were fishing, and some women gathering herbs as medicine. They all felt happy and content, a situation quite impossible for our world to emulate. I made an inquiry, and one person came up and bowed to me, saying: "Our clan originally came from China. The Son of Heaven sent Xu Fu to find the immortals, and we arrived here after one year's voyage. We were those young boys and girls. Now Xu Fu was a devious man, and he knew that it was impossible to find the immortals or the magic mountain of Peng Lai, so he decided to end here when we reached this place. We took the grains from our boat and sowed them, so we have crops every year; we catch fish from the water, so we have daily meals; we also choose and gather flowers on the island, so our clan survives. We bury our dead in the water; we raise the newborn on this island; and emotionally we have severed all ties with the old country. We have never heard about send-ing soldiers to the five garrison towns, or forced labor in building the Great Walls, or hardships in constructing the Ah Fang Palace. So what can they do to us, even though they levy heavy taxes and have their cruel penal laws?[77]

Although a very short text, this fictional letter supposedly written by a "barbarian seafarer" is rather intriguing in a number of ways. First, it has the typical utopian element of a sea voyage and the discovery of a peaceful community after a terrible storm, which is often the necessary passage of initiation in a utopian narrative. Second, it describes a society and a way of life superior to reality and yet unmistakably human, a community of human beings on earth rather than a fairyland of deities or immortals. Third, it suggests a communal way of life that has people act together collectively, though as individuals they enjoy their lives in leisure and simple entertain-ment. And finally, the utopian vision expressed in such descriptions has an inherently critical function, for it serves as a measure against which the defects of social life and political reality become glaringly visible. All these elements were later developed in a few other works, notably the late Qing novel, Li Ruzhen's *Romance of Flowers in the Mirror,* which is a fantastic jour-ney combining social satire with positive models of imaginary societies; it is often thought to be "China's equivalent of *Gulliver's Travels.*"[78] Of all the ancient texts that contain some elements of utopian ideas, however, the pas-sage in the *Records of Rites* on Great Unity remains arguably the most signif-icant and most inspiring, and it forms an important background for many works that contain some utopian elements. In more recent history, it becomes even more famous when the political reformer Kang Youwei (1858–1927) made use of the idea in writing his utopian work entitled *Datong shu* or the *Book of Great Unity.*

Kang Youwei and Utopianism in Modern China

The Opium Wars in the 1840s marked the starting point of China's acute crisis in modern history, which saw a rapid movement from political reform to radical revolution. Growing up at a time when the last imperial dynasty was about to collapse in China because of widespread corruption

77. Wang Yucheng, "Record of a Letter Written by a Barbarian Seafarer," in *Wang Yucheng shi wen xuan,* p. 227.
78. Richard J. Smith, *China's Cultural Heritage: The Qing Dynasty, 1644–1912,* p. 238. See also Wang An-chi, *Gulliver's Travels and Ching-hua Yuan Revisited: A Menippean Approach.*

inside and the pressure of Western imperialist powers from the outside, Kang Youwei deeply felt the malaise of the time and became leader of the reformist movement. He first made his fame in 1888 when he wrote a letter of petition to the emperor for political reform, and then again in 1895 when he gathered many scholars who were in Beijing for national civil service examinations to send another petition to the emperor in advocacy of reform. Finally in 1898, emperor Guangxu summoned him to the royal palace for consultation, and Kang Youwei became a leading figure in the short-lived reform that only lasted for about a hundred days.

Conservatives congregated under the aegis of the powerful Empress Dowager Cixi and put a stop to the reform, rescinded almost all of Guangxu's reform edicts, and executed several leading reformers. As the political situation deteriorated quickly, Kang Youwei fled to Japan with his student Liang Qichao, and remained a royalist for the rest of his life, even after the Qing empire was toppled by the 1911 Revolution. Thus Kang Youwei was first and foremost a political activist rather than a devoted student of Confucian classics, and all his voluminous writings were composed to serve certain political agendas. In the rapid transformation from reform to revolution, however, Kang Youwei quickly became identified, in the increasing radicalization of political life in twentieth-century China, not as a progressive thinker, but as a conservative and even reactionary political figure. His reformist argument and utopian vision presented in several of his works, especially in the *Book of Great Unity*, got easily lost in the much more radical call to political action and revolutionary rhetoric, and thus had a rather limited impact on Chinese politics in his time.

As a political reformer, Kang Youwei's utopian vision was very much influenced by his reading of Western works that had been introduced and translated since the late Ming and particularly the late Qing period, and was shaped by his observations of social conditions outside China when he visited Hong Kong as a young man and, later, Europe and North America when he was in exile. Hence he articulated his utopian vision through his innovative reinterpretation of old ideas in terms of the new knowledge and new experience he acquired about the world outside. At the same time, as a scholar in late imperial China, he expressed his utopian ideas in a traditional form and in the traditional language of Confucianism. He adopted ideas in the so-called New Text School in Confucian classical studies, particularly the notion of three different ages or different worlds taken from the Gongyang school of interpretation of the Confucian classic, the *Spring and Autumn Annuals*, i.e., the "World of Disturbance (*juluan shi*)," the "World of Stability (*shengping shi*)," and the

"World of Great Equality (*taiping shi*)." These three worlds form a series of gradually ascending stages of social conditions, and Kang collated the three worlds with the ideas of Great Unity and Small Prosperity found in the *Records of Rites*, and arranged them in a succession of stages in evolutionary progress, arguing that the future world of Great Unity would correspond with the coming age of Great Equality.

He understood the evolutionary process as not only temporal but also spatial, for he located China in a lower stage, while Europe and North America were said to have entered a higher stage of social evolution. "For the last two thousand years in China, whether it was Han or Tang or Song or Ming dynasty, and whether it was a time of stability or chaos, thriving or decline, all in all it was always a world of Small Prosperity," Kang wrote in commenting on the famous passage on Great Unity in the *Records of Rites*. "For all the teachings of ancient scholars in the last two thousand years in China, whether it was Xunzi, Liu Xin, or Zhu Xi, and whether the teaching was true or false, refined or crude, good or bad, all in all it was the way to Small Prosperity."[79] That is to say, for Kang Youwei at that time, China had only reached the stage of the World of Stability, which was correspondent with the social condition of Small Prosperity, while Great Unity or the World of Great Equality was yet to be realized in the future. As Tang Zhijun also remarks, Kang saw all of China's two-thousand-year history as the history of the World of Stability, while the World of Great Equality was something yet to come, modeled on the West, because for Kang "it was only the establishment of a capitalist system based on constitutional monarchy that would move China gradually into the realm of Great Unity."[80]

After the failed reform, however, when he traveled to Europe and North America and saw the reality of Western countries, Kang realized that the ideal World of Great Unity was still far from social reality anywhere in the world; so he slightly revised his three world theory accordingly and argued that China had always remained in the first or the lowest stage, the World of Disturbance, while Western countries had mostly entered the second stage, the World of Stability, whereas the highest stage, the World of Great Unity, was the ideal society yet to be realized in the future for the entire human race.

Whatever the theoretical confusion or logical inconsistency, the way Kang Youwei interpreted traditional Confucian ideas of Great Unity,

79. Kang Youwei, "Preface to *Notes on the Li yun Chapter of the Records of Rites*," in *Kang Youwei zhenglun ji*, p. 193.

80. Tang Zhijun, *Gailiang yu geming de Zhongguo qinghuai—Kang Youwei yu Zhang Taiyan*, p. 92.

Great Equality, and the like was obviously not traditional, but very much influenced by his understanding of Western ideas and Western social and political systems. Even a very generous and sympathetic reader of his work observed that Kang Youwei had, in as early as 1886, "already drawn up a blueprint of development for Chinese society to enter modernity and to move further toward Great Unity through constitutional monarchy. Such an idea later became an inalterable article of faith for the rest of his life, while the so-called 'Gongyang school three world theory' and the like were nothing but an outer form in which that basic idea manifested itself."[81]

In form and organization, as Zhu Weizheng points out, Kang's short and early utopian work, the *Comprehensive Book of Solid Reason and Public Laws*, was "in complete imitation of Euclid's *Elements of Geometry*," of which the first six chapters had been translated and published in 1607 by Xu Guangqi in collaboration with Matteo Ricci, and the remaining nine chapters were translated by Li Shanlan in collaboration with Alexander Wylie in the 1850s. These translators would never have anticipated that, in the 1880s, Euclid's *Geometry* "should provide a young scholar living in obscurity in Canton with the form of expression for his utopian ideas."[82] Indeed, Kang Youwei appealed to the authority of science to lend legitimacy and persuasion to his social and political theory, and he claimed, for example, that basic principles such as "human beings have the right of autonomy" and that all societies should be organized on the basis of "human equality" were all "geometric axioms."[83] By using the language of geometry for his argument, Kang wanted to present his theory of autonomous and equal society as the implementation of some sort of an indisputable scientific law, something as self-evident and verifiable as geometric relationships.

Similarly for his *Book of Great Unity*, Western ideas and works provided Kang Youwei with sources of information, including information and ideas about utopia in such texts as Edward Bellamy's *Looking Backward*, which began to appear in a serial Chinese translation in 1891 and was described by its translator as presenting the picture of a "World of Great Unity."[84] Ironically, therefore, the first thing to notice about Kang Youwei's *Datong shu* or *Book of Great Unity* is that it actually has very little to do with the passage about *datong* or Great Unity from the *Records of*

81. Dong Shiwei, *Kang Youwei pingzhuan*, p. 33.
82. Zhu Weizheng, "From the *Comprehensive Book of Solid Reason and Public Laws* to the *Book of Great Unity*," in *Qiusuo zhen wenming*, pp. 233, 233–34.
83. Kang Youwei, *Shili gongfa quan shu* [*The Comprehensive Book of Solid Reason and Public Laws*], in *Kang Youwei datong lun er zhong*, p. 7.
84. See Zhu Weizheng, *Qiusuo zhen wenming*, p. 246.

Rites, despite its eye-catching title. Of the one hundred or so characters in that famous passage, he quoted only a few words. As Zhu Weizheng observes, "though this should not be reason enough to deny the relationship between the idea of Great Unity in the *Records of Rites* and Kang Youwei's utopianism, it does prove that the doctrine attributed to Confucius in that classic was not the real ideal Kang tried to advocate when he was constructing his world of Great Unity."[85] Far more significant is the influence of Western works, even though Kang's knowledge and understanding of the West was rather limited—as seen in particular from the historical distance of more than a hundred years.

In his book, Kang mentioned a certain "Mr. Fu," actually the French utopian socialist Charles Fourier, though he mistook him for an Englishman. He even mentioned the term utopia, but he had made a totally mistaken attribution when he maintained that the world had already shown a general tendency toward Great Unity, so much so that "Confucius's world of Great Equality, Buddha's world of Lotus Flowers, Liezi's Mountain of Danping, and Darwin's Utopia are all realities, not mere fantasies."[86] It is typical in Kang to mix up a number of Chinese sources with information he acquired from reading Chinese translations of Western books, or from his personal observations of Western societies. However, in his time, Kang certainly was among the first to incorporate Western learning in his discussion of traditional ideas and Confucian classics, and such clear signs of Western influence did not escape his conservative opponents' attention, hence offering them an excellent excuse to attack his political views and social ideas in terms of "paying respect to Confucius on the surface, but surreptitiously following Jesus."[87] Such a tendentious statement is surely a deliberate exaggeration, but when we look at Kang Youwei's text, we do see the use of Confucian terminology as an acceptable front or vehicle for carrying new ideas that largely derived from the West. As Wong Young-tsu observes, "he obviously borrowed Confucius's way of Great Unity in support of his evolutionary theory and

85. Ibid., p. 256, no. 51. But Zhu Weizheng is mistaken to say that Kang Youwei quoted just three characters from that passage, because in addition to the three characters which is the equivalent of "women all found good families through marriage," Kang also quoted some more words, the equivalent of "They hated to see goods discarded on the ground, but they kept those goods not for their own use; they hated to see efforts made not by themselves, but they made efforts not in their own interests." See Kang Youwei, *Datong shu* [*The Book of Great Unity*], in *Datong lun er zhong,* pp. 190, 351.

86. Kang Youwei, *Datong shu* [*The Book of Great Unity*], in ibid., p. 120.

87. This is Kang Youwei's own summary of the attacks launched by his opponents, particularly Zhu Yixin. See Zhu Weizheng, "Kang Youwei and Zhu Yixin," in *Yindiao weiding de chuantong,* p. 246.

in service of his political ideas."[88] Zhu Weizheng also notes that "on the surface Kang never stepped out of the frame of the Gongyang school theory of the three worlds, but he was evidently pouring a new wine into an old bottle, and what he poured in was social Darwinism."[89] For Kang Youwei as for many other scholars of his time, social Darwinism appeared extremely attractive because it seemed to put a social theory on the solid foundation of scientific discovery and truth, and because it seemed to provide the hope or even the promise that social progress would come about as assuredly as the natural progress of the evolution of species.

Just as he was fascinated by Euclid's geometric axioms, Kang Youwei found the Darwinian theory of evolution powerful and scientifically persuasive when applied to human life and society. In the *Book of Great Unity*, he argued for the eventual abolition of state boundaries and the unification of all nations on earth, and the way he envisioned to achieve that goal was indeed influenced by social Darwinist ideas of competition and survival of the fittest. "Division and unification are courses of natural selection," Kang wrote.

> The annexation of the small to the great and the elimination of the weak by the strong would serve well as preliminary steps toward Great Unity. The federation of states in Germany and the United States offers a particularly excellent strategy for unification that makes the lesser states forget their demise. Isn't this perhaps going to be the basis on which the United States will take over the entire Americas and Germany will take over the various European states? This is indeed the route by which Great Unity will be gradually achieved.[90]

With the historical hindsight of knowing what has happened in the twentieth century, particularly during the two World Wars, the route to Great Unity as Kang Youwei imagined has a horribly ominous ring to it in our ears, but for him writing at the turn of the century, social Darwinism was attractive because of its scientific appeal, even if its social implications were impossible for him to detect at the time. In Kang's imagination, nations would first form a loose federation and then merge into one unified entity governed by one common authority. He designed a "Table of the Three Worlds Showing the Merging of Nations in Great Unity," in which we find a detailed list of the differences among the three worlds, that of Disturbance, of Stability, and of Great Equality, all lined

88. Wong Young-tsu, *Kang Zhang helun*, p. 26.
89. Zhu Weizheng, *Qiusuo zhen wenming*, p. 245.
90. Kang Youwei, *Datong shu* [*The Book of Great Unity*], in *Datong lun er zhong*, p. 121.

up in a neat gradation of social progress. He even drew up a "Table of Human Evolution" that presents the three worlds as progressive steps leading toward the ideal condition of Great Unity, in which racial differences would gradually disappear when "all races will merge into one, and there will be no distinction of the intelligent and the ignorant"; and eventually "all people will be equal, and there will be neither slaves nor servants."[91] If readers today are more sensitive to the implications of the ways and means with which Kang Youwei's imaginary world of Great Unity was to be achieved, for Kang himself writing about a hundred years ago, it was the final end, the ultimate utopian ideal of equality, unity, and harmony for all humanity that held out the hope of a better way of being.

The imaginary world of Great Unity that Kang Youwei envisioned does have features of a typical utopia. Like More's *Utopia*, Kang's work begins with the description of various sufferings and miseries he saw in reality, both in China and abroad, in history and the contemporary world. He made use of rich materials of Chinese history and classics, and also from what he had learned about other countries in portraying the human condition as fundamentally miserable. The picture of human suffering he presented and his critique of the many defects and evils in the Chinese society were rather impressive, so much so that Zhu Weizheng thought of them as more valuable in the *Book of Great Unity* than Kang's utopianism.[92] Again, as in More's *Utopia*, the representation of human suffering in Kang's book laid the ground for presenting the utopian ideal of Great Unity as the only rescue. "Looking at all possible remedies," he said, "there is no way we can rid human beings of their miseries in order to seek joy and pleasure except by following the way of Great Unity."[93] He then went on to specify concrete ways leading toward Great Unity: the abolition of state boundaries to unify all land; the erasing of racial differences to unify humanity; the freeing of all women from male-domination to accomplish total equality of the sexes; the abolition of families to cultivate world citizenship; the elimination of private ownership to achieve public management of agriculture, industry, commerce, transportation; and so on and so forth. In his world of Great Unity, everyone will enjoy the same equal rights and have satisfaction of all natural desires, including sexual desires, without encroaching on the liberty and rights of others.

91. Ibid., pp. 142–59, 176–78.
92. See Zhu Weizheng, *Qiusuo zhen wenming*, p. 247.
93. Kang Youwei, *Datong shu* [*The Book of Great Unity*], in *Datong lun er zhong*, p. 54.

Given the heavily patriarchal structure of the Chinese society at the time, Kang's liberal views on love, sex, and marriage are particularly noteworthy. He would have marriage abolished and replaced with an agreement or contract between two partners. "In matters of sex and copulation," he says, "the two will come together when there is love, but they will part from one another when there is incompatibility." Sex, he argued, "will be a matter of each individual's gratification of desires and the willingness to give such gratification to others, with no formal denomination or capacity, no limits or boundaries, but agreed upon through mutual affection." He even gave homosexuality the equal status as heterosexuality when he maintained that "in the world of Great Unity, men and women will be equal and everyone will be independent and free. They will be dressed in similar attire and hold similar jobs, and there will be no difference between male and female. As for sex, there will be no difference whether it is between a man and a woman, or between a man and another man."[94] Finally, in the ideal world of Great Unity according to Kang Youwei, there will be no individual or group differences; there will be no separate nations but all humanity living under one common government subdivided into autonomous regions; there will be no army or navy, though police will still exist to maintain order; there will be no private property, no racial difference, no gender discrimination, and all will be equal and free.

Kang's utopian vision, however, does have its blind spots. For example, his understanding of racial difference is marked by the influence of nineteenth-century European ideas of racism and social Darwinism, for he saw different races as inhabiting different stages on the scale of evolution, with the white and the yellow races on top of the chain of evolution, while the brown, the red, and the black were seen as remnants of a primitive stage, precariously poised on the verge of extinction in accordance with the social Darwinist principle of "survival of the fittest." Evolution was hierarchical, and different races were understood as occupying different stages in the progress of the human species. "At the present, all nations are competing with one another," says Kang, "so it will perforce take hundreds and thousands of years to gradually enter the sphere of Great Unity. After going through gradual elimination of the weak by the strong for hundreds and thousands of years, the black and brown races will sadly lose out and probably would not have their genus left in the new world of Great Unity." Kang went on to say even more explicitly: "Therefore when the world of Great Unity is finally reached, only the

94. Ibid., pp. 346, 347.

white and the yellow races will exist, whereas the black and the brown ones will all disappear. Only a small number of Indians will survive, but they will mostly migrate to places all over the world and the color of their race will also change to some extent." In the merging of races, therefore, what would happen in Kang Youwei's imagination is the disappearance of the brown and the black through a gradual process of turning them into the yellow, and then the "mixing of the yellow and the white into one, with no distinction of the noble and the poor."[95] This is perhaps the most alarmingly ominous aspect of Kang Youwei's utopian vision of the future world, in which social Darwinist ideas served to justify draconian measures of unification and uniformity that may turn out to be, if implemented as a kind of eugenic program, a most dangerous and repressive social engineering far from any possible vision of an ideal society. After the 1911 Revolution and the overthrow of the last imperial dynasty of Qing, Kang Youwei's reformist and royalist ideology became passé as the political situation in twentieth-century China quickly moved in a direction favorable for the growth of socialism and communism.

In the eyes of Marxist revolutionaries, utopia is a mere fantasy and the ideal of Great Unity an empty dream with no real chance of fulfillment. Armed with a Hegelian concept of historical teleology and the kind of confidence typical of nineteenth-century scientism, Marx and Engels distinguished their own socialism as a scientific theory of history and society from the theories of all earlier socialists such as Saint-Simon, Charles Fourier, and Robert Owen as "utopian," that is, dreamy and unrealistic, mere "fantastic pictures of future society," and imaginary "castles in the air."[96] According to Marx and Engels, the utopian socialists could hardly present anything better than "fantastic pictures" not because their philosophy was any less systematic or coherent than the Marxist theory of historical materialism, but because their philosophy could not have the solid foundation in social and economic reality, and because at the time of these pre-Marxist socialists, "the proletariat, as yet in its infancy, offers to them the spectacle of a class without any historical initiative or any independent political movement."[97] It was therefore time or history itself beyond any individual human will or intention that had brought socialism out of its pre-Marxist infancy of fantasies to the maturity of a scientific theory and social practice. With Marx's discovery of a materialist conception of history, and especially his discovery of surplus value as the key to

95. Ibid., pp. 171, 178.
96. Marx and Engels, *Manifesto of the Communist Party*, in *Selected Works*, p. 60.
97. Ibid., p. 61.

understanding the intricacies of the capitalist mode of production, so Engels declared, "socialism became a science."[98] As Engels explained in his essay entitled *Socialism: Utopian and Scientific*, Marxism is a science because it has discovered the laws of historical development, the impersonal laws that govern the operation of the "final causes" of social changes and political revolutions. Such "final causes," says Engels, are to be found "not in men's brains, nor in men's better insight into eternal truth and justice, but in changes in the modes of production and exchange. They are to be sought not in the *philosophy*, but in the *economics* of each particular epoch."[99]

In China, Mao Zedong made much the same claim with regard to Kang Youwei's utopianism. "From the time of China's defeat in the Opium War of 1840," says Mao, "Chinese progressives went through untold hardships in their quest for truth from the Western countries. Hung Hsiu-chuan, Kang Yu-wei, Yen Fu and Sun Yat-sen were representative of those who had looked to the West for truth before the Communist Party of China was born." According to Mao, all those who looked to the West before the birth of the Chinese Communist Party necessarily failed, for the truth of Marxism came to China via Russia. "It was through the Russians that the Chinese found Marxism. Before the October Revolution, the Chinese were not only ignorant of Lenin and Stalin, they did not even know of Marx and Engels. The salvoes of the October Revolution brought us Marxism-Leninism." Once the Chinese communists found truth, "this has made it possible to achieve socialism and communism through the people's republic, to abolish classes and enter a world of Great Unity." Then he went to say: "Kang Yu-wei wrote *Ta Tung Shu*, or the *Book of Great Unity*, but he did not and could not find the way to achieve Great Unity. . . . The only way is through a people's republic led by the working class."[100] For Mao, it was only the "dictatorship of the proletariat" as a form of state and institutionalized political power that could accomplish what Kang Youwei did not and could not achieve. At the same time, however, he also saw communism as a way—a better way—to achieve what Kang Youwei and the other "Chinese progressives" had failed, namely, the realization of the ancient ideal of Great Unity.

98. Engels, *Socialism: Utopian and Scientific*, in ibid., p. 416.

99. Ibid., p. 417.

100. Mao Tse-tung, "On the People's Democratic Dictatorship," in *Selected Works*, pp. 412, 413, 414. In the English translation quoted here, the term *datong* is rendered as "Great Harmony," which I have amended to read "Great Unity" in order to be consistent with the way I have translated this term in this book.

Just as Engels considered early utopian thinkers as precursors of modern scientific socialism, so Mao regarded Kang Youwei and other pre-communist thinkers as pioneers in a failed and yet commendable effort to find truth. In presenting socialism as the political means to achieve Great Unity as the end, Mao preserved the core of the Chinese utopian vision in his grand design of a "people's republic" and the "dictatorship of the proletariat." This is of course wholly in keeping with the Marxist dialectic, a perfect *Aufhebung* of the old utopian idea in the new ideology. "Socialism, and more particularly communism," as Gregory Claeys remarks, "is the characteristic form that utopian aspirations have assumed in the modern world."[101] In such an *Aufhebung*, however, not only are utopian aspirations turned into socialist and communist ideologies, or fantasy into "science," but utopia as an idea becomes materialized as social and political realities. If utopia articulates the ideal of a good society as a social allegory, socialism as realized utopia collapses the ideal into the real and brings about a whole new set of problems for the utopian vision.

Corruptio optimi

Utopia as a social allegory is by definition a fiction. In its Greek etymological sense, the word means "no place," though also playing on another rather tantalizing sense of "good place" (*eutopia*). The name of the narrator in More's *Utopia*, Hythloday, means something like a "nonsense peddler." These words point to the fictive nature of utopia as a literary tradition; and indeed utopia is ideal only because it is not real. In the nineteenth century, when socialism, especially Marxism, started to realize the ideal of a good society by means of political organization and economic restructuring of existent systems rather than imagining the good society as a literary fiction, "utopia was consigned to the dustbin of history, as the wish-fulfillment of ages that could only dream of the good society." Consequently, as Krishan Kumar observes, the first half of the nineteenth century saw the decline of literary utopias: "Utopian social theory, and the experimental utopian community, not the literary utopia, became all the rage."[102] But socialism itself also gave rise to some new literary utopias in the late nineteenth century and the early twentieth, such as Edward Bellamy's *Looking Backward* (1888), William Morris's *News*

101. Claeys, "Socialism and Utopia," in *Utopia: The Search*, p. 206.
102. Kumar, "Utopia and Anti-Utopia in the Twentieth Century," in *Utopia: The Search*, p. 251.

from Nowhere (1890), and H. G. Wells's *A Modern Utopia* (1905). After the Russian revolution, early Soviet novels such as Aleksey Tolstoy's *Aelita* (1923) and Konstantin Fedin's *Cities and Years* (1924) are all utopian in structure and purpose.

As Jurij Striedter points out, if Soviet novelists saw a world fallen apart after World War I, they would not just present a picture of disillusionment and ruins, but would "perceive and present the crisis as a transition from a disintegrating past to a better, reintegrated future. After all, a happy humanity, glued together, remains the final aim of the revolution and its product, the Soviet Union."[103] Revolution and the new Soviet regime would offer the fallen world the new hope of reconstruction. Despite the Marxist dismissal of utopian socialism, Striedter goes on to argue, utopian novels emerged as an important form of post-revolutionary Russian literature.

> The Communist revolution itself favored the reactivation and adaptation of old utopian traditions as well as the creation of new utopian visions, from chiliastic hopes including the resurrection of the dead, to projects of political economists disguised or popularized as utopian novels; from the renewed myths and programs of rural Russia to the urban and proletarian pamphlets and poems of the futurists and the *Proletkult;* from strictly *Russian* messianism to internationalism and cosmism; from anarchist dreams to constructivist models.[104]

Thus from the fervor of revolution came the euphoria of utopian aspirations, which filled early Soviet literature with attempts at imagining a better new world yet to rise from the ashes of war and devastation, a brave new world to be constructed by the proletariat equipped with the technologies made possible by industrialization and modernization, by the advancement of science, and inspired by Lenin's idea of communism as the Soviet system plus electric engineering.

At the same time, however, utopia's negative mirror image, the anti-utopia or dystopia, also began to develop in the nineteenth century and became particularly significant in the twentieth as a response to the often too optimistic views of the fundamental malleability of human nature, the unrealistic expectations of an impending good society, and the confidence in the efficacy of machines and technological advancement. In France, Charles Nodier published several anti-utopian novels in the 1830s, and Emile Souvestre's *Le Monde tel qu'il sera* (1845) offered

---

103. Striedter, "Journeys Through Utopia," *Poetics Today* 3:1 (Spring 1982): 34.
104. Ibid., p. 36.

its readers a "prescient cautionary tale about the dangers of mechanization, thought control, and the inhumanity of a society obsessed with material possessions." Therefore, as Laurent Portes observes, in as early as 1845, "a novelist had come forward to denounce a future 'in which man would be enslaved by the machine and self-interest would replace love.'"[105] In England, such works as Richard Jefferies's *After London* (1885), Ignatius Donnelly's *Caesar's Column* (1890), and Eugene Richter's *Pictures of a Socialist Future* (1893) were all anti-utopian novels as social commentaries, which seemed to suggest, as Kumar argues, that "Utopia and anti-utopia support each other; they are two sides of the same literary genre. They gain sustenance from each other's energy and power. The one paints the future in glowing tones; the other colors it black."[106] But it is certainly more than just the internal dynamic of challenge and response in the literary genre itself that underlies the tug of war between utopia and anti-utopia and determines the undeniable victory of the latter in the twentieth century.

It was social reality itself that had forced upon the literary imagination, as it were, the relevance and cogency of anti-utopian novels. "For literary intellectuals and humanists in particular," as Kumar also notes, "World War I, the rise of Fascism, the descent of Soviet communism into Stalinism, the failure of Western capitalism in the 1930s: all these were mocking commentaries on utopian hopes. . . . So far as utopia itself was concerned, the dominant mood and mode seemed to be unequivocally dystopian."[107] In other words, it was the social and political reality at the turn of the century that had produced, as responses and commentaries in the literary form, such powerful and influential anti-utopias as Yevgeny Zamyatin's *We* (1924), Aldous Huxley's *Brave New World* (1932), and George Orwell's *Nineteen Eighty-Four* (1949). It is such direct and yet disguised connection of the utopian or anti-utopian text with the social and political reality as context that constitutes the allegorical double structure in the tradition of utopian and anti-utopian novels. In reading such novels, we must understand not only what the text says literally, but also what it means allegorically, either as the expression of a positive utopian vision or as its ironic parody or critique.

But what exactly is the problem with utopia as an imaginary good society, to which the anti-utopian writers felt necessary to respond? Or more importantly, is there anything in the very idea of utopia itself that tends to degenerate, almost of necessity, into its anti-utopian reverse? Despite the

---

105. Portes, "Utopia and Nineteenth-century French Literature," in *Utopia: The Search*, p. 245.
106. Kumar, "Utopia and Anti-Utopia," in *Utopia: The Search*, p. 253.
107. Ibid., p. 255.

many variations and internal differences, one major problem with the utopian ideal for the communal good is the tendency to favor collectivity at the expense of individuality. It is in this context that we can fully appreciate the meaning of the title of Zamyatin's anti-utopian novel *We* in which all the inhabitants of a dystopian "OneState" are identified not by individual names, but as Numbers, as mere statistics. In a fictional "self-interview" about the state of Soviet letters in the 1920s, Zamyatin told an imaginary French interviewer that "the problem uppermost was still that of the individual personality versus the collective," and that his novel *We* "was the first to expose this problem."[108] The substitution of personal names by "numerals," as Renata Galtseva and Irina Rodnyanskaya observe, "inevitably evokes the memory of the bookkeeping practices of the Stalinist and Hitlerian 'archipelagos.'" And yet, what is remarkable here is not just the novelist's uncanny anticipation of the reality of the Stalinist or Hitlerian totalitarian state, since Zamyatin wrote *We* in 1920–21, but his insight into the very logic of totalitarianism that diminishes the individual in the name of the collective: "By means of voluntarily renouncing one's previous self and assuming attributes of a different guise, the individual prepares for namelessness—for becoming identical with a numbered place in a collective formation."[109]

We may trace the problem of the collective versus the individual in the utopian tradition back to early utopian works, to More's *Utopia*, in which individual rights and interests are already sacrificed in the utopian social planning and regulation as systematic control of everyday life and severe restrictions on personal freedom. More's utopians, for example, cannot travel freely and individually, but they "travel in groups, taking a letter from the governor granting leave to travel and fixing a day of return. . . . Anyone who takes upon himself to leave his district without permission, and is caught without the governor's letter, is treated with contempt, brought back as a runaway, and severely punished. If he is bold enough to try it a second time, he is made a slave."[110] This is, to put it mildly, a disturbing dark side of utopia that remains a threatening shadow so long as it is only a literary fiction, but it becomes unbearably depressing when it is materialized as the political reality of a totalitarian society. That is, of course, what many people perceive to have happened in China under Mao's iron rule, in the former Soviet Union and Eastern Europe, and also

108. Clarence Brown, introduction to *We* by Zamyatin, p. xxvii.
109. Renata Galtseva and Irina Rodnyanskaya, "The Obstacle: The Human Being, or the Twentieth Century in the Mirror of Dystopia," in *Late Soviet Culture*, ed. Luhusen with Kuperman, p. 80.
110. More, *Utopia*, p. 145.

what great twentieth-century anti-utopian novels try to depict as the nightmarish image of dystopia. If utopia begins in the basic human desire for a better way of being and sets that desire to full bloom in a literary form, the sacrifice of individual freedom in the name of collective interest is like a worm lurking and nibbling at the core of utopia until it is completely ruined.

The individual versus the collective is thus the fundamental problem in all utopias, and I would like to discuss this problem with reference to Zamyatin's *We*, not only because it is the earliest of great twentieth-century anti-utopian novels and has exerted some influence on Huxley and Orwell, but also because the problem of the individual versus the collective is depicted in this novel with extraordinary imaginative and analytic power, compelling imagery, and profound insight. *We* is a novel set in the distant future, from which D-503, the narrator, writes down everything in a series of records to report what happens in a technologically highly developed OneState, a sort of science-fiction chronicle intended for his unknown readers in the ancient past, i.e., back in our own time. In the dystopian world of OneState, life is strictly regulated by a "Table of Hours," which determines what exactly D-503 and all the other Numbers will do at each precise moment, an all-inclusive and prescriptive table the narrator calls "a system of scientific ethics—that is, one based on subtraction, addition, and multiplication."[111]

The idea of unregulated act, i.e., freedom, is considered an abomination, frequently held up to ridicule as something primitive, irregular and irrational, even criminal. "Freedom and criminality are just as indissolubly linked as . . . well, as the movement of an aero and its velocity," writes D-503 in his diary. "When the velocity of an aero is reduced to 0, it is not in motion; when a man's freedom is reduced to zero, he commits no crimes. That's clear. The only means to rid man of crime is to rid him of freedom."[112] In this context, Zamyatin's reinterpretation of the biblical story of the fall of man would appear extremely significant as it brings out, perhaps without consciously intending it, the old pre-Augustinian meaning of the genesis story, and reads it as a story about individual choice and human freedom.

Of course, that reinterpretation is presented ironically through the distorting lens of a dystopian perspective. "The old legend about Paradise—that was about us, about right now," says R-13, the appointed poet of OneState, when he reflected on the execution of a rebel Number the day

---

111. Zamyatin, *We*, p. 14.
112. Ibid., p. 36.

before and the nature of happiness as understood in his dystopian world. "Those two in Paradise, they were offered a choice: happiness without freedom, or freedom without happiness, nothing else. Those idiots chose freedom. And then what? Then for centuries they were homesick for the chains." In this reinterpretation of the story of the fall of man, OneState reaches the truly dystopian goal of total elimination of individual choice by redefining happiness as non-freedom, that is, as severe restriction and total control. Speaking as the mouthpiece of OneState in his capacity of the official poet, R-13 thus continues,

> Yes! We helped God finally overcome the Devil—because that's who it was that pushed people to break the commandment and taste freedom and be ruined. It was him, the wily serpent. But we gave him a boot to the head! Crack! And it was all over: Paradise was back. And we're simple and innocent again, like Adam and Eve. None of those complications about good and evil: Everything is very simple, childishly simple—Paradise! The Benefactor, the Machine, the Cube, the Gas Bell, the Guardians: All those things represent good, all that is sublime, splendid, noble, elevated, crystal pure. Because that is what protects our nonfreedom, which is to say, our happiness.[113]

In the dystopian OneState, to feel "happy" thus means to give up choice, personal freedom, and individual rights so as to be completely identified with the collective. As the narrator puts it in a characteristically mathematical way of expression, the relation of the individual and the collective can be measured in a simple calculation.

> So, take some scales and put on one side a gram, on the other a ton; on one side "I" and on the other "We," OneState. It's clear, isn't it?—to assert that "I" has certain "rights" with respect to the State is exactly the same as asserting that a gram weighs the same as a ton. That explains the way things are divided up: To the ton go the rights, to the gram the duties. And the natural path from nullity to greatness is this: Forget that you're a gram and feel yourself a millionth part of a ton.[114]

This passage effectively exposes the logic of the totalitarian state, which is always the logic of the insignificance of the individual vis-à-vis the all-important collective; the expression of that logic by way of a simple calculation is typical of Zamyatin's ironic style, particularly his ironic use of mathematics as a symbol of control in anti-utopia. Alluding to a

---

113. Ibid., p. 61.
114. Ibid., p. 111.

similar mathematical reference in Dostoevsky's *Notes from the Underground*, Zamyatin puts the logic of control in the form of a simple equation and has the narrator singing the praise of the "multiplication table" which "never—repeat, never—makes a mistake." D-503 goes on to add, "And there's nothing happier than figures that live according to the elegant and eternal laws of the multiplication table. No wavering, no wandering. Truth is one, and the true path is one. And that truth is two times two and that true path is four."[115] In the literary context of the anti-utopian novel, the simple mathematical truth of "two times two equals four" signifies much more than just complete control, for the "scientific ethics" it exemplifies reduces human life, and indeed humanity itself, to an abstraction, to an empty zero, represented with as much assurance as a linear teleology, an impersonal, icy-cold logic of arithmetic. By means of his ironic use of mathematics, Zamyatin thus puts in question the relentless scientism prevalent in the socialist ideology and socialist state as he saw at the time, and alerts us to the danger of dehumanization in the sacrifice of personal freedom for a collective cause—the danger of utopian pretensions of rationality, scientific progress, and the communal good.

The novel, however, as Mikhail Bakhtin argues, is by nature polyphonic, containing "a diversity of social speech types (sometimes even diversity of languages) and a diversity of individual voices, artistically organized." That is to say, the novel is always a microcosm of social and ideological "heteroglossia."[116] Even if the discourse of authority and control is deliberately represented as prevailing in the anti-utopian novel, as is the case with Zamyatin's *We*, the novel as a polyphonic genre must develop in such a way as to lead to the inevitable collapse of the authoritarian word. "The novel is the expression of a Galilean perception of language, one that denies the absolutism of a single and unitary language," says Bakhtin. "The novel begins by presuming a verbal and semantic decentering of the ideological world, a certain linguistic homelessness of literary consciousness, which no longer possesses a sacrosanct and unitary linguistic medium for containing ideological thought."[117] Drawing on Bakhtin's concept of the polyphonic novel, Striedter shows how, in Zamyatin's *We*, the narrator's "linguistic consciousness" moves from a mindless echoing of the official, authoritarian word to a discovery of "the possibility of *different* words and voices, including its own," and thus

---

115. Ibid., p. 65–66.
116. Bakhtin, "Discourse in the Novel," in *The Dialogic Imagination*, trans. Michael Holquist, pp. 262, 263.
117. Ibid., pp. 366, 367.

"begins to discover the polyphony of the surrounding society." Gradually, the authoritarian word loses its grip on the narrator as the novel moves on and becomes ineluctably more and more polyphonic. "This polyphony," says Striedter, "challenges and erodes the authoritarian political language, as well as the absolute language of algebra or mathematics so familiar to the mathematician D-503 (and the Engineer Zamyatin) and canonized by the absolute state out of its commitment to clear rationalism."[118]

That is indeed how language and tone move and change in Zamyatin's *We:* even though life in the totalitarian OneState is regulated with mathematical precision and kept under surveillance in total transparency, the regulation and control cannot be really complete or total. For a while, it does seem that everything is under control in the totalitarian OneState, and there are no variables, no surprises. As the story unfolds, however, it is precisely the irregular and unpredictable, represented by the enigmatic female figure I-330 and her alluring mysteries and wayward behaviors, that threaten to bring down the almost perfect control of the anti-utopia.

Zamyatin did not, however, promise liberation from the totalitarian control at the end of his novel. Though the seemingly unbreakable machine of OneState is finally broken and proves to be less perfect in its control than it first appeared, it is by no means dead. After an unsuccessful revolt, the rebel Numbers are being killed and executed, and the rest are all ordered to have the last vestige of humanity removed from the brain in a compulsory Operation. Having gone through such an Operation, D-503, who was momentarily drawn to the rebels' side by I-330 and through his own awakened humanity, now comes back to the side of the establishment, betrays all rebel Numbers, and even sits with the omnipotent Benefactor to watch the torture and execution of rebels. The suppression of the revolt and execution of rebels must be done swiftly, says the repentant D-503:

> It can't be put off, because in the western quarters there is still chaos, roaring, corpses, animals, and, unfortunately, quite a lot of Numbers who have betrayed reason.
> But on Fortieth Avenue, which runs crosstown, they've managed to build a temporary wall of high-voltage waves. And I hope we'll win. More—I'm certain we'll win. Because reason has to win.[119]

With these lines the novel comes to its end, and readers are left with the impression that the totalitarian state is regaining control over the riot

118. Striedter, "Journeys Through Utopia," p. 43.
119. Zamyatin, *We,* p. 221.

and chaos, and there is very little hope for the rebels to overthrow the all-powerful Benefactor and his efficient killing machine. Given the political situation in the 1920s, Zamyatin's refusal to satisfy the reader's sense of poetic justice by granting the false hope of an unlikely victory for the individual only testifies to his sober analysis of political reality at the time and his insights into the danger of utopian pretensions. The dark ending of the novel shows not so much Zamyatin's pessimism as his sensitive response to social and political reality. "The anti-utopia," as Krishan Kumar argues, "can indeed be thought of as an invention to combat socialism, in so far as socialism was seen to be the fullest and most sophisticated expression of the modern worship of science, technology and organization. In that sense, both utopia and anti-utopia in the past hundred years have come to express and reflect the most significant political phenomenon of modern times, the rise of socialism as an ideology and as a movement."[120]

If anti-utopia as the ghostly *Doppelgänger* of the utopian vision emerged as a response and critique of socialism, as both ideology and political reality, then the tremendous changes at the end of the twentieth century might put an end to both utopias and anti-utopias. The highly symbolic demolition of the Berlin Wall in 1989, the disintegration of the Soviet Union, and the remarkable changes taking place in China since the 1990s all clearly demonstrate that socialism as state-planned economy and "dictatorship of the proletariat" has failed. Perhaps the twentieth century has provided enough evidence to show the irony of history that the utopian vision of a good society has the nasty tendency of turning into its ugly opposite. Frédéric Rouvillois cites many examples to support his argument that utopia has some sort of a natural affinity with totalitarianism. "The proximity is too frequent to be accidental," says Rouvillois. "Utopia and totalitarianism are both engaged in a mirroring game, tirelessly sending the same image back and forth as if utopia were nothing more than the premonition of totalitarianism and totalitarianism the tragic execution of the utopian dream. Only the distance that separates a dream from its realization seems to stand between the two."[121]

The most fundamental connection between the two, as I have discussed earlier, is the disregard of the individual in the name of the collective. Since the collective in political reality cannot remain an abstract, it must function through human agency and be represented by real human beings, and most likely, by a man, a supreme leader. To put it in Zamyatin's mathematical

---

120. Kumar, *Utopia and Anti-Utopia*, p. 49.
121. Rouvillois, "Utopia and Totalitarianism," in *Utopia: The Search*, p. 316.

terms, the powerful leader is the ton that has all the weight, whereas each individual becomes an insignificant gram in comparison. In anti-utopian novels, that leader becomes a god-like figure such as the Benefactor in Zamyatin's *We* or Big Brother in Orwell's *Nineteen Eighty-Four.* "Fundamentally, utopia and totalitarianism share a similar conception of man, nature, and history. They understand history as a necessary and perpetual progress with conscious, rational man as its principal actor and propelling force," says Rouvillois. "And what we see beyond the common project of seeing 'the kingdom of heaven fulfilled at last upon earth' is a similar wish, inherently linking utopia and totalitarianism, to put man in God's place, even if he must endure all the torments of hell to reach it."[122] The utopian wish "to put man in God's place" may remind us of Kumar's discussion of the genesis of More's *Utopia* in the secularized context of the Renaissance and the Reformation, especially the idea that utopia is a critique of, and a rebellion against, the Augustinian concept of original sin and bad human nature. After experiences of utopian pretensions and anti-utopian critiques, we may perhaps now realize that man is not God after all, and that more importantly, man cannot be put in God's place. This does not mean a return to religious pietism, but certainly to a deeper sense of humility and modesty, a more sober-minded realization of our own limitations and vulnerability as human beings.

Utopia, however, need not be completely identified with socialism, nor is socialism the sole target of anti-utopian critiques. To blame utopia for all the failings of socialist countries, as Kumar insists, "is like blaming Christianity for the Inquisition."[123] Ultimately, utopia is the desire for change and a vision of that change. It "confronts reality not with a measured assessment of the possibilities of change but with the demand for change."[124] At the beginning of the twenty-first century, not only utopia, but anti-utopia is also disappearing. "There has been no successor to Wells, none even to Huxley or Orwell," says Kumar. "Anti-utopia has fared almost as badly as utopia, though some novelists and science-fiction writers have drawn up its modes and techniques to conjure up their particular nightmare visions of the future."[125] And yet, to proclaim the end of utopia is as pretentious as the proclamation of the end of history. The best we can do is to rid utopia of all the elements that turn it into its nightmarish opposite, even though we fully understand the difficulty. History goes on, and the future still needs to be constructed one way or another. "Our

122. Ibid., p. 331.
123. Kumar, *Utopianism*, p. 99.
124. Ibid., p. 107.
125. Kumar, "Utopia and Anti-Utopia," in *Utopia: The Search*, p. 265.

situation could very well be a paradoxical one," as Roland Schaer puts it elegantly, "we know that, in actual fact, we do construct the future; whether we like it or not, we know that the purely human choices we make today will have lasting consequences for the world for generations to come. Unless we are willing to accept that these are blind choices and that the destiny of the world we are constructing is subject to laws that are entirely beyond our grasp, we have no choice but to opt for utopia, in the spirit, as it were, of Sartre's statement, 'We are condemned to be free.'"[126]

Utopia, in other words, is our imagined future. That is to say, after all the development in the last five hundred years since Thomas More, the concept of utopia finally comes back to its most basic starting point, namely, the very human desire for a better society beyond reality or, as Levitas puts it, "the desire for a better way of being." In that sense, of course, utopia or the ideal of a good society will always be alive and will always sustain our hope and determination to work for the future. Given what we have witnessed in the twentieth century, however, we must always be alert to the danger of grand ideas, including that of utopia, which deprive human beings of their individuality in the name of collective interest; and we must realize that there should always be a gap between the ideal and the real, between utopia as a concept and the reality of social and political life. Perhaps it is one of the most cruel ironies or dialectics in history that the hope for a perfect society contains the very seed of its negation, that the belief in human nature as essentially good should have elicited the worst of human greed for power and domination. And yet, humanity cannot give up the hope for a better society and better life, even though there will always be a gap between the ideal and the real. How to bridge that gap, to reach an equilibrium, and to achieve a good balance between individual rights and collective responsibilities: that is not just a question for politicians, but an important question for everyone of us to think about as we move into a new century and a new millennium.

A future without vision is unthinkable, so the utopian vision will live on. If the reality of this world has not been as desirable as the imagined ideal society, it is not the ideal society that we have to blame. Let us then conclude on an optimistic note that the utopian vision of an ideal society will lead us on, and that with so much experience of failed projects and frustrated expectations, we may just do it better in the future as we build a more open, tolerant, and humane society respectful of individual rights as well as collective interests, a society that combines the best of the visions of hope and the political wisdom of the East and the West.

126. Schaer, "Utopia: Space, Time, History," in *Utopia: The Search*, p. 6.

5

Conclusion: Reading and Politics

Thus far in this book we have examined allegory as a mode of writing and allegoresis as a mode of interpretation, particularly allegorical interpretation of canonical literature exemplified by commentaries on the Song of Songs in the Bible and the Confucian classic, *the Book of Poetry*. If utopia and its double, anti-utopia, are consciously constructed allegories of a social ideal or its corruption into a totalitarian nightmare, allegorical interpretation of the Song of Songs and the love poems in the *Book of Poetry* are often tendentious and ideological readings imposed on texts that in themselves are not allegorical. To guard against such an imposition of tendentious misreading and misinterpretations, I have emphasized the importance of the literal sense and the integrity of the text, even though these are not unrelated to the reader's necessarily subjective stance and horizon of expectations. It is true that our reading always begins with certain preconceived notions about the text we are about to read. Yet the process of reading is not a circular movement of self-confirmation, but rather an open-ended process of exchange and communication in which our preconceived notions are being challenged by the text, constantly revised and adjusted until we come to a better and more adequate understanding. The point of the hermeneutic circle is not that we all move in circles, but that we can work out the process of understanding by reaching out to the text and the world outside the circle so that we may learn something significant and valuable.

It is on the grounds of the literal sense and textual integrity that we can challenge an abuse of language such as Zhao Gao's devious scheme to call a stag a horse, or a distortion of literary texts such as the political mis-reading of Su Shi's poem on the juniper trees, or Wang Wei's on the Zhongnan Mountain. To expose such tendentious misreading is in itself a political action, a necessary critical intervention with political implica-tions. It is necessary because such political misreading is not just some-thing far away and long ago, not of immediate danger or concern. It is, rather, very much part of the reality of our times. In a society where there is no law to protect the freedom and autonomy of literary and artistic expressions and no legal ways to redress the abuse of power in the perse-cution of writers, allegorical interpretation in political terms may indeed have serious consequences. Here the discrepancies in political and insti-tutional structures among different types of societies, or more precisely between a democratic society subjected to the rule of law and a totalitar-ian or authoritarian society controlled by the whim and will of the all-powerful ruling few, cannot be overemphasized. The relationship between reading and politics will thus be the topic with which I conclude my discussion, though the examples I shall discuss will make our subject more immediate perhaps than the cases drawn from far away and long ago, cases written by ancient Chinese writers whose names are, to most readers in the West, unfamiliar and even exotic sounding.

I would like to examine some of the discrepancies between reading and politics in order to show how they make a world of difference by giving the very concept of "political interpretation" radically different meanings and implications. There is no denying that "political interpretation" is very much emphasized in the academic discourse of contemporary criti-cism in the West, and that it is even regarded by some as the absolute horizon of all interpretations.[1] Therefore it may be useful and instructive to take a close look at the nature of such interpretations and their impli-cations, so that we can see clearly the different consequences they may have under different social and political conditions.

One example that concerns such discrepancies is the introduction to a special issue of *Representations* (Winter 1995) on "Identifying Histories: Eastern Europe Before and After 1989." The special issue grew out of the contact and collaboration between two American professors at Berkeley and a Hungarian historian in Budapest, and the three of them co-edited a

1. See, for example, Fredric Jameson's influential argument for "the priority of the political interpretation of literary texts," which "conceives of the political perspective not as some supplementary method, nor as an optional auxiliary to other interpretive methods current today—the psychoanalytic or the myth-critical, the stylistic, the ethical, the struc-tural—but rather as the absolute horizon of all reading and all interpretation." *The Political Unconscious*, p. 17.

collection of interesting and richly informative essays that deal with "the linked problems of censorship, secrecy, memory, and dissent."[2] In writing the introduction to the special issue, however, the co-editors did not collaborate to have one introduction with three signatures, but they wrote three separate sections instead, in which each spoke of his own experiences and ideas, "'each according to his own needs,' to borrow a still-serviceable phrase from Marx." The reason for such a less than perfect collaboration is spelled out in the introduction itself. The co-editors realized that their "interests and experiences varied, too," and so they "decided to let differences show from the very beginning in this introduction," and "to acknowledge [their] inability or unwillingness to smooth over the complex life-world of Eastern Europe and of [their] engagement with it."[3] The candid acknowledgment of differences with regard to "the complex life-world of Eastern Europe" (and, by implication, of the West as well) suggests a sense of discrepancy as mentioned above, a sense shaped first and foremost by their "engagement with" different social and political realities, and ultimately by the different environments of their daily lives.

The fact that the "inability or unwillingness" to come to agreement for the introduction happens with three scholars from different political situations, two Americans and an Eastern European, speaks for itself. Our life experience or engagement with reality definitely has a way to influence our use of language and our understanding of the meaning of words. Concepts and terms, especially those charged with ethical and political values, tend to carry very different meanings for people living under different social and political conditions. Here difference rather than similarity becomes crucial for adequate understanding. As Boris Kagarlitsky argues, terms like "left," "right," "radical," and "conservative" can be very confusing and practically inapplicable to social realities across the boundaries of the East and the West. The "characteristic notable feature of the left movement in the West," says Kagarlitsky, "has always been the struggle for the democratic participation of the workers in the management of the economy," but countries that claim to be socialist, like the former Soviet Union, can hardly fit into that concept of the left precisely because there is no democracy in those countries, which claim to fight "'limited bourgeois democracy' in the name of the interests of the workers, while simultaneously denying democratic rights to the workers themselves."[4] What we find in those places is

2. Stephen Greenblatt, István Rév, and Randolph Starn, Introduction, *Representations* 49 (Winter 1995): 1.

3. Ibid., p. 2.

4. Kagarlitsky, "A Step to the Left, a Step to the Right," in *Late Soviet Culture: From Perestroika to Novostroika,* ed. Thomas Lahusen with Gene Kuperman, pp. 22–23.

nothing like a democratic reality, and the term "left" becomes totally misleading when applied to its politics. "By definition, a totalitarian regime can
be neither right nor left," says Kagarlitsky. It may "use left or right terminology, depending on which 'works' better in a given situation," but it
"cannot *occupy* some portion of the political spectrum because it *replaces the
entire spectrum.*"[5]

Indeed, when "left" becomes the state monopoly, how is it possible to
form a "left" in such socialist states as an opposition to the state? Obviously, the concept of the "left" does not mean the same in different societies, nor does the concept of "political interpretation." Such concepts do
not travel across boundaries between democracy and totalitarianism without fundamentally changing their meaning and significance. I want to
illustrate the point by discussing examples of politicized readings and to
show how the predilection for political interpretation can have very different implications in different types of societies. That is to say, moral
and political allegoresis may have very different consequences in societies
and political realities East and West.

Reading for Political Subversiveness

In the introduction to *The Power of Forms in the English Renaissance*,
Stephen Greenblatt makes some programmatic statements about new
historicism as a critical approach "set apart from both the dominant historical scholarship of the past and the formalist criticism that partially
displaced this scholarship in the decades after World War Two."[6] Old

5. Ibid., p. 23.
6. *The Power of Forms in the English Renaissance*, ed. Greenblatt, p. 5. To define new historicism is certainly no easy matter. Perhaps it is better to speak, as Louis Montrose suggests, "of a new historical *orientation* because those identified with it, by themselves or by
others, are heterogeneous in their practices and often reticent in their theorization of those
practices." "Renaissance Literary Studies and the Subject of History," *English Literary
Renaissance* 16 (Winter 1986): 6. New historicism is mainly an American term, while in
Britain, the same kind of orientation, represented by the works of Jonathan Dollimore and
Alan Sinfield, is known as cultural materialism. Edward Pechter understands new historicism as "a kind of 'Marxist criticism'" in "The New Historicism and Its Discontents: Politicizing Renaissance Drama," *PMLA* 102 (May 1987): 292; Joseph Litvak sees new
historicism as related to both Marxism and deconstruction, and argues that "it is the latter
relationship that accounts more powerfully not only for the rapidity with which the new
historicism has established itself in literary studies but also for what is most interesting—
and most problematic—in this growing body of work" in "Back to the Future: A Review-
Article on the New Historicism, Deconstruction, and Nineteenth-Century Fiction," *Texas
Studies in Literature and Language* 30 (Spring 1988): 122; while Judith Newton calls for a
revision of the histories of new historicism so that feminist critics can be credited for their

historical scholarship, from which new historicism differentiates itself and thereby acquires its identity, is represented, in Greenblatt's introductory essay, by Dover Wilson, especially his 1939 essay, "The Political Background of Shakespeare's *Richard II* and *Henry IV.*" The difference between Wilson and Greenblatt, between old and new historicism, comes to light with regard to a remark Queen Elizabeth made on August 4, 1601 when she made the comment on a performance of Shakespeare's play that dramatized the deposing and killing of King Richard II. "I am Richard II. Know ye not that?" the Queen responded to the play which had been staged one day before the abortive Essex rising. In his essay, Dover Wilson argued that the Queen should not have worried, because the play was not at all politically subversive. For Greenblatt, however, Queen Elizabeth's remark is a much more adequate response than Wilson's to the political significance of Shakespeare's work precisely because the Queen's remark discloses the potential subversiveness residing in the play and its performance. Wilson's interpretation may have covered up all the subversive impulses and elements, thus making the play look like a representation of a politically orthodox view, "a hymn to Tudor order." But, says Greenblatt,

> The Queen is clearly responding to something else: to the presence of any representation of deposition, whether regarded as sacrilegious or not; to the choice of this particular story at this particular time; to the place of the performance; to her own identity as it is present in the public sphere and as it fuses with the figure of the murdered king. Dover Wilson is not a New Critic: he does not conceive of the text as an iconic object whose meaning is perfectly contained within its own formal structure. Yet for him historical research has the effect of conferring autonomy and fixity upon the text, and it is precisely this fixity that is denied by Elizabeth's response.[7]

According to Greenblatt, Wilson's reading of the play tends to obscure and smooth over the traces of diverse competing political forces, especially the subversive implications that might jeopardize the sovereign power of the Queen. It makes Shakespeare's play politically harmless, if

---

contribution to, or their anticipation of, the ideas of new historicism in "History as Usual?: Feminism and the 'New Historicism,'" *The New Historicism*, ed. Veeser (New York: Routledge, 1989), pp. 152–167. In my discussion, I focus on Greenblatt's works as the most representative of new historicist scholarship not only because he is the most prominent of the new historicists but also because he has, to my mind, provided the most clearly articulated propositions of this new critical approach.

7. *The Power of Forms in the English Renaissance*, pp. 4–5.

not altogether non-political. It is therefore not Dover Wilson the literary historian but her majesty the Queen who had the insight to discern the political implications of the play, and shrewdly "understood the performance as a threat."[8] In "clearly responding to something else," the Queen obviously understood the play and its performance as a political allegory, a dramatization of the deposition of the monarch with other than just the literal and historical sense of the Shakespearean text.

In Greenblatt's essay, the critique of the old historicist's simplistic view of the politics of literary production is forcefully argued with eloquence and persuasion. Unlike old historicism and its formalist concern to establish the organic unity of literary works, new historicism is much more interested in seeing literary texts as discontinuous and fragmented, as fields of forces engaged in the perpetual struggle for political power and ideological control, "as fields of force, places of dissension and shifting interests, occasions for the jostling of orthodox and subversive impulses."[9] In the light of such a new perspective focused on political implications of literary and dramatic art, Queen Elizabeth, herself a political figure whose survival depended on the constant watching over and successful suppression of treason and subversion, emerges as a much better critic of the Shakespearean play than Dover Wilson, a much more insightful decipherer of the Renaissance drama as a sign in the total structure of the English society and its political *energia*, a decipherer with an adequate understanding of the power of literary form, or the nature of literature as a form of power.

New historicism, says Greenblatt, "challenges the assumptions that guarantee a secure distinction between 'literary foreground' and 'political background' or, more generally, between artistic production and other kinds of social production."[10] If Dover Wilson in his essay on the political background of Shakespeare's plays has sought to foreground Shakespeare's aesthetic transcendence of politics and ideology, new historicism now refuses to honor such a transcendent Shakespeare, but instead reads his plays as politically conditioned and engaged, as "Renaissance modes of aesthetic empowerment."[11] Grounded in the influential works of Michel Foucault and other postmodern theorists, new historicism joins

8. Ibid., p. 4.
9. Ibid., p. 6.
10. Ibid.
11. Greenblatt, *Shakespearean Negotiations*, p. 5. Cf. Louis Montrose's remark that New Historicism is "new in its refusal of unproblematized distinctions between 'literature' and 'history,' between 'text' and 'context'; new in resisting a prevalent tendency to posit and privilege a unified and autonomous individual—whether an Author or a Work—to be set against a social or literary background." "Renaissance Literary Studies," p. 6.

other major critical approaches in contemporary literary theory in seeing literary texts as fields of political confrontation, the symbolic battlefields of competing forces for power and domination.

Compared with new historicism and its self-reflective awareness of the power of forms, including the power of its own discourse and politicized rhetoric, old historical scholarship as exemplified by Dover Wilson's essay may appear to a contemporary reader as hopelessly antiquated with its allegedly simplistic, "monological" view of history, its reconstruction of a holistic, single political vision presumed to be held by the entire literate class or even the entire nation, and its search for aesthetic autonomy and fixity of the literary work. What puts such an uncritical view of history and politics into question and finally deconstructs it, according to the new historicist, is the presence of political subversiveness in the literary work itself, subversiveness that has been obscured, covered up, and ignored by old historicists, but revealed and immediately brought to the point by Queen Elizabeth's telling remark: "I am Richard II. Know ye not that?" Here again, the crucial means to read the literary text or dramatic performance politically is the Queen's identification of the figure of Richard II in the play with herself as a political figure in reality. Once the identification is in place, the subversiveness of the play can be clearly exposed.

The new historicist fully acknowledges the Queen's political insight in a learned and innovative way. After the long influence of New Criticism and old historicism, new historicism can now map out some new paradigms for the study of literature of the past, and its success has been spectacular. Indeed, as Louis Montrose claims, American new historicism, especially in the field of Renaissance studies, is "on its way to becoming the newest academic orthodoxy."[12] One must admire the precision with which this statement was made as a sort of prophecy more than a decade ago, for new historicism now offers an enabling paradigm in literary and cultural studies for many students of literature: in a word, it has indeed become a new academic orthodoxy.

Amidst the excitement over the advent of a new theoretical model and methodological innovation, however, some nagging questions still remain and are difficult to exorcise. Steven Justice aptly formulated a crucial question in an article published in *Representations*, the premier journal of new historicism, a question that evolves out of the very political emphasis of new historicism itself:

---

12. Montrose, "Renaissance Literary Studies," p. 7.

The historical study of dissent and its antagonists—of rebellion and repression, heresy and orthodoxy, criticism and authority—almost irresistibly demand of the historian now what they demanded of everyone then: *take sides*. But where, and with whom, does the historian stand?[13]

The last question is perhaps meant to put the very demand of taking sides into question, but taking such a demand seriously, one can almost sense a sort of moral anxiety over the new historicist's own stance in a conflict of forces, the ethical concern that the correct side to choose should be the side of the vulnerable, the powerless, the accused, and the victimized, rather than the side that has the power of a sovereign or the political establishment. But if literary historians and critics are to honor kings and queens for their political sensibility (but what other sensibility can we expect of them in their capacity as kings and queens?), to cultivate the same kind of sensibility, and to find subversive impulses everywhere in all works of literature, as Elizabeth did in *Richard II*, then, are we not unwittingly making a wrong moral choice, that is, stepping on the wrong side in matters of political antagonism and alliance? Here one cannot, however, talk about a choice made uniformly by a scholarly community or any collective entity. If there is a concrete choice to be made, it is to be made by each individual in a distinct cultural and historical context. The historicity of each person will ultimately determine what choice, political and otherwise, that person is going to make because, contrary to what old historicism seems to propagate and as Greenblatt already points out, there is no single political vision universally shared by the entire literate class, let alone an entire population.

Nonetheless, individual choices and decisions are also influenced in important ways by the cultural and political conditions of a given society, and that may explain why it is felt to be necessary for Greenblatt and his two co-editors of the special issue of *Representations* on Eastern Europe to acknowledge their differences in the introduction. Moral knowledge and understanding of the concept of political subversion are all grounded in real life-experiences and constitute a kind of *phronesis*, filled with contingencies and limited by one's horizon of expectations. Any decision of taking sides in a historical investigation of political conflict becomes, of necessity, a negotiation between individual predilections and social conditions, but such decisions are also fraught with consequences: it is almost impossible in making such decisions not to take on some ethical and political responsibilities.

13. Justice, "Inquisition, Speech, and Writing: A Case from Late-Medieval Norwich," *Representations* 48 (Fall 1994): 1.

It is precisely this question of taking sides that makes one wonder how new historicism measures up in its obsession with subversiveness in literature and its endorsement of Queen Elizabeth's political interpretation. Annabel Patterson has also discussed Queen Elizabeth's comment on *Richard II* in terms of what she calls a "hermeneutics of censorship." Such a political interpretation, she observes, depends on an "implied analogy" between the current situation and the historical past depicted in a play, and those who saw the play as politically subversive were not "at all bothered by the inexactness or the incompleteness of the parallel." History thus became a dangerous subject and, as Patterson reminds us,

> It was for this reason, among others, that the writing of history was specifically included in the province of official censorship by the Bishops' Order of 1599, which included, along with its prohibition of satire, the direction that "noe English historyes be printed excepte they bee allowed by some of her majesties privie Counsell."[14]

Before I raise the question in a different cultural and political context, let me add yet another example of how moral anxiety may arise in reading the kind of criticism that finds subversiveness in Renaissance literature. This time, the work in question is Greenblatt's discussion of the charge of atheism brought against Christopher Marlowe in a notorious secret police file and, in relation to that, the reputation of Thomas Harriot as an atheist.[15] Because atheism was considered a horrible crime and heavily punished in England in the sixteenth and seventeenth centuries, public declarations of atheism were virtually nonexistent, but accusations of atheism were often used as smear tactics by both Catholics and Protestants against each other and against anyone thought to be an enemy of the religious as well as secular authority. Not surprisingly, then, nothing in Harriot's writing, either of his private correspondence or his public discourse, can be found to substantiate the charge of atheism. However, "if we look closely at *A Brief and True Report of the New Found Land of Virginia* (1588), the only work Harriot published in his life time and hence the work in which he was presumably the most cautious," Greenblatt argues, "we can find traces of material that could lead to the remark

14. Annabel Patterson, *Censorship and Interpretation*, p. 55.
15. See Greenblatt, *Shakespearean Negotiations*, pp. 21–39. Greenblatt seems to give a normative significance to the interpretation of Harriot's otherwise obscure text for the critical approach of new historicism. The importance of "understanding the relation between orthodoxy and subversion in Harriot's text," he remarks, lies in the promise that it "will enable us to construct an interpretive model that may be used to understand the far more complex problem posed by Shakespeare's history plays," p. 23.

attributed to Marlowe, that 'Moses was but a juggler, and that one Heriot being Sir W Raleighs man Can do more than he.'"[16] Sure enough, under the new historicist's careful scrutiny, Harriot's *Report* is found to contain traces that can be logically concluded as suggestions of atheism.

Sent by Raleigh to make a record of the first Virginia colony, Harriot learned the language of the Algonquian Indians and described in great detail their native culture: their social life and their religious beliefs. In describing the Other, Harriot had to use the language of his own culture, translating, for example, the Algonquian *weroan* as "great Lord," and using terms like "the chief Ladies," "a young gentlewoman," and so forth. Therefore, wittingly or unwittingly, his writing is penetrated and implicated by an alien, pagan culture that reflects back on his own. As Greenblatt observes, "There is an easy, indeed almost irresistible, analogy in the period between accounts of Indian and European social structure, so that Harriot's description of the inward mechanisms of Algonquian society implies a description of comparable mechanisms in his own culture."[17] But the problem with Harriot's *Report* is not just the unavoidable Indian-European analogy caused, as it were, by linguistic contamination. The analogy is at most implicit, and it is unlikely that Harriot's *Report* would be taken primarily as a social satire on England instead of a first-hand account of the native Indians in the colony of Virginia. Perhaps that *Report* can be better described as what Mikhail Bakhtin calls a "gifted, creative exposition defining alien world views," and as such, it is "always a free stylistic variation on another's discourse; it expounds another's thought in the style of that thought even while applying it to new material, to another way of posing the problem; it conducts experiments and gets solutions in the language of another's discourse."[18] That is to say, a report on the alien culture in the colony is necessarily a mixture of discourses and languages, in which the discourse of the colonized Other is at least as visible as the implicit analogy with the European self.

Like so many other reports and travelogue literature at the time, Harriot's account of the Algonquian Indians represents the interest, in all senses of the word, of aggressive European expansionism and colonialism; it would have seemed, as Greenblatt remarks, "even for readers who sensed something odd about it, closer to confirmation than to subversion of religious orthodoxy."[19] Nevertheless, in a sort of self-congratulating observation of how the simple Indians marveled at the various little

16. Ibid., p. 23.
17. Ibid., p. 27.
18. Bakhtin, "Discourse in the Novel," in *The Dialogic Imagination*, p. 347.
19. Greenblatt, *Shakespearean Negotiations*, p. 34.

things and instruments the English had brought with them, and how such technological superiority made the Indians revere the Europeans as divine, Harriot seems to have confirmed one of the Machiavellian theses most feared and hated by the Renaissance Church and state—"the very core of the Machiavellian anthropology that posited the origin of religion in an imposition of socially coercive doctrines by an educated and sophisticated lawgiver on a simple people."[20] In other words, Harriot seems to have exposed the coercive power of religion as based on the ignorance and fear of a primitive people, as tricks played by the sophisticated on the simple and the naive. In his very evangelical zeal to colonize the New World and to persuade the Indians to accept and obey the Christian God as all-powerful, Harriot, according to Greenblatt, "seems to confirm the most radically subversive hypothesis in his culture about the origin and function of religion." And this subversiveness, Greenblatt goes on to say, resides in the very paradoxical nature of religion, since it is a self-generated consequence of the power of religious colonialism:

> Thus the subversiveness that is genuine and radical—sufficiently disturbing so that to be suspected of it could lead to imprisonment and torture—is at the same time contained by the power it would appear to threaten. Indeed the subversiveness is the very product of that power and furthers its ends. One may go still further and suggest that the power Harriot both serves and embodies not only produces its own subversion but is actively built upon it: the project of evangelical colonialism is not set over against the skeptical critique of religious coercion but battens on the very confirmation of that critique.[21]

This is indeed an interesting and shrewd observation of the nature of religious conversion. It can be read as a powerful indictment of evangelical colonialism, a devastating unfolding of its inherent inconsistency and self-contradiction. Perhaps we may say that such inconsistency is inherent in *all* forms of totalizing and totalitarian power, so much so that a thorough implementation of its policies would often lead to the exposure of its irrationality, and that may also explain why many who began as the monarch's favorite servants would end their political life in jail, exile, or on the gibbet. Out of its own insistent claims to reason, justice, and truth, the irrationality of the totalitarian power and its political rhetoric are often exposed. Greenblatt calls this phenomenon "a strange paradox," but it is important to remember that such a paradox appears strange only

20. Ibid., p. 27.
21. Ibid., p. 30.

to us who are not, or no longer, directly under the control of that power, whereas the paradox may well remain a blind spot in the political vision of those who are subject to that control, or who have an interest in keeping that paradox unexplored and invisible. Greenblatt admits that the subversiveness of what he calls Harriot's confirmation of the Machiavellian hypothesis "is invisible not only to those on whom the religion is supposedly imposed but also to most readers and quite possibly to Harriot himself." And yet he proceeds to argue that Harriot's *Report* is a subversive "coded report," pregnant with its "latent heterodoxy."[22]

In order to decide whether the subversiveness in Harriot's account remained a blind spot for himself or was indeed a conscious, albeit a surreptitiously performed, act of insinuation, it is crucial to know what Harriot intended to do in writing his *Report*. That intention is of course difficult to ascertain. "Yet it is misleading," says Greenblatt with a certain degree of assurance, "to conclude without qualification that the radical doubt implicit in Harriot's account is *entirely* contained. . . . if we should be wary of naively accepting a version of reality proffered by the secret police, we cannot at the same time dismiss that version altogether."[23] It is from this indecision and uncertainty, from this suspicion and a there-is-no-smoke-without-fire attitude, that some serious moral questions arise. "We simply do not know," says Greenblatt, "what was thought in silence, what was written and then carefully burned, what was whispered by Harriot to Ralegh. . . . In Harriot's text the relation between orthodoxy and subversion seems, at the same interpretive moment, to be both perfectly stable and dangerously volatile."[24]

By imagining silent, hidden thoughts, secretly burned documents, and conspiratorial whispers, however, Greenblatt makes Harriot's subversion more real and more certain than he explicitly acknowledges it to be. The vivid imagining takes on the color of a graphic literary representation. In fact, one of the fascinating things about Greenblatt's writing is a sense of discovery, the excitement of a kind of intellectual detection at work, which reveals the secret force of subversion at work in Renaissance texts where such a subversive force is least expected and hardly detectable. The force of Greenblatt's own text, the force of his learned and imaginative reasoning, thus tends to lead the reader to conclude, perhaps tentatively and with some degree of ambivalence, that the suspicion of atheism in Harriot and the charge against Marlowe are not just smear tactics after

22. Ibid., p. 31.
23. Ibid., pp. 34–35.
24. Ibid., p. 35.

all, and that the Elizabethan secret police had good reason to conclude, probably based on some reports not available to us about those silent thoughts, burned documents, and eavesdropped whispers, that Harriot and Marlowe were indeed guilty of holding heretic, atheistic ideas. In that case, then, such a political reading proposed by the new historicist may eventually turn out to be not an indictment of the institutional power Harriot served, but an indictment of Harriot as the writer of a secret and subversive message encrypted in his *Report*.

Of course, such an "indictment" four hundred years later cannot be used against Harriot, and therefore it hardly matters either to him or to Queen Elizabeth's secret police. But if what actually happened in Harriot's mind, his intention in writing what he did in the *Report* cannot in any case be known for certain, one may wonder why is it that the new historicist in his reinterpretation tends to endorse the suspicion and the charge against Harriot and others like him, and therefore to lean toward an agreement with the Queen and the conclusion reached by the royal police? Does not this sound like taking the wrong side and making a wrong choice in political alliance? Isn't it possible for the political establishment to use the detection of subversiveness in literary texts to bring writers and artists under control by the state?

Greenblatt, however, has already an answer as though in anticipation of the question. Though the new historicist invariably focuses his attention on power relations and the efficacy of political discourse, those power relations and efficacy of political discourse in past history are somehow insulated, so to speak, from our own historical moment. Greenblatt writes,

> The answer, I think, is that the term *subversive* for us designates those elements in Renaissance culture that contemporary audiences tried to contain or, when containment seemed impossible, to destroy and that now conform to our own sense of truth and reality. That is, we find "subversive" in the past precisely those things that are *not* subversive to ourselves, that pose no threat to the order by which we live and allocate resources . . . What we find in Harriot's *Brief and True Report* can best be described by adapting a remark about the possibility of hope that Kafka once made to Max Brod: There is subversion, no end of subversion, only not for us.[25]

The self-conscious acknowledgment of the safe distance from the "subversive" and "volatile" historical events under investigation is rather revealing. Greenblatt has ridiculed old historicism's simplistic view of

25. Ibid., p. 39.

mimesis: "Literature is conceived to mirror the period's beliefs, but to mirror them, as it were, from a safe distance."[26] In a strangely ironic way, new historicism also conceives of the much emphasized political subversiveness as detached from the present political order, "from a safe distance." At the end of his essay on inquisition and heresy trial in late-medieval Norwich, Steven Justice also realizes that if the new historicist engages with the accused heretics at all, he only engages with them "from the safety of privilege and inconsequence."[27] Whatever torture and forced confession that went on in medieval inquisition pose no present danger. So we realize that it is only in the protected academic environment of an American university that the new historicist can aestheticize political subversion, and indeed aestheticize politics in general. What is called "subversive" is nothing serious or dangerous, but becomes something almost glamorous. Gerald Graff calls the repetitive and almost meaningless use of "subversive" as a "form of cant," and relates it to "the decline of socialism as a realistic social alternative," when there is no longer a shared criterion for evaluating cultural phenomena as progressive or regressive. "'Subversive' has become little more than a plus-mark," Graff observes, "a gold star awarded to whatever a critic happens to approve of, rather the way an earlier generation of critics used words like 'beautiful' and 'noble.'"[28]

But is "subversive" equivalent to "beautiful"? What if one takes "subversive" more seriously than a mere "form of cant," and, indeed, take historical events more seriously than merely something gone by and done with in the remote past, something that "poses no threat to the order by which we live and allocate resources"? The "safety of privilege and inconsequence" that Steven Justice mentioned seems to apply only to the academic discourse in the study of history and literature in American universities, but that peculiar American-style inconsequence of historical study is more an exception than the rule when we consider the social and political situations in our world today, in places where political subversiveness is anything but "a gold star" to be awarded to a literary or artistic work. It is almost irresistible for me to ask, what happens if the subversiveness is found in our time, or more exactly, what if it is perceived to pose a threat to the power of a political establishment that exists today, in our own society?

26. Greenblatt, *The Power of Forms in the English Renaissance*, p. 5.
27. Justice, "Inquisition, Speech, and Writing," p. 27.
28. Graff, "Co-optation," in *The New Historicism*, ed. Veeser, pp. 173–74.

Political Reading and Its Consequences

Whether reading for political subversiveness in a literary work may have any real consequence or lead to anything in a real life situation—that is not a totally imaginary or hypothetical question. A real case in recent Chinese history, the case of Wu Han, whose play *Hai Rui Dismissed from Office* marked an initial moment of the Chinese Cultural Revolution in the mid-1960s, may provide an example of political interpretation that has very different implications from that in the new historicist reading of a Shakespearean play or a Renaissance document. I should strongly emphasize, however, that the case of Wu Han and his play is in many ways a special case, a case that is quickly slipping into oblivion, if it has not already gone out of the collective Chinese memory completely, even before it has been thoroughly studied and examined by historians and literary scholars. In many ways, Maoist China during the Cultural Revolution was almost unique and extreme in its claims to absolute truth and its legitimization of violence in the name of that truth, and therefore political interpretation of literary works under such circumstances cannot be simply equated with political interpretation advocated in new historicism and other contemporary Western approaches to literature. Even in China, the political situation has gone through a series of tremendous changes, which make the Wu Han case even less representative or relevant today. By showing the danger of political interpretation in the Wu Han case, therefore, what I am suggesting is precisely the difference between the academic advocacy of political interpretation in the American university and the persecution of writers in a special period of time in China.

That very difference, however, needs to be kept in perspective, for the suppression of literary expression and the persecution of writers are not totally extinct, after all, in our world today. The Chinese case may then serve to remind us of the ominous implications of political interpretation, particularly the assertion of subversiveness in literary works, in places where the political and the aesthetic do not have a sufficiently safe distance from one another. Moreover, the Chinese Cultural Revolution, which had such a tremendous influence not just in China, but also in the West during the 1960s with a romaniticized image of radical Maoism and a revolutionary East, remains suppressed as a topic in China today; therefore, an inquiry into the case of Wu Han may have more than just an antiquarian interest merely forty years later. What we learn from that case may be helpful in our effort to understand the Cultural Revolution and its aftermath.

Wu Han (1909–1969) was a noted historian, a member of the Chinese communist party, and deputy mayor of Beijing. He wrote a number of scholarly works, but he also wrote a play in 1961 about Hai Rui (1515–1587), a historical figure famous for his uprightness and moral integrity, whom the play eulogized for his courage to punish a local despot even at the cost of losing his own position in the government office under Emperor Jiaqing of the Ming Dynasty (whose reign lasted from 1522 to 1566). The dramatic action unfolds around Hai Rui's determination to bring the wicked but well-connected man to justice, his courage in opposing the powerful landed gentry, and his eventual dismissal by the emperor, who was corrupted by the forces of evil at court. When Hai Rui left office, the local people sent him off with tears and praise, and through their mouths as a sort of chorus at the end, Wu Han expressed great admiration for Hai Rui as an incorruptible administrator or a "clean official" [*qing guan*], one that was willing to sacrifice his career and even his life for the benefit of the common people.

The play was staged in Beijing with some modest success. Then, in November 1965, Yao Wenyuan, at that time a relatively minor functionary in the propaganda department of the Municipal Party Committee in Shanghai, published an article accusing Wu Han's play of political subversion. At the time of its publication, Yao's article had gone through nine revisions during a period of two months, and every revision was secretly sent from Shanghai to Beijing for comments by Jiang Qing or Madame Mao.[29] In the politically charged atmosphere of China in the 1960s, Yao's critique of the play was not literary criticism in the usual sense, but part of a carefully orchestrated campaign against "bourgeois intellectuals," a critique which, in the words of an editorial of *Red Flag*, the theoretical organ of the Central Committee of the Chinese Communist Party, "sounded the clarion call for the great proletarian cultural revolution."[30] With that article to his credit, Yao Wenyuan won the favor of Mao Zedong, quickly rose to the powerful Politburo of the Central Committee, and later became a member of the notorious "Gang of Four," headed

29. See Zi Lin and Zi Zhen, "Wu Han and *Hai Rui Dismissed from Office*," in *Wu Han he Hai Rui baguan*, ed. Renmin chubanshe [People's Press], p.7.
30. *Hongqi* [*Red Flag*] editorial, no. 9, 1966; for the English translation, I quote from the Chinese official publication, *Peking Review*, no. 28, July 8, 1966, p. 32. I have followed the *pinyin* system for the spelling of Chinese names. For a study in English of the Wu Han case and its relationship with the Cultural Revolution, see James R. Pusey, *Wu Han: Attacking the Present through the Past*. For English translations of Wu Han's play as well as discussion of its critique by the Chinese authorities, see Clive Ansley, *The Heresy of Wu Han: His Play 'Hai Jui's Dismissal' and its Role in China's Cultural Revolution*; and *Hai Jui Dismissed from Office*, trans. C. C. Huang.

by Madame Mao herself. To numerous Chinese writers and scholars in those days, Yao became the angel of death whose touch was deadly and lethal, because anyone named and denounced by him as producing plays or literary works that were branded as "anti-Party and anti-socialist poisonous weeds" would immediately face public humiliation, ostracism, physical harm, and even death. Once attacked in official publications like *Red Flag* or the *People's Daily* by Yao and the other crusaders of Mao's Cultural Revolution, the accused would soon be physically abused by radical young students, known as the Red Guards. Such mental and physical attacks were the direct cause of many deaths and suicides during the ten years of Cultural Revolution from 1966 to 1977, and among these Wu Han was one of the first casualties.

Yao Wenyuan's article on *Hai Rui Dismissed from Office* focuses its critique on Wu Han's alleged excessive praise of Hai Rui as a "clean official." Using the highly reductionist method of class analysis popular in Mao's China, Yao argues that all officials in China's pre-communist past, whether corrupt or not, dirty or clean, all served the interests of the feudal landlord class and could not possibly have done anything good for the poor peasants. Therefore Wu Han is guilty of fabricating a pseudo-historical figure that has somehow transcended class differences and become a "savior" of the oppressed peasant class in Ming China. Like the image of the dragon in Su Shi's poem on juniper trees tendentiously interpreted by his political enemy, the image of the savior in Yao's article was also overdetermined, for "savior" (literally "saving star," *jiu xing*) had long become, at least in the official parlance, a sacred word in mainland China reserved almost exclusively for Chairman Mao himself, who was likened to the red sun and called the Great Savior of the Chinese people, celebrated in an immensely popular song, "The East Is Red." Therefore, to say that Wu Han had made Hai Rui the "savior" of the poor peasants, that he had turned an official in the "feudal" society of the Ming dynasty into a hero of the people, was in fact making a serious charge that the writer-historian was guilty of sacrilege, of denying indirectly that only Chairman Mao and the Communist Party could save China.

At the same time, Wu Han was also guilty of whitewashing the "feudal" society and its master, the reactionary landlord class. "Isn't this taking the state machine of the landlord class completely for an instrument for the protection of the peasants?" asks Yao by posing a loaded question. "Isn't this erasing at one stroke the nature of the dictatorship of the landlord class as the oppressor of the peasants?" Putting the play in the political context of 1961 when Mao pushed for class struggle among the Chinese, Yao's article ended on a rather ominous note, suggesting that

Wu Han's play was a manifestation of class struggle waged by the bourgeoisie against the proletariat; and it concluded, in the encoded language of political allegory of the time, that Wu Han's play was "not a fragrant flower but a poisonous weed."[31]

By December 1965, Yao Wenyuan's attack on Wu Han had started a nationwide condemnation of "clean officials" in Chinese history and their modern advocates, but a much more serious charge was soon brought against Wu Han and other writers who had written on Hai Rui or any other historical figure that had the courage to petition the emperor for redressing wrongdoings. This charge originated from none other than Chairman Mao himself, who remarked on December 21, 1965, that "the crux of *Hai Rui Dismissed from Office* was the question of dismissal from office. The Emperor Jiaqing dismissed Hai Rui from office. In 1959 we dismissed Peng Dehuai from office. And Peng Dehuai is 'Hai Rui' too."[32] Such an interpretation immediately linked Wu Han's work with an internal power struggle at the top level within the Chinese Communist Party that had happened two years before the appearance of the play. On July 14, 1959, Peng Dehuai, then the Minister of Defense, sent a letter to Mao to express his doubts and misgivings about the party's policies both in cities and rural areas, raising questions about the disasters created by Mao's unrealistic movements of the Great Leap Forward and the too hasty establishment of people's communes. One month later, at the Central Committee's plenary session at Lushan, Peng Dehuai and a number of his supporters were accused of forming an anti-party clique, labeled as "right opportunists," and dismissed from their leading positions in the party, the army, and the state government.

Wu Han's *Hai Rui Dismissed from Office*, which was performed as a Beijing opera and published in 1961, was interpreted by Mao not as a historical play but a political allegory that used the dismissal of Hai Rui as a shadow for referring to the dismissal of Peng Dehuai in actual political fact, thus directly engaging in a power struggle by attacking politics of the present through a seditious use of past history. "After the enemies with guns have been wiped out," an editorial of the *Liberation Army Daily* warned its readers by quoting Chairman Mao, "there will be enemies without guns; they are bound to struggle desperately against us; we must never regard these enemies lightly."[33] Wu Han, and the other intellectuals

31. Yao Wenyuan, "On the new historical play *Hai Rui Dismissed from Office*," *Wenhui bao*, November 10, 1965.

32. Quoted in "Two Diametrically Opposed Documents," *Hongqi* [*Red Flag*] editorial, no. 9, 1967; English trans. in *Peking Review*, no. 23, June 2, 1967, p. 22.

33. "Never Forget the Class Struggle," *Jiefangjun bao* [*Liberation Army Daily*] editorial,

labeled as "bourgeois scholars," were thus regarded as "enemies without guns," who allegedly conspired with "the imperialists, modern revisionists and the reactionaries of all countries," "the overthrown reactionary classes within the country," and "the Right opportunist elements within the Party," to oppose Chairman Mao, his political authority, and his revolutionary directives. The army newspaper editorial sternly admonished its readers that struggle with such enemies was "a life-and-death struggle," and it emphatically pointed out the subversive nature of all literature, art, and academic scholarship, connecting them firmly with the politics of domestic and international "counter-revolution."

The perceived danger of subversion by writers and artists, says the editorial, is not "merely a 'scholar's rebellion,'" but a serious threat to the political structure of the state.

> "Every counter-revolutionary restoration starts in the realm of the mind—including ideology, the superstructure, theoretical and academic work, literature and art—so as to win over public opinion." This was the way Khrushchov revisionism usurped the leadership of the Soviet Communist Party. Likewise, in Hungary in 1956, it was a number of revisionist and bourgeois writers, artists and intellectuals who organized the Petofi Club and acted as the shock force in the counter-revolutionary riots.[34]

Having connected Wu Han's play with enemies at home and abroad, the critique of the playwright amounts to the charge of treason with fatal consequences for Wu Han and his family. He was not only verbally criticized in all the Chinese news media but also repeatedly beaten by the Red Guards in many public gatherings. In the violent mass movement of the "Cultural Revolution," we witness a dangerous process in which political overinterpretation often led to physical abuse and torture. After one of those beatings, on October 11, 1969, according to a biography of Wu Han, "his liver and bladder broke; deeply wronged and falsely accused, he died after spitting a good deal of blood."[35] But Wu Han was not the only one relentlessly persecuted and driven to death in disgrace, for the same misfortune fell on his wife and daughter, the famous actor Ma Lianliang who played the part of Hai Rui in the Beijing opera performance, and a number of other people involved in the production of Wu Han's play. For those who did not live through such terrible madness of a mass movement

---

May 4, 1966; quoted from *Peking Review*, no. 20, May 13, 1966, p. 41.

34. Ibid., pp. 41, 42.

35. Su Shuangbi and Wang Hongzhi, "Life of Wu Han," appendix to Wu Han, *Wu Han shixue lunzhu xuanji*, 4:463.

out of control, the whole thing can hardly be imagined, let alone believed, but even for those who did witness the violence during the Cultural Revolution in China, the cruelty and stupidity of those dark days would seem unreal and implausible some forty years after.

Looking back at those tumultuous years of political convulsion and mass persecution, the case of Wu Han now seems just a prelude to the high drama of the split and war between the factions within the party, the tragi-comic corruption of utopian passion into nightmarish dystopian reality. The ten years of the Cultural Revolution (1966–1976) was indeed an insane episode in history that wiped out so many powerful figures on the very top, including Liu Shaoqi, Chairman of the People's Republic, Lin Biao, Mao's hand-picked successor, and many of China's top intellectuals and scholars. It was a decade of such brutal self-destruction that took so heavy a toll of the people that the death of Wu Han seems almost insignificant in comparison, "a mere pawn in a series of power struggles," as one scholar put it.[36] On the personal level, however, the misery and anguish of a wronged individual are not rendered any less painful by the suffering of an entire nation, and the loss of one life cannot be ignored and obscured by the huge shadow of history that affected so many lives of a whole population.

Speaking of history and historical analogies, it would be rather revealing if we put together Queen Elizabeth's response to *Richard II* and Chairman Mao's response to *Hai Rui Dismissed from Office*. Just as the Queen identified herself with the deposed king, the Chairman likewise identified himself with the disproved Emperor Jiaqing. We can almost borrow Greenblatt's words and say, *mutatis mutandis*, that Chairman Mao was responding to the presence of *any* representation of dismissal; to the choice of this particular story at this particular time; to the place of the performance; to his own identity as it is present in the public sphere and as it fuses with the figure of the discredited Emperor. Here again, identification or the displacement of a literary character by a real person in history constitutes the crucial interpretive strategy to read a literary work as a political satire or allegory. Of course, the identification in Mao's reading was not so much to equate himself with Emperor Jiaqing, but to identify Hai Rui as Marshal Peng Dehuai, which resembles in some ways the identification of Bullingbrook with the Earl of Essex in a political reading of Shakespeare's play.

Once a character is seen as an encoded signifier for a real political figure as the signified, the whole work can then be interpreted as a fictive

36. Kwok, introduction to *Hai Jui Dismissed from Office*, p. 4.

retelling of a real story in history, but a retelling motivated by a certain interest and serving the purpose of a particular political group. All elements that fit in with such an interpretive framework will be seen as essential and relevant, whereas elements that do not fit in will be ignored as irrelevant and dispensable. Such a strategy of selective identification becomes the key factor of political interpretation, and the validity of such an interpretation can in turn be proved by pointing at the identification. The premise and the conclusion are thus mutually implicated in a most vicious hermeneutic circle. "I am Richard II. Know ye not that?" says Queen Elizabeth. This statement at once offers an interpretation of the Shakespearean play and serves as proof of the play's subversive impulses perceived in such an interpretation. "Peng Dehuai is 'Hai Rui' too," says Chairman Mao. Likewise, this serves as the key to expose the play's subversiveness and also as proof of the play's political subversion. The identification of Peng Dehuai as Hai Rui formed a self-contained, circular argument that seems to support its own claim to truth, and it seems to make Wu Han's subversive use of history so glaringly obvious that even some American scholars accepted this version of the Wu Han story without much questioning.[37]

But is such identification valid? Is Elizabeth Richard II? Is Peng Dehuai really Hai Rui? In her remark, the Queen apparently meant to ask a rhetorical question, but it would be unwise to surrender one's critical alertness too quickly and take its implied answer for granted. The Chairman's remark is less rhetorical and more prosaic, presented as a statement of fact, but it is every bit as authoritative as a royal decree, of which the claim to truth is not subject to negotiations. But again, I would not take Mao's words at face value as a simple statement of truth. For one thing, the dismissal of Peng Dehuai in the summer of 1959 was kept as top secret at the time, and the official document concerning his dismissal was not made public until 1967, six years after Wu Han's play was put on the stage in Beijing. It is highly unlikely that in late 1959 when Wu Han began to work on the play, he could have any knowledge about Peng Dehuai's dismissal. Moreover, Wu Han's seemingly suspicious article, "Hai Rui Scolds the Emperor," which was interpreted during the Cultural Revolution as an attack on Mao and heavily criticized, was published in *People's Daily* on June 16, 1959, two months *before* the dismissal of Peng Dehuai. Unless we believe that Wu Han possessed some sort of an uncanny presentiment worthy of a Teiresias, it would be quite impossible to argue that he meant Peng Dehuai when he wrote Hai Rui. In the

37. See Kwok, and also Pusey, *Wu Han: Attacking the Present through the Past.*

"hermeneutics of censorship," however, as Annabel Patterson argues, "Disclaimers of topical intention are not to be trusted, and are more likely to be entry codes to precisely that kind of reading they protest against."[38] Mao's reading of the play, just like John Chamberlain's questioning about the timing of Sir John Hayward's *Life of Henry IV*, builds its suspicion on the grounds of historical chronology, the coincidence of the performance of the play with a certain political event. Chamberlain's question—"Why such a storie shold come out at this time"—as Patterson remarks, constitutes a principle in political interpretation: "That is, the importance of an exact chronology in determining what any given text was likely to mean to its audience at the time of its appearance."[39] It is this chronology and its political implications, not the exact parallel between Wu Han's play and the dismissal of Peng Dehuai, that has made the play look suspiciously like a political satire.

Wu Han was not, however, a simple victim, an innocent lamb sacrificed on the altar of an ultra-leftist political hermeneutics, nor was his writing on Hai Rui a purely academic exercise in the study of history. He declared unabashedly that scholarship was not a pure pursuit of knowledge for its own sake, but the purpose of historical studies was to serve the present, "to use the past for the present" (*gu wei jin yong*).[40] Although he claimed to be faithful to historical records, he did not write the play about Hai Rui for a mere historical interest, because he considered it useful and relevant to the situation in contemporary China. "This play," he wrote in the prefatory note, "emphasizes Hai Rui's strong will that held to his uprightness; he never yielded to violence and power, he could never be scared off by failure, and he was ready to try again even if he failed. . . . Hai Rui's place in history should be affirmed, and what is good in his character deserves our emulation today."[41] In an essay on Hai Rui published in September 1959, Wu Han called for a modern Hai Rui that would fight for the cause of socialism.[42]

Of all the historical figures more or less known for being upright and honest, why did Wu Han, one may wonder, choose Hai Rui to be the model for emulation in modern China? Why did he want to emphasize Hai Rui's strong will and unyielding spirit? To be sure, as a historian, Wu Han was particularly interested and knowledgeable in the Ming dynasty, the period in which the real Hai Rui lived, but the true answer to the

38. Annabel Patterson, *Censorship and Interpretation*, p. 65.
39. Ibid., 55.
40. Wu Han, "Emphasize More the Present than the Past and Use the Past for the Present," in *Wu Han shixue lunzhu xuanji*, 3:45.
41. Wu Han, *Hai Rui ba guan* [*Hai Rui Dismissed from Office*], in ibid., 3:542.
42. See Wu Han, "On Hai Rui," in ibid., 3:179.

question is rather pathetically ironic, because Wu Han did all his work on Hai Rui not to oppose Chairman Mao, but to please him. It was Mao who had proposed, at a party meeting one year earlier in 1958, that the Chinese communists should dare to think, dare to speak, dare to act, and should learn from "the spirit of Hai Rui."[43] It is Mao who first made Hai Rui a model of courage and urged the Chinese not to fear the emperor: "He who is not afraid of death by a thousand cuts dares to unhorse the emperor," said Mao approvingly.[44] In writing about Hai Rui as courageous enough to scold the emperor and to fight the high officials at court, Wu Han was indeed using the past to serve the present, but his purpose was to confirm rather than oppose what Chairman Mao had said about Hai Rui as a historical model for contemporary China. That is to say, Wu Han's writings on Hai Rui, and the play in particular, are indeed allegorical in nature, as they all have an intended meaning beyond the historical content, a meaning fully comprehensible only when it is understood in the political context of China in the late 1950s.

Such a topical use of historical figures and events and their political allegorization, however, pose a basic problem—namely, the fundamental ambiguity and indeterminacy, the potentially uncontrollable plurality of interpretation. Wu Han might have every intention to write his play as a footnote to Chairman Mao's positive remarks on Hai Rui, but the political situation in the last few months of 1965 put Mao in a totally different mood, which made him interpret Wu Han's play as subversive rather than confirmative. When Mao encouraged the Chinese to learn from "the spirit of Hai Rui" and be daring enough to "unhorse the emperor," he had Liu Shaoqi and his other political rivals in mind, but the representation of dismissal of Hai Rui in Wu Han's play made him think of his own dismissal of Peng Dehuai instead. All these were of course quite beyond the knowledge of Wu Han, and his use of past history to please Mao was completely turned around in a political interpretation that found nothing but subversiveness at work. Indeed, during the Cultural Revolution, the whole of history and culture became suspect, and at the peak of such political paranoia, nothing was safe from the charge of subversion, and nothing from the historical past or from a foreign culture could have any positive value in a China spellbound by its own revolutionary fervor.

43. See Su Shuangbi and Wang Hongzhi, "Life of Wu Han," in ibid., 4:462.
44. Mao Zedong, "Speech at the Chinese Communist Party's National Conference on Propaganda Work," quoted in Yao Wenyuan, "On 'Three-Family Village': The Reactionary Nature of 'Evening Talks at Yenshan' and 'Notes from Three-Family Village,'" *Peking Review*, no. 22, May 27, 1966, p. 18. This remark was widely quoted in many other newspaper articles and editorials during the Cultural Revolution.

It is no exaggeration to say that Mao's political reading of Wu Han's play was severely paranoid, because he smelled subversion everywhere: not just in the present but also in the past, not just in the world of reality but also in the world of thoughts and ideas—in history and philosophy, in literature and arts, in the humanities in general. For a long period of time, except for Mao's own works, no book was exempt from suspicion in China, and virtually all literary works were condemned as reactionary and poisonous, because they were either "feudalist" (traditional Chinese literature), or "capitalist" (Western literature), or "revisionist" (Soviet and Eastern European literature). For a long time, the eight hundred million Chinese had only eight "revolutionary model plays" to watch, plays that were authorized to provide them with ideological indoctrination. Mao's China had a long record of anti-intellectualism, a history of incessant campaigns against writers, scholars, and their works, and the critique of Wu Han led to the extreme of such anti-intellectualism during the Cultural Revolution. This tendency put an extraordinary emphasis on class struggle in the sphere of ideas and saw every literary work as a potential ideological bomb ticking away in the system. One of the frequently quoted passages from Mao conceives of literature as a form of power that always paves the way to political subversion: "The use of the novel for anti-Party activities is quite an invention," says Chairman Mao. "To overthrow a political power, it is always necessary, first of all, to create public opinion, to do work in the ideological sphere. This is true for the revolutionary class as well as for the counter-revolutionary class."[45]

To see the novel or any other kind of literary work as politically subversive, however, is not quite an invention in China. We have seen the heavily moral and political emphasis in traditional Chinese criticism, and the inglorious tradition of anti-intellectualism can be traced back to the First Emperor's draconian measures to control thinking by burning books and burying scholars alive, an infamous incident that Mao himself often cited as an analogy with his own cultural policies. The darker side of this anti-intellectual tradition entails not just the condemnation of literature as politically subversive, but also the persecution of poets and writers, an ancient practice known as *wenzi yu*, literally "imprisonment on account of words," which has been rendered into English rather elegantly as *literary inquisition*.[46] In the practice of such "literary inquisition," politically motivated allegoresis has always been the main strategy, and in that context, as

45. Quoted in "Great Truth, Sharp Weapon," *Hongqi* [*Red Flag*] editorial, no. 9, 1967; also see *Peking Review*, no. 23, June 2, 1967, p. 17.
46. For a pioneer study in English, see Goodrich, *The Literary Inquisition of Ch'ien-lung*.

the example of Wu Han shows, subversiveness allegedly detected in literary works often has consequences that are far more serious and dangerous than anything one can find in the new historicist reading of Renaissance literature, the equating of "political" with "beautiful" or "valuable." The comparison here is not meant to show the similarity, but rather the important differences of social and political conditions that are not always brought into conscious reflection in new historicist readings.

From this one may conclude that the finding of subversive impulses in literature has been a familiar way for political and religious powers to suppress literary expression, whether intended to be subversive or not. This happens not just in China or the European past, for not so very long ago, the Ayatollah Khomeini's *fatwa* to all Muslims to seek out and execute Salman Rushdie, author of *The Satanic Verses*, can serve as yet another reminder of this hermeneutics of terror in more recent history. One may perhaps endlessly debate whether the work of Rushdie, Wu Han, Harriot, Shakespeare or any other writer is subversive morally, politically, or religiously, but such a debate becomes an intellectual luxury many writers and scholars outside Western academia cannot afford, since in the real world of political contingencies, such a debate has consequences that are not altogether academic. When critical discourse tends to privilege and celebrate "subversiveness" in literature, let us not forget the question of taking sides, the moral responsibility of making claims about the political intention of a writer or a text. Ironically, the politicization of interpretation and the celebration of subversive force in literature become possible only when literature and literary scholarship are effectively insulated from the power of the state and can discourse on the subversive from a safe distance. That insulation, let us bear in mind, is also an important aspect of the politics of interpretation.

Bibliography

WORKS IN WESTERN LANGUAGES

Aaron, Daniel. "What Can You Learn from a Historical Novel?" *American Heritage* 43 (October 1992): 55–62.

——. *American Notes: Selected Essays*. Boston: Northeastern University Press, 1994.

Alter, Robert and Frank Kermode, eds. *The Literary Guide to the Bible*. Cambridge: Harvard University Press, 1987.

Altmann, Alexander, ed. *Biblical Motifs: Origins and Transformations*. Cambridge: Harvard University Press, 1966.

Ansley, Clive. *The Heresy of Wu Han: His Play "Hai Jui's Dismissal" and its Role in China's Cultural Revolution*. Toronto: University of Toronto Press, 1971.

apRoberts, Ruth. *The Biblical Web*. Ann Arbor: University of Michigan Press, 1994.

Aquinas, Thomas. *Basic Writings of St. Thomas Aquinas*. 2 vols. Edited by Anton Pegis. New York: Random House, 1945.

Aristotle. *The Basic Works of Aristotle*. Edited by Richard McKeon. New York: Random House, 1941.

——. *Poetics* I with *the Tractatus Coislinianus*, reconstruction of *Poetics II*, and the Fragments of the *On Poets*. Translated by Richard Janko. Indianapolis: Hackett, 1987.

Auerbach, Erich. *Mimesis: The Representation of Reality in Western Literature*. Translated by Willard R. Trask. Princeton: Princeton University Press, 1953.

——. *Scenes from the Drama of European Literature: Six Essays*. New York: Meridian Books, 1959.

Augustine, Saint. *The City of God*. Translated by Marcus Dods. New York: The Modern Library, 1993.

——. *On Christian Doctrine*. Translated by D. W. Robertson, Jr. Indianapolis: Bobbs-Merrill, 1958.

Baker-Smith, Dominic. *More's Utopia*. London: HarperCollins, 1991.

Bakhtin, M. M. *The Dialogic Imagination: Four Essays*. Translated by Caryl Emerson and Michael Holquist. Austin: University of Texas Press, 1981.

Barney, Stephen A. *Allegories of History, Allegories of Love*. Hamden, Conn.: Archon Books, 1979.

Bell, Ian E. A., ed. *Ezra Pound: Tactics for Reading*. London: Vision, 1982.

Benjamin, Walter. *The Origin of German Tragic Drama.* Translated by John Osborne. London: Verso, 1985.

Berman, Antoine. *The Experience of the Foreign: Culture and Translation in Romantic Germany.* Translated by S. Heyvaert. Albany: State University of New York Press, 1992.

Bernstein, Richard J. *Beyond Objectivism and Relativism: Science, Hermeneutics, and Praxis.* Philadelphia: University of Pennsylvania Press, 1983.

Bloom, Harold, ed. *Modern Critical Interpretations: Virgil's Aeneid.* New York: Chelsea, 1987.

Bloomfield, Morton W. "Allegory as Interpretation." *New Literary History* 1 (Winter 1972): 301–317.

Bokenkamp, Stephen R. "Chinese Metaphor Again: Reading—and Understanding—Imagery in the Chinese Poetic Tradition." *Journal of the American Oriental Society* 109 (April–June 1989): 211–221.

Boyarin, Daniel. "The Song of Songs: Lock or Key? Intertextuality, Allegory and Midrash." In *The Book and the Text: The Bible and Literary Theory,* edited by Schwartz, pp. 214–230.

Bruns, Gerald L. *Hermeneutics Ancient and Modern.* New Haven: Yale University Press, 1992.

Buck, David. "Forum on Universalism and Relativism in Asian Studies, Editor's Introduction." *The Journal of Asian Studies* 50 (February 1991): 29–34.

Budick, Sanford, and Geoffrey H. Hartman, eds. *Midrash and Literature.* New Haven: Yale University Press, 1986.

Cain, T. G. S., and Ken Robinson, eds. *Into Another Mould: Change and Continuity in English Culture 1625–1700.* London: Routledge, 1992.

Cairns, Francis. *Virgil's Augustan Epic.* Cambridge: Harvard University Press, 1989.

Cassirer, Ernst. *Language and Myth.* Translated by Susanne K. Langer. New York: Harper and Brothers, 1946.

Chan, Wing-tsit. *Chu Hsi: Life and Thought.* Hong Kong: The Chinese University Press, 1987.

——, ed. *Chu Hsi and Neo-Confucianism.* Honolulu: University of Hawaii Press, 1986.

Chang, Kwang-chih. *Art, Myth, and Ritual: The Path to Political Authority in Ancient China.* Cambridge: Harvard University Press, 1983.

Chesneaux, Jean. "Egalitarian and Utopian Traditions in the East." *Diogenes* 62 (Summer 1968): 76–102.

Claeys, Gregory. "Socialism and Utopia." In *Utopia: The Search for the Ideal Society in the Western World,* edited by Roland Schaer et al., pp. 206–240.

Confucius. *The Analects.* Translated by D. C. Lau. Harmondsworth: Penguin, 1979.

Couvreur, S., trans. *Cheu King: texte chinois avec une double traduction en français et en latin.* 3rd ed. Sien Hien: Imprimerie de la mission catholique, 1934.

Curtius, Ernst Robert. *European Literature and the Latin Middle Ages.* Translated by Willard R. Trask. Princeton: Princeton University Press, 1973.

Daniélou, Jean. *Origen.* Translated by Walter Mitchell. New York: Sheed and Ward, 1955.

——. *From Shadow to Reality: Studies in the Biblical Typology of the Fathers.* Translated by Wulstan Hibberd. Westminster, Md.: Newman, 1960.

Dawson, Raymond. *Confucius.* Oxford: Oxford University Press, 1981.

Derrida, Jacques. *Of Grammatology.* Translated by Gayatri Chakravorty Spivak. Baltimore: Johns Hopkins University Press, 1976.

Eckermann, Johann Peter. *Conversations with Goethe.* Translated by John Oxenford. London: Dent, 1970.

Eco, Umberto. *The Aesthetics of Thomas Aquinas.* Translated by Hugh Bredin. Cambridge: Harvard University Press, 1988.

——. *Art and Beauty in the Middle Ages.* Translated by Hugh Bredin. New Haven: Yale University Press, 1986.

Eco, Umberto, with Richard Rorty, Jonathan Culler, and Christine Brooke-Rose. *Interpretation and Overinterpretation*. Edited by Stefan Collini. Cambridge: Cambridge University Press, 1992.

Egan, Ronald C. "Narratives in *Tso chuan*." *Harvard Journal of Asiatic Studies* 37 (December 1977): 323–352.

Emerson, Ralph Waldo. *The Complete Works of Ralph Waldo Emerson*. 12 vols. Edited by E. W. Emerson. Boston: Houghton Mifflin, 1903–1904.

Fenollosa, Ernest. *The Chinese Written Character as a Medium for Poetry*. Edited by Ezra Pound. San Francisco: City Lights Books, 1969.

Fichter, Andrew. *Poets Historical: Dynastic Epic in the Renaissance*. New Haven: Yale University Press, 1982.

Fletcher, Angus. *Allegory: The Theory of a Symbolic Mode*. Ithaca: Cornell University Press, 1964.

Foucault, Michel. *The Order of Things: An Archaeology of the Human Sciences*. New York: Vintage, 1973.

Freedman, H., and Maurice Simon, eds. *The Midrash Rabbah*. 5 vols. London: Soncino, 1977.

Frei, Hans W. "The 'Literal Reading' of Biblical Narrative in the Christian Tradition: Does It Stretch or Will It Bend?" In *The Bible and the Narrative Tradition*, edited by McConnell, pp. 36–77.

Froehlich, Karlfried. "'Always to Keep the Literal Sense in Holy Scripture Means to Kill One's Soul': The State of Biblical Hermeneutics at the Beginning of the Fifteenth Century." In *Literary Uses of Typology from the Late Middle Ages to the Present*, edited by Miner, pp. 20–48.

——, ed. and trans. *Biblical Interpretation in the Early Church*. Philadelphia: Fortress Press, 1984.

——. "Problems of Lutheran Hermeneutics." In *Studies in Lutheran Hermeneutics*, edited by Reumann et al., pp. 127–141.

Frye, Northrop. *Anatomy of Criticism: Four Essays*. Princeton: Princeton University Press, 1957.

——. *Fearful Symmetry: A Study of William Blake*. Princeton: Princeton University Press, 1947.

Gadamer, Hans-Georg. *Truth and Method*. English trans. revised by Joel Weinsheimer and Donald G. Marshall. 2nd rev. ed. New York: Crossroad, 1989.

Géfin, Laszlo. *Ideogram: History of a Poetic Method*. Austin: University of Texas Press, 1982.

Gernet, Jacques. *China and the Christian Impact: A Conflict of Cultures*. Translated by Janet Lloyd. Cambridge: Cambridge University Press, 1985.

Gollwitzer, Helmut. *Das hohe Lied der Liebe*. Munich: Chr. Kaiser, 1978.

Goodrich, Luther C. *The Literary Inquisition of Ch'ien-lung*. New York: Paragon Book Reprint Corp., 1966.

Graff, Gerald. "Co-optation." In *The New Historicism*, edited by A. Veeser, pp. 168–181.

Graham, A. C. *Disputers of the Tao: Philosophical Arguments in Ancient China*. La Salle, Ill.: Open Court, 1989.

——. *Chuang-tzŭ: The Inner Chapters*. London: George Allen & Unwin, 1981.

Grant, Robert, with David Tracy. *A Short History of the Interpretation of the Bible*. 2nd rev. ed. Philadelphia: Fortress Press, 1984.

Green, Garrett, ed. *Scriptural Authority and Narrative Interpretation*. Philadelphia: Fortress Press, 1987.

Greenblatt, Stephen, ed. *The Power of Forms in the English Renaissance*. Norman, Okla.: Pilgrim Books, 1982.

———. *Shakespearean Negotiations: The Circulation of Social Energy in Renaissance England.* Berkeley: University of California Press, 1988.

Hall, David L., and Roger Amers. *Thinking Through Confucius.* Albany: State University of New York Press, 1987.

Hansen, Chad. *Language and Logic in Ancient China.* Ann Arbor: University of Michigan Press, 1983.

Hartman, Charles. "Images of Allegory: A Review Article." *Early China* 14 (1989): 183–200.

———. "Poetry and Politics in 1079: The Crow Terrace Poetry Case of Su Shi." *Chinese Literature: Essays, Articles, Reviews* 12 (December 1990): 15–44.

Hartman, Geoffrey H., and Sanford Budick, eds. *Midrash and Literature.* New Haven: Yale University Press, 1986.

Heine, Heinrich. *Selected Works.* Edited and translated by Helen M. Mustard. New York: Vintage, 1973.

Henderson, John B. *Scripture, Canon, and Commentary: A Comparison of Confucian and Western Exegesis.* Princeton: Princeton University Press, 1991.

Hill, Christopher. *Milton and the English Revolution.* London: Faber and Faber, 1979.

Huang, C. C., trans. *Hai Jui Dismissed from Office.* Honolulu: The University Press of Hawaii, 1972.

Irwin, John T. *American Hieroglyphics: The Symbol of the Egyptian Hieroglyphics in the American Renaissance.* New Haven: Yale University Press, 1980.

Jameson, Fredric. *The Political Unconscious: Narrative as a Socially Symbolic Act.* Ithaca: Cornell University Press, 1982.

Jensen, Lionel M. "The Invention of 'Confucius' and His Chinese Other, 'Kon Fuzi.'" *Positions* 1 (Fall 1993): 414–449.

———. *Manufacturing Confucianism: Chinese Traditions and Universal Civilization.* Durham: Duke University Press, 1997.

Jullien, François. *Detour and Access: Strategies of Meaning in China and Greece.* Translated by Sophie Hawkes. New York: Zone Books, 2000.

———. "Naissance de l'«imagination»: Essai de problématique au travers de la réflexion littéraire de la Chine et de l'Occident." *Extrême-Orient—Extrême-Occident* 7 (1985): 23–81.

———. *La valeur allusive: Des catégories originales de l'interprétation poétique dans la tradition chinoise (Contribution à une réflexion sur l'altérité interculturelle).* Paris: École française d'Extrême-Orient, 1985.

Jullien, François, with Thierry Marchaisse. *Penser d'un Dehors (la Chine): Entretiens d'Extrême-Occident.* Paris: Éditions du Seuil, 2000.

Jung, Hwa Yol. "Misreading the Ideogram: From Fenollosa to Derrida and McLuhan." *Paideuma* 13 (Fall 1984): 211–227.

Justice, Steven. "Inquisition, Speech, and Writing: A Case from Late-Medieval Norwich." *Representations* 48 (Fall 1994): 1–29.

Karlgren, Bernhard, trans. *The Book of Odes.* Stockholm: The Museum of Far Eastern Antiquities, 1950.

Kelly, J. N. D. *Jerome: His Life, Writings, and Controversies.* London: Duckworth, 1975.

Kermode, Frank. "The Plain Sense of Things." In *Midrash and Literature*, edited by Geoffrey H. Hartman and Sanford Budick, pp. 179–194.

Krieger, Murray. *Ekphrasis: The Illusion of the Natural Sign.* Baltimore: Johns Hopkins University Press, 1992.

Kugel, James. "The 'Bible as Literature' in Late Antiquity and the Middle Ages." *Hebrew University Studies in Literature and the Arts* 11 (Spring 1983): 20–70.

———. *The Idea of Biblical Poetry: Parallelism and Its History.* New Haven: Yale University Press, 1981.

———. "Two Introductions to Midrash." *Prooftexts* 3 (May 1983): 131–155.

Kumar, Krishan. *Utopia and Anti-Utopia in Modern Times.* Oxford: Basil Blackwell, 1987.

——. "Utopia and Anti-Utopia in the Twentieth Century." In *Utopia: The Search for the Ideal Society in the Western World,* edited by Roland Schaer, pp. 251–267.

——. *Utopianism.* Minneapolis: University of Minnesota Press, 1991.

Lahusen, Thomas, with Gene Kuperman, eds. *Late Soviet Culture: From Perestroika to Novostroika.* Durham: Duke University Press, 1993.

Lamberton, Robert. *Homer the Theologian: Neoplatonist Allegorical Reading and the Growth of the Epic Tradition.* Berkeley: University of California Press, 1986.

Lampe, G. W. H., and K. J. Woollcombe, eds. *Essays on Typology.* Naperville, Ill.: Alec R. Allenson, 1957.

Laursen, John Christian, ed. *Religious Toleration: "The Variety of Rites" from Cyrus to Defoe.* New York: St. Martin's Press, 1999.

Laws, G. Malcolm, Jr. *The British Literary Ballad: A Study in Poetic Imitation.* Carbondale: Southern Illinois University Press, 1972.

Lee, Peter H. *Songs of Flying Dragons: A Critical Reading.* Cambridge: Harvard University Press, 1975.

Legge, James, trans. *The She King or the Book of Ancient Poetry.* London: Trubner, 1976.

Levitas, Ruth. *The Concept of Utopia.* New York: Philip Allan, 1990.

Lewis, C. S. *The Allegory of Love: A Study of Medieval Tradition.* New York: Oxford University Press, 1958.

Lieberman, Saul. *Hellenism in Jewish Palestine: Studies in the Literary Transmission, Beliefs and Manners of Palestine in the I Century B.C.E.–IV Century C.E.* New York: Jewish Theological Seminary of America, 1950.

Litvak, Joseph. "Back to the Future: A Review-Article on the New Historicism, Deconstruction, and Nineteenth-Century Fiction." *Texas Studies in Literature and Language* 30 (Spring 1988): 120–149.

Liu, James J. Y. *The Art of Chinese Poetry.* Chicago: University of Chicago Press, 1962.

——. *Chinese Theories of Literature.* Chicago: University of Chicago Press, 1975.

——. *Language-Paradox-Poetics: A Chinese Perspective.* Edited by Richard John Lynn. Princeton: Princeton University Press, 1988.

Lloyd, G. E. R. *Adversaries and Authorities: Investigations into Ancient Greek and Chinese Science.* Cambridge: Cambridge University Press, 1996.

Lovejoy, Arthur O. *Essays in the History of Ideas.* Baltimore: Johns Hopkins University Press, 1948.

Loewe, Raphael J. "Apologetic Motifs in the Targum to the Song of Songs." In *Biblical Motifs: Origins and Transformations,* edited by Altmann, pp. 159–196.

Lowth, Robert. *Lectures on the Sacred Poetry of the Hebrews.* Translated by G. Gregory. London: S. Chadwick, 1847.

Lynn, Richard John. "Chu Hsi as Literary Theorist and Critic." In *Chu Hsi and Neo-Confucianism,* edited by Wing-tsit Chan, pp. 337–354.

——, trans. *The Classic of Changes: A New Translation of the I Ching as Interpreted by Wang Bi.* New York: Columbia University Press, 1994.

Mao Tse-tung. *Selected Works.* Vol. 5. New York: International Publishers, 1956.

Marx, Karl, and Friedrich Engels. *Selected Works in One Volume.* New York: International Publishers, 1968.

Maspero, Henri. *China in Antiquity.* Translated by Frank A. Kierman Jr. Amherst: University of Massachusetts Press, 1978.

McConnell, Frank, ed. *The Bible and the Narrative Tradition.* New York: Oxford University Press, 1986.

Minamiki, George. *The Chinese Rites Controversy from Its Beginning to Modern Times.* Chicago: Loyola University Press, 1985.

Miner, Earl, ed. *Literary Uses of Typology from the Late Middle Ages to the Present*. Princeton: Princeton University Press, 1977.

Montaigne, Michel Eyquem de. *The Complete Essays of Montaigne*. Translated by Donald M. Frame. Stanford: Stanford University Press, 1958.

Montrose, Louis. "Renaissance Literary Studies and the Subject of History." *English Literary Renaissance* 16 (Winter 1986): 5–12.

More, Thomas. *Utopia: Latin Text and English Translation*. Edited by George M. Logan, Robert M. Adams, and Clarence H. Miller. Cambridge: Cambridge University Press, 1995.

Mueller-Vollmer, Kurt, ed. *The Hermeneutics Reader: Texts of the German Tradition from the Enlightenment to the Present*. New York: Continuum. 1985.

Newton, Judith. "History as Usual?: Feminism and the 'New Historicism.'" In *The New Historicism*, edited by A. Veeser, pp. 152–167.

Nussbaum, Martha. "Human Functioning and Social Justice: In Defense of Aristotelian Essentialism." *Political Theory* 20 (May 1992): 202–246.

Origen. "On First Principles: Book Four." In *Biblical Interpretation in the Early Church*, edited and translated by Froehlich, pp. 48–78.

——. *The Song of Songs: Commentary and Homilies*. Translated by R. P. Lawson. Westminster, Md.: Newman, 1957.

Owen, Stephen. "Poetry and Its Historical Ground." *Chinese Literature: Essays, Articles, Reviews* 12 (December 1990): 107–118.

——. *Remembrances: The Experience of the Past in Classical Chinese Literature*. Cambridge: Harvard University Press, 1986.

——. *Traditional Chinese Poetry and Poetics: Omen of the World*. Madison: University of Wisconsin Press, 1985.

Pagels, Elaine. *Adam, Eve, and the Serpent*. New York: Vintage, 1989.

Patterson, Annabel. *Censorship and Interpretation: The Conditions of Writing and Reading in Early Modern England*. Madison: The University of Wisconsin Press, 1984.

Patterson, Lee. Introduction. In *Commentary as Cultural Artifact*, edited by Lee Patterson. *South Atlantic Quarterly* 91 (Fall 1992): 787–791.

Pechter, Edward. "The New Historicism and Its Discontents: Politicizing Renaissance Drama." *PMLA* 102 (May 1987): 292–303.

Perkins, David. *A History of Modern Poetry: From the 1890s to the High Modernist Mode*. Cambridge: Harvard University Press, 1976.

Plato. *The Collected Dialogues, Including the Letters*. Edited by Edith Hamilton and Huntington Cairns. Princeton: Princeton University Press, 1963.

Pope, Marvin, ed. and trans. *The Anchor Bible: Song of Songs*. Garden City: Doubleday, 1977.

Portes, Laurent. "Utopia and Nineteenth-century French Literature." Translated by Nadia Benabid. In *Utopia: The Search for the Ideal Society in the Western World*, edited by Roland Schaer et al., pp. 241–247.

Pusey, James R. *Wu Han: Attacking the Present through the Past*. Cambridge: Harvard University Press, 1969.

Quintillian. *Institutio Oratoria*. 4 vols. Translated by H. E. Butler. Cambridge: Harvard University Press, 1953.

Reichwein, Adolf. *China and Europe: Intellectual and Artistic Contacts in the Eighteenth Century*. Translated by J. C. Powell. New York: A. A. Knopf, 1925.

Reumann, John, with Samuel H. Nafzger, and Harold H. Ditmanson, eds. *Studies in Lutheran Hermeneutics*. Philadelphia: Fortress Press, 1979.

Ricci, Matteo. *China in the Sixteenth Century: The Journals of Matthew Ricci: 1583–1610*. Translated by Louis J. Gallagher. New York: Random House, 1953.

Rickett, Adele Austin, ed. *Chinese Approaches to Literature from Confucius to Liang Ch'i-ch'ao*. Princeton: Princeton University Press, 1978.

Ricoeur, Paul. *Interpretation Theory: Discourse and the Surplus of Meaning*. Fort Worth: Texas Christian University Press, 1976.

Ronan, Charles E., and Bonnie B. C. Oh, eds. *East Meets West: The Jesuits in China*. Chicago: Loyola University Press, 1988.

Rouvillois, Frédéric. "Utopia and Totalitarianism." Translated by Nadia Benabid. In *Utopia: The Search for the Ideal Society in the Western World*, edited by Roland Schaer et al., pp. 316–331.

Saintsbury, George. *Miscellaneous Essays*. London: Percival, 1892.

Sargent, Lyman Tower. "Utopian Traditions: Themes and Variations." In *Utopia: The Search for the Ideal Society in the Western World*, edited by Roland Schaer et al., pp. 8–17.

Saussure, Ferdinand de. *Course in General Linguistics*. Translated by Wade Baskin. New York: Philosophical Library, 1959.

Saussy, Haun. *The Problem of a Chinese Aesthetic*. Stanford: Stanford University Press, 1993.

Schaer, Roland, Gregory Claeys, and Lyman Tower Sargent, eds. *Utopia: The Search for the Ideal Society in the Western World*. New York, Oxford: The New York Public Library, Oxford University Press, 2000.

——. "Utopia: Space, Time, History." In *Utopia: The Search for the Ideal Society in the Western World*, edited by Roland Schaer et al., pp. 3–7.

Schleiermacher, Friedrich. *Hermeneutics: The Handwritten Manuscripts*. Translated by James Duke and Jack Forstman. Missoula, Mont.: Scholars Press, 1977.

Schneider, Laurence A. *Ku Chieh-kang and China's New History: Nationalism and the Quest for Alternative Traditions*. Berkeley: University of California Press, 1971.

Schwartz, Regina, ed. *The Book and the Text: The Bible and Literary Theory*. Oxford: Basil Blackwell, 1990.

Smith, Richard J. *China's Cultural Heritage: The Qing Dynasty, 1644–1912*. 2nd ed. Boulder: Westview, 1994.

Steiner, George. *After Babel: Aspects of Language and Translation*. Oxford: Oxford University Press, 1975.

Stern, David. *Midrash and Theory: Ancient Jewish Exegesis and Contemporary Literary Studies*. Evanston: Northwestern University Press, 1996.

——. *Parables in Midrash: Narrative and Exegesis in Rabbinic Literature*. Cambridge: Harvard University Press, 1991.

Striedter, Jurij. "Journeys Through Utopia: Introductory Remarks to the Post-Revolutionary Russian Utopian Novel." *Poetics Today* 3:1 (Spring 1982): 33–60.

Svensson, Martin. "Hermeneutica / Hermetica Serica: A Study of the *Shijing* and the Mao School of Confucian Hermeneutics." Ph. D. dissertation. Stockholm University, 1996.

Tanner, Kathryn E. "Theology and the Plain Sense." In *Scriptural Authority and Narrative Interpretation*, edited by Garrett Green, pp. 59–78.

Tate, J. "On the History of Allegorism." *The Classical Quarterly* 28 (April 1934): 105–114.

Todorov, Tzvetan. *Literature and Its Theorists: A Personal View of Twentieth-Century Criticism*. Translated by Catherine Porter. Ithaca: Cornell University Press, 1987.

Touraine, Alan. "Society as Utopia." Translated by Susan Emanuel. In *Utopia: The Search for the Ideal Society in the Western World*, edited by Roland Schaer et al., pp 18–31.

Veeser, H. Aram, ed. *The New Historicism*. New York: Routledge, 1989.

Vendler, Helen. *The Poetry of George Herbert*. Cambridge: Harvard University Press, 1975.

Vico, Giambattista. *The New Science*. Edited and Translated by Thomas G. Bergin and Max H. Fisch. Ithaca: Cornell University Press, 1976.

Virgil. *The Aeneid*. Translated by Robert Fitzgerald. New York: Random House, 1981.

Waley, Arthur, trans. *The Book of Songs*. 2nd ed. London: Allen & Unwin, 1954.

Wang An-chi. *Gulliver's Travels and Ching-hua Yuan Revisited: A Menippean Approach*. New York: Peter Lang, 1995.

Wang, C. H. *The Bell and the Drum: Shih Ching as Formulaic Poetry in an Oral Tradition*. Berkeley: University of California Press, 1974.

———. *From Ritual to Allegory: Seven Essays in Early Chinese Poetry*. Hong Kong: The Chinese University Press, 1988.

Warnke, Georgia. *Gadamer: Hermeneutics, Tradition and Reason*. Stanford: Stanford University Press, 1987.

Watson, Burton. *Early Chinese Literature*. New York: Columbia University Press, 1962.

Wegemer, Gerard. "*The City of God* in Thomas More's *Utopia*." *Renascence* 44 (Winter 1992): 115–135.

White, Hayden. *Tropics of Discourse: Essays in Cultural Criticism*. Baltimore: Johns Hopkins University Press, 1978.

Whitman, Jon. *Allegory: The Dynamics of an Ancient and Medieval Technique*. Cambridge: Harvard University Press, 1987.

Wilde, Oscar. *Plays, Prose Writings and Poems*. Edited by Anthony Fothergill. London: J. M. Dent, 1996.

Winch, Peter. *The Idea of a Social Science and Its Relation to Philosophy*. London: Routledge and Kegan Paul, 1958.

———. *Ethics and Action*. London: Routledge & Kegan Paul, 1972.

Wolfson, Harry Austryn. *Philo: Foundations of Religious Philosophy in Judaism, Christianity, and Islam*. 2 vols. Cambridge: Harvard University Press, 1948.

Wright, Arthur F., ed. *Studies in Chinese Thought*. *The American Anthropologist* 55, no. 5, part 2, memoir no. 75 (December 1953).

Yu, Anthony C. *Rereading the Stone: Desire and the Making of Fiction in Dream of the Red Chamber*. Princeton: Princeton University Press, 1997.

Yu, Pauline R. *The Reading of Imagery in the Chinese Poetic Tradition*. Princeton: Princeton University Press, 1987.

Zamyatin, Yevgeny. *We*. Translated and introduced by Clarence Brown. Harmondsworth: Penguin, 1993.

Zhang Longxi. *Mighty Opposites: From Dichotomies to Differences in the Comparative Study of China*. Stanford: Stanford University Press, 1998.

———. *The Tao and the Logos: Literary Hermeneutics, East and West*. Durham: Duke University Press, 1992.

———. "Toleration, Accommodation, and the East-West Dialogue." In *Religious Toleration: "The Variety of Rites" from Cyrus to Defoe*, edited by Laursen, pp. 37–57.

WORKS IN CHINESE

Cai Zhengsun 蔡正孫 (fl. 1279). *Shilin guangji* 詩林廣記 [*In the Woods of Poetry*]. Beijing: Zhonghua, 1982.

Chunqiu zuozhuan zhengyi 春秋左傳正義 [*The Correct Meaning of Zuo's Commentaries on the Spring and Autumn Annals*]. In vol. 2 of *Shisan jing zhushu*, edited by Ruan Yuan.

Confucius 孔子. *Lunyu* 論語 [*The Analects*]. See Liu Baonan.

Ding Fubao 丁福保 (ed.). *Lidai shihua xubian* 歷代詩話續編 [*A Sequel to Remarks on Poetry from Various Dynasties*]. 3 vols. Beijing: Zhonghua, 1983.

Dong Shiwei 董士偉. *Kang Youwei pingzhuan* 康有為評傳 [*A Critical Biography of Kang Youwei*]. Nanchang: Baihuazhou wenyi chubanshe, 1994.

Feng Youlan 馮友蘭. *Zhongguo zhexue shi* 中國哲學史 [*History of Chinese Philosophy*]. 2 vols. Beijing: Zhonghua, 1961.

Ge Zhaoguang 葛兆光. *Qi shiji qian Zhongguo de zhishi, sixiang yu xinyang shijie: Zhongguo sixiang shi, di yi juan* 七世紀前中國的知識、思想與信仰世界：中國思想史，第一卷 [*The World of Knowledge, Thought and Beliefs in China before the Seventh Century: Chinese History of Ideas, Volume One*]. Shanghai: Fudan University Press, 1998.

——. *Qi shiji zhi shijiu shiji Zhongguo de zhishi, sixiang yu xinyang: Zhongguo sixiang shi, di er juan* 七世紀至十九世紀中國的知識、思想與信仰：中國思想史，第二卷 [*Knowledge, Thought and Beliefs in China from the Seventh Century to the Nineteenth Century: Chinese History of Ideas, Volume Two*]. Shanghai: Fudan University Press, 2000.

Gu Jiegang 顧頡剛 (1893–1980) et al. (eds.). *Gu shi bian* 古史辨 [*Discriminations of Ancient History*]. 7 vols. Shanghai: Shanghai guji, 1982.

Guo Qingfan 郭慶藩 (1844–95?). *Zhuangzi jishi* 莊子集釋 [*Variorum Edition of the Zhuangzi*], in vol. 3 of *Zhuzi jicheng*.

Guo Shaoyu 郭紹虞. *Song shihua kao* 宋詩話考 [*Textual Notes on Song Dynasty Remarks on Poetry*]. Beijing: Zhonghua, 1979.

Guo Shaoyu 郭紹虞 and Wang Wensheng 王文生 (eds.). *Zhongguo lidai wenlun xuan* 中國歷代文論選 [*Selections of Chinese Literary Criticism from the Various Dynasties*]. 4 vols. Shanghai: Shanghai guji, 1979.

Han Yu 韓愈 (768–824). *Han Changli quanji* 韓昌黎全集 [*Complete Works of Han Yu*]. Beijing: Zhongguo shudian, 1991.

He Wenhuan 何文煥 (1732–1809) (ed.). *Lidai shihua* 歷代詩話 [*Remarks on Poetry from Various Dynasties*]. 2 vols. Beijing: Zhonghua, 1981.

Ji Kang 嵇康 (224–263). *Ji Kang ji zhu* 嵇康集注 [*Ji Kang's Works with Commentaries*], eds. Yin Xiang 殷翔 and Guo Quanzhi 郭全芝. Hefei: Huangshan shushe, 1986.

Ji Yougong 計有功 (fl. 1126). *Tang shi jishi* 唐詩紀事 [*Records of Tang Poetry*]. 2 vols. Beijing: Zhonghua, 1965.

Jiang Boqian 蔣伯潛. *Shisan jing gailun* 十三經概論 [*Outlines of the Thirteen Classics*]. Shanghai: Shanghai guji, 1983.

Jiao Xun 焦循 (1763–1820). *Mengzi zhengyi* 孟子正義 [*The Correct Meaning of the Works of Mencius*]. In vol. 1 of *Zhuzi jicheng*.

Kang Youwei 康有為 (1858–1927). *Kang Youwei zhenglun ji* 康有為政論集 [*Kang Youwei's Political Writings*]. Edited by Tang Zhijun 湯志鈞. Beijing: Zhonghua, 1981.

——. *Kang Youwei datong lun er zhong* 康有為大同論二種 [*Kang Youwei's Two Works on the Doctrine of Great Unity*]. Edited by Zhu Weizheng 朱維錚. Beijing: Sanlian, 1998.

Li Bai 李白 (701–762). *Li Taibai quanji* 李太白全集 [*Complete Works of Li Bai*]. 3 vols. Edited by Wang Qi 王琦 (fl. 1723). Beijing: Zhonghua, 1977.

Liji zhengyi 禮記正義 [*The Correct Meaning of the Records of Rites*]. In *Shisan jing zhushu*, edited by Ruan Yuan.

Li Tiangang 李天綱. *Zhongguo liyi zhi zheng: lishi, wenxian he yiyi* 中國禮儀之爭：歷史、文獻和意義 [*The Chinese Rites Controversy: History, Documents and Meaning*]. Shanghai: Shanghai guji, 1998.

Liu Baonan 劉寶楠 (1791–1855). *Lunyu zhengyi* 論語正義 [*The Correct Meaning of the Analects*]. In vol. 1 of *Zhuzi jicheng*.

Liu Xie 劉勰 (465?–522). See Zhou Zhenfu.

Liu Yuxi 劉禹錫 (772–842). *Liu Yuxi ji* 劉禹錫集 [*Works of Liu Yuxi*]. Edited by Bian Xiaoxuan 卞孝萱. Beijing: Zhonghua, 1990.

Luo Genze 羅根澤. *Zhongguo wenxue piping shi* 中國文學批評史 [*History of Chinese Literary Criticism*]. 3 vols. Shanghai: Gudian wenxue, 1961.

Mao shi zhengyi 毛詩正義 [*The Correct Meaning of the Mao Text of the Book of Poetry*]. In vol. 1 of *Shisan jing zhushu*, edited by Ruan Yuan.

Mencius 孟子. See Jiao Xun 焦循.

Meng Haoran 孟浩然 (689–740). *Meng Haoran ji jiaozhu* 孟浩然集校注 [*Critical Edition of Meng Haoran's Works*]. Beijing: Renmin wenxue, 1989.

Qian Mu 錢穆. *Zhuzi xin xue'an* 朱子新學案 [*New Scholarly Records of Master Zhu*]. 3 vols. Chengdu: Bashu shushe, 1987.

Qian Zhongshu 錢鍾書 (1910–1998). *Guan zhui bian* 管錐編 [*The Tube and Awl Chapters*]. 5 vols. Beijing: Zhonghua, 1986.

———. *Qi zhui ji* 七綴集 [*Collection of Seven Essays*]. Shanghai: Shanghai guji, 1985.

———. *Song shi xuanzhu* 宋詩選注 [*Selected Poems from the Song Dynasty with Annotations*]. Beijing: Renmin wenxue, 1982.

———. *Tan yi lu* 談藝錄 [*Discourses on the Literary Art*]. Enlarged ed. Beijing: Zhonghua, 1984.

Qiu Zhao'ao 仇兆鰲 (fl. 1685). *Du shi xiangzhu* 杜詩詳注 [*Du Fu's Poems with Detailed Annotations*]. 5 vols. Beijing: Zhonghua, 1979.

Renmin chubanshe 人民出版社 (ed.). *Wu Han he Hai Rui baguan* 吳晗和海瑞罷官 [*Wu Han and Hai Rui Dismissed from Office*]. Beijing: Renmin chubanshe, 1979.

Ruan Ji 阮籍 (210–263). *Ruan Ji ji jiaozhu* 阮籍集校注 [*Ruan Ji's Works with Annotations*]. Edited by Chen Bojun 陳伯君. Beijing: Zhonghua, 1987.

Ruan Yuan 阮元 (1764–1849) (ed.). *Shisan jing zhushu* 十三經注疏 [*The Thirteen Classics with Annotations*]. 2 vols. Beijing: Zhonghua, 1980.

Sima Qian 司馬遷 (145?–190? B.C.E.). *Shi ji* 史記 [*Records of the Grand Historian*]. 10 vols. Beijing: Zhonghua, 1959.

Su Shi 蘇軾 (1037–1101). *Su shi shiji* 蘇軾詩集 [*Collected Poems of Su Shi*]. Edited by Wang Wen'gao 王文誥 (1764–?). 8 vols. Beijing: Zhonghua, 1987.

Tang Zhijun 湯志鈞. *Gailiang yu geming de Zhongguo qinghuai: Kang Youwei yu Zhang Taiyan* 改良與革命的中國情懷：康有為與章太炎 [*Concerns about China in Reform and Revolution: Kang Youwei and Zhang Taiyan*]. Hong Kong: Shangwu, 1990.

Tao Yuanming 陶淵明 (365–427). *Tao Yuanming ji* 陶淵明集 [*Tao Yuanming's Works*]. Edited by Lu Qinli 逯欽立. Beijing: Zhonghua, 1979.

Wang Anshi 王安石 (1021–1086). *Wang Anshi shixuan* 王安石詩選 [*Wang Anshi's Selected Poems*]. Edited by Liu Yisheng 劉逸生. Hong Kong: Sanlian, 1983.

Wang Chong 王充 (27–100?). *Lun heng* 論衡 [*Discourses of Equilibrium*]. In vol. 7 of *Zhuzi jicheng*.

Wang Dajin 王達津 (ed.). *Wang Wei Meng Haoran xuanji* 王維孟浩然選集 [*Selected Works of Wang Wei and Meng Haoran*]. Shanghai: Shanghai guji, 1990.

Wang Jun 王筠 (1784–1854). *Shuowen judou* 說文句讀 [*Notes on the Explanation of Words*]. 4 vols. Shanghai: Shanghai guji, 1983.

Wang Ming 王明 (ed.). *Taiping jing hejiao* 太平經合校 [*The Collated Classic of Great Equality*]. 2 vols. Beijing: Zhonghua, 1960.

Wang Ping 王平. *Taiping jing yanjiu* 太平經研究 [*A Study of the Classic of Great Equality*]. Taipei: Wenjin, 1995.

Wang Wei 王維 (701?–761). *Wang Youcheng ji jianzhu* 王右丞集箋注 [*Wang Wei's Works with Annotations*]. Annotated by Zhao Dianchen 趙殿成 (1683–1756). Shanghai: Shanghai guji, 1961.

Wang Yuanhua 王元化. *Wenxin diaolong jiangshu* 文心雕龍講疏 [*Commentaries on the Literary Mind or the Carving of Dragons*]. Shanghai: Shanghai guji, 1992.

Wang Yucheng 王禹偁 (954–1001). *Wang Yucheng shiwen xuan* 王禹偁詩文選 [*Wang Yucheng's Selected Poetry and Prose*]. Edited by Wang Yanti 王延梯. Beijing: Renmin wenxue, 1996.

Wang Yunxi 王運熙 and Yang Ming 楊明. *Wei Jin Nan Bei chao wenxue piping shi* 魏晉南北朝文學批評史 [*History of Literary Criticism in the Wei, Jin, and the Southern and the Northern Dynasties*]. Shanghai: Shanghai guji, 1989.

Wen Yiduo 聞一多. *Shenhua yu shi* 神話與詩 [*Myth and Poetry*]. Beijing: Guji chubanshe, 1956.

Wong Young-tsu 汪榮祖. *Kang Zhang helun* 康章合論 [*A Critical Study of Kang Youwei and Zhang Taiyan*]. Taipei: Lianjing, 1988.

Wu Han 吳晗. *Wu Han shixue lunzhu xuanji* 吳晗史學論著選集 [*Wu Han's Selected Writings on History*]. 4 vols. Beijing: Renmin chuban she, 1988.

Xu Fuguan 徐復觀. *Zhongguo renxinglun shi: Xian Qin pian* 中國人性論史：先秦篇 [*History of Chinese Views on Human Nature: The Pre-Qin Period*]. Taipei: The Commercial Press, 1969.

Yu Guanying 余冠英 (ed.). *San Cao shixuan* 三曹詩選 [*Selected Poems by the Three Cao's*]. Beijing: Zuojia chubanshe, 1956.

Yu Ying-shi 余英時. *Shixue yu chuantong* 史學與傳統 [*Historiography and Tradition*]. Taipei: Shibao wenhua, 1982.

Zheng Zhenduo 鄭振鐸. *Chatu ben Zhongguo wenxue shi* 插圖本中國文學史 [*Illustrated History of Chinese Literature*]. 4 vols. Beijing: Zuojia chubanshe, 1957.

Zhong Rong 鍾嶸 (468?–518). *Shipin zhu* 詩品注 [*Ranking of Poetry with Annotations*]. Edited by Chen Tingjie 陳廷傑. Beijing: Renmin wenxue, 1961.

Zhou Yutong 周予同 (1898–1981). *Zhou Yutong jingxueshi lunzhu xuanji* 周予同經學史論著選集 [*Selected Papers on the History of Classical Studies*]. Edited by Zhu Weizheng 朱維錚. Shanghai: Shanghai renmin, 1983.

Zhou Zhenfu 周振甫. *Wenxin diaolong zhushi* 文心雕龍注釋 [*The Literary Mind or the Carving of Dragons with Annotations*]. Beijing: Renmin wenxue, 1981.

Zhouyi zhengyi 周易正義 [*The Correct Meaning of the Book of Changes*]. In vol. 1 of *Shisan jing zhushu*, edited by Ruan Yuan.

Zhu Weizheng 朱維錚. *Yindiao weiding de chuantong* 音調未定的傳統 [*The Tradition without a Definite Tone*]. Shenyang: Liaoning jiaoyu chubanshe, 1995.

——. *Qiusuo zhen wenming: Wan Qing xueshushi lun* 求索真文明：晚清學術史論 [*In Search of True Civilization: Essays on the History of Scholarship in the Late Qing Dynasty*]. Shanghai: Shanghai guji, 1996.

Zhu Xi 朱熹 (1130–1200). *Shi jizhuan* 詩集傳 [*The Book of Poetry with Collected Commentaries*]. Shanghai: Shanghai guji, 1980.

——. *Zhuzi yulei* 朱子語類 [*Classified Sayings of Master Zhu*]. Originally edited by Li Jingde 黎靖德 (fl. 1270). Subsequently edited by Wang Xingxian 王星賢. 8 vols. Beijing: Zhonghua, 1986.

Zhuangzi 莊子 (369?–286? B.C.E). See Guo Qingfan.

Zhuzi jicheng 諸子集成 [*Collection of Distinguished Philosophical Works*]. 8 vols. Beijing: Zhonghua, 1954.

Index